AND THE
UNIVERSE
HINDU PERSPECTIVES

GW01417580

MAN

AND THE
UNIVERSE

HINDU PERSPECTIVES

by
Prof. R R Pandey

PILGRIMS

PILGRIMS PUBLISHING
Varanasi◆Kathmandu

Man and the Universe: Hindu Perspectives
Prof. R R Pandey

Published by:
PILGRIMS PUBLISHING

An imprint of:
PILGRIMS BOOK HOUSE
B 27/98 A-8, Nawabganj Road
Durga Kund, Varanasi-221010, India
Tel: 91-542-314060, 312456
E-mail: pilgrims@satyam.net.in
Website: www.pilgrimsbooks.com

Distributed in India by:
PILGRIMS BOOK HOUSE
B 27/98 A-8, Nawabganj Road
Durga Kund, Varanasi-221010, India
Tel: 91-542-314060, 312456
E-mail: pilgrims@satyam.net.in
Website: www.pilgrimsbooks.com

Distributed in Nepal by:
PILGRIMS BOOK HOUSE
P O Box 3872, Thamel,
Kathmandu, Nepal
Tel: 977-1-424942
Fax: 977-1-424943
E-mail: pilgrims@wlink.com.np

Copyright © 2002, Pilgrims Publishing
All Rights Reserved

Edited by Christopher N Burchett
Cover design by Sasya
Layout by Asha

ISBN: 81-7769-182-1
Rs. 210/-

The contents of this book may not be reproduced, stored or copied in any form—printed, electronic, photocopied, or otherwise—except for excerpts used in review, without the written permission of the publisher.

Printed in India

Dedicated
to
My revered parents

PREFACE TO THE NEW EDITION

The age of cybernetics and molecular biology is now in vogue. Their methodologies are formalistic, analytical, grammatical, and semiological—each of them stemming from an alphabet of elements. After the discovery of the biological basis of heredity, encoded in DNA, living tissue is no more a mystery it is a product of molecular combinations, the rules of which are open to decipherment. Is this discovery of biochemistry, masquerading as a universal science of character, really the last word? Now, as it claims there is nothing like a mysterious noumenon? Indeed, the post-Heideggerean life sciences along with cybernetics have bewildered the human intelligibility in defining and delimiting the human existentiell. Even Heideggerean Dasein freed from its prison of *Being* ultimately lands into a new mysticism of philosophical linguistics. Richard Rorty in his "Philosophy and the Mirror of Nature" has described all the methods of philosophy starting from Descartes till Husserl as self-deception and grand illusion. The post-Heideggereans like Richard Rorty, Jurgen Habermas, Michel Foucault and Jaques Derrida usually designated as postmodernists deny the very foundations of truth, knowledge and morals and emphasize 'historicism', 'skepticism', 'nihilism' and 'relativism' by applying the method of deconstruction or depth hermeneutics. Is not the concept of construction implied in the deconstruction of logocentrism by Derrida? Can Logos, Consciousness or Subjectivity be at all negated by deconstruction or depth heremeneutics? What is deconstruction or depth hermeneutics other than rigorous analysis? Their negation itself is their affirmation. These postmodernists, through their deconstruction or depth hermeneutics, exploded the very myth of Hegelean theoria or reason on which the Eurocentric edifice starting from Plato to Husserl was constructed. The emergence of postmodernism is the collapse of Europe as the cape and brain of the world and it remains only the 'land of sunset' from which the morning of a new world history has already prepared to dawn. Eurocentrism has surrendered to globalism and postmodernism. After the collapse of Soviet Russia in the late eighties, their was now only one super power in the world, and it was the USA till the morning of Black Tuesday, the 11th of September 2001, its Pearl Harbour, which had remained untouched for over seven decades and the World Trade Centre of New York, the real pearl of the USA, which was truly the cape and brain of the entire globe was reduced to a heap of rubbles within minutes and thereby turned the idiom darkness at dawn into literal truth. The World Trade Centre, the symbol of the supremacy of USA collapsed like a castle of sand. The full implications of this event will take years to sink in but what became immediately clear was that invincibility built on material foundations is a myth. It is an irony of history that in 1945, Hiroshima and Nagasaki bore the brunt of the first atomic attack and a permanent terror struck the heart of humanity. Now the architect of that terror is facing the wall because now what has struck is not an atomic or nuclear bomb but a human bomb. Is it not an indication of the collapse of globalism? Terrorism is the most dangerous evil rooted in religious fundamentalism. It must be eradicated. Globalism has various dimensions—economic, scientific, cultural and political. It believes in domination by using any means. But no unscrupulous mammonism can survive for long. It is destined to collapse. The collapse of globalism and postmodernism will lead to the new dawn of World history. J.L. Metha's suggestion is prophetic that the Upanishadic tradition of India can contribute more substantially towards the preparation of that new dawn than has seemed possible so far. Man and the Universe in Hindu philosophy is a blue print of that dawn by making subtle enquiries into the various inner layers of human subjectivity, finally leading to the realization of the absolute Reality.

FOREWORD

The question concerning man and universe is the most important question of philosophy. In fact it may be said to be the central problem of philosophy in the sense that man's concern about his true nature and destiny is the only question that makes philosophy relevant to life. All over the world there have been speculations about man and his place in the world. But in Indian philosophy there is a certain peculiarity. In spite of differences in their metaphysical outlook the Indian systems have an undercurrent of unity. They all believe that philosophy starts with the problem of suffering and that suffering is due to the ignorance of reality or truth, especially the truth about one's self. It is ignorance that involves us in Karma which gives rise to the cycle of birth and death or suffering. All the systems hold that ignorance and hence suffering can be finally and completely eradicated by knowledge alone and so the attainment of that knowledge is the supreme goal of life.

The most difficult question concerning man and the universe is the question, how man as a spiritual being comes to be involved in Nature or *Prakriti*. It is here that Indian philosophy makes a distinct contribution not to be found in Western philosophy. Nature here is conceived not as something independent of man. The whole play of Nature is due to the Karmas of living beings. But not only that, the whole of Nature is operating for the spiritual evolution of man. Dr. Pandey has very ably shown that Nature is no doubt governed by its own laws but it is subservient to the law of karma. Nature provides the necessary environment and organs for the liquidation of man's karmas, which ultimately lead to the development and purification of his mind (which is itself part of Nature) and man becomes fit for that kind of knowledge that brings about liberation. So Nature is not indifferent, much less cruel to man as it is taken to be in the West; it has a spiritual role to play in the evolution of man.

Dr. Pandey has considered the views of the orthodox systems of Indian philosophy concerning man and the universe in a very systematic and coherent manner. He has not failed to pay attention to the Vedic and Upanishadic thought to which all the orthodox systems owe allegiance. He has so arranged the chapters that after a critical examination of the different systems one is led to the Vedantic view at the end. He has successfully shown that behind the system of physical facts called Nature there is a moral system in the form of the law of karma operating. The world is not left merely to the care of physical laws without any goal or direction; the law of karma gives a direction to the whole process. The operation of the law of karma through process of Nature is meant to take every living being in the direction of the supreme goal of life, which is the discovery of the true nature of the self. Dr. Pandey has rightly considered the different conceptions of the self and has come to the Vedantic view as the most satisfactory. The speciality of Advaita Vedanta in this connection is two-fold. First, it is shown here that Nature is not only not an enemy of man but also that Nature cannot be an enemy, because it has no ontologically independent status; it is ultimately false. Secondly, unlike other systems, Advaita Vedanta emphasizes not only the essential unity of all men but also the unity of man with the supreme reality. It is quite appropriate to conclude the study with Advaita Vedanta as Dr. Pandey has done.

I have had the pleasure of going through the whole book and also of discussing certain points with Dr. Pandey. I am happy to say that Dr. Pandey has presented the different systems with an insight and perspective, which we cannot get merely from text books on Indian philosophy. His language is lucid and arguments are clear. His study is based on the first hand knowledge of the texts and is, therefore, quite authentic. His approach is critical and comparative. I am sure it is a very welcome addition to the literature on Indian philosophy and will be well received by both, laymen and scholars.

R. K. Tripathi
Professor of Philosophy
Ex-Director of Centre of Advanced Study in Philosophy
Banaras Hindu University
Varanasi

ACKNOWLEDGMENT

It is a pleasure to record my gratitude to the eminent scholars, both Indian and Western, from whom I have learnt philosophy. My deepest obligations are due to Dr. S. Datta, former Head of the Department of Philosophy, University of Allahabad, who not only suggested the subject for research but also kindly agreed to guide me. I do not know how to express my deep gratitude to Prof. R. K. Tripathi, ex-Director, Centre for Advanced Study in Philosophy, B.H.U., from whom I have had the privilege to learn and with whom I have been working for a few years. He has very kindly read the entire manuscript, discussed it word by word and has offered valuable suggestions and criticisms. But for him this little monograph would not have been what it is.

My revered uncle Acharya Pt. Ram Karan Pandey, Principal Shri R. D. Mahavidyalaya, Jaunpur has been throughout a source of inspiration to me. I believe that without his blessings, I would have not been what I am today.

I am thankful to Prof. T. R. V. Murti, and Pt. Badari Nath Shukla who have been kind enough to discuss some important texts with me. Pt. Vidya Niwas Mishra also has inspired me throughout in the course of my research.

I have had the opportunity to discuss Philosophy with some top German Indologists when I was in W. Germany (1972-1974). I was lucky to work with Prof. Dr. Lambert Schmithausen of Hamburg University. It is he who initiated me into German philological methodology. Prof. Dr. A. Welzer, Direktor, Seminar Fur Geschichte und Kultur Indiens, der Universitat Hamburg was equally affectionate to me in discussing the Yoga philosophy. My obligations are due to Prof. Paul Hacker, Direktor des Indologisches Seminar der Universitat Munster who discussed with me some Advaitic and Pauranic texts. Prof. Dr. K. Ruping and Dr. S. N. Sharma of Munster University were also very helpful to me. From Frieburg University Dr. G. C. Tripathi provided me very helpful suggestions to work out a plan of higher studies in Germany.

I owe a great debt to my teachers of the University of Allahabad. They include late Prof. A. C. Mukherjee, Late Prof. R. N. Kaul, Prof. S. C. Biswas, Prof. S. S. Roy, Prof. V. S. Naravane, Shri S. L. Pandey and Shri S. K. Seth.

I must thank Prof. N. S. S. Raman, the present Head of Department of Philosophy, B.H.U., for his affectionate encouragement.

I cannot forget Dr. Mrs. L. Saxena, Head of the Department of Philosophy, Gorakhpur University with whom I have had the privilege to work for about eight years at the University of Gorakhpur.

My thanks are due to Prof. N. K. Devaraja, Prof. R. S. Mishra, Dr. S. Basu, Dr. A. K. Chatterjee, Dr. R. R. Dravid, Dr. L. N. Sharma, Shri Kamalakar Mishra, Shri K. N. Mishra and Dr. Harsh Narain of B.H.U. with whom I have the pleasure to work at present. I also thank Prof. G. J. Larson of the University of California with whom I had very useful discussions on problems of Indian philosophy during his stay at B.H.U. (1976-77).

Among my friends who have directly or indirectly moulded my thinking, a few who may be mentioned are Dr. R. C. Tripathi, Dr. D. N. Dwivedi, Dr. R. L. Singh of the University of Allahabad, Dr. S. Mishra of the University of Gorakhpur and Satyapal Verma of Kurukshetra University. I am really grateful to my friend Dr. R. K. Shukla of the Department of

English, B.H.U., who helped me in improving the language of the manuscript of this work.

In the present work I have depended as far as possible on the basic texts of different systems. I have also considered the views of some modern interpreters. However, the way of looking at different systems is all my own and so whatever merit or demerit is there is due to me. My only attempt is to present the different views clearly and critically leading ultimately to the Advaitic point of view. I do not know how far I have succeeded in presenting a certain perspective but I do believe that such an attempt was worthwhile and was probably not made before.

Rewati Raman Pandey
Varanasi

ABBREVIATIONS

AS	—Agama Shastras
AV	—Atharva Veda
BHP	—Bhashapariccheda
KU	—Kiranavali of Udayana
MS	—Mimamsa Sutra of Jaimini
NBS	—Nimbarka on Brahma Sutra
NK	—Nyayakandali
NLV	—Nyayalilavati of Vallbha
NLVK	—Kanthabharana of Shamkara Misra, a comm. on NLV
NLVP	—Nyayalilavatiprakasha of Vardhamana, a comm. on NLV
NS	—Nyaya Sutra
N-V	—Nyaya-vaisheshika
NV	—Nyaya Vartika
NVT	—Nyaya Vartika Tatparya Tika
PYD	—Patanjala Yoga Dipika
RBG	—Ramanuja (bhashya) on Bhagavadgita
RBS	—Ramanuja (bhashya) on Brahma Sutra
RV	—Rigveda
PPBH	—Prashastapada Bhashya
SB or SBS	—Sariraka Bhashya
SBG	—Shamkara (bhashya) on Bhagavadgita
SDS	—Sarva Darshana Shamgraha
SK	—Samkhya Karika
SM	—Siddhanta Muktavali
SPS	—Samkhya Pravacana Bhashya
SS	—Samkhya Sutra
STK	—Samkhya Tattva Kaumudi
SV	—Shloka Vartika
SY	—Samkhya-yoga
TBH	—Tarka Bhasha of Keshava Misra
VBS	—Vallabha on Brahma Sutra
VKT	—Vedanta Kalpa Taru of Amalananda Sarasvati, a comm. on Bhamati
VPS	—Vivarana Prameya-Samgraha

CONTENTS

INTRODUCTION:

In Indian philosophical systems there are discussions of creation and human soul but these discussions do not take into account the nature of man and his place in the universe. The present work was undertaken with a view to approaching Indian Philosophy in this perspective as is found in some of the Western systems. This is probably the first attempt to reconstruct Indian Philosophy from this angle. We must hasten to mention that we have considered here only the orthodox systems of Indian Philosophy for fear of making the dissertation unduly voluminous. We have deliberately excluded the views of such systems as Charvaka, Buddhism, Jainism, Saivism, and Tantra etc. All the same, we have not omitted the consideration of Vedic and Upanishadic thought, as the Vedas and Upanishads are the starting point of the orthodox systems of Indian philosophy.

Looking at the universe and man in it, we observe one feature, which seems to be the most striking, i.e., change. Everything in the universe seems to be constantly changing. This phenomenon of change raises certain questions. Is the universe changing according to its own nature or is there some other force responsible for this change? Is the change going on in some direction or not? In other words, is change teleological? Again, is there also something which remains unchanged in the midst of this change and if so, what is the relation between the changing and the unchanging and how does that relationship help or hinder man in his struggle to attain the goal of his life?

This change is an important subject, which has been discussed by philosophers everywhere, both ancient and modern.

In the earliest period of Indian thought we find the view that the mighty forces of Nature, which are, no doubt, responsible for change and variety are, controlled by deities. We get a conception of Nature, which is something living and dynamic and not dead and inert. But at a later stage a universal principle operating behind these forces was discovered and named *Rita*. *Prakriti* is considered as having her own laws. Though a clear sense of teleology has not yet emerged, the picture of *Prakriti* is very fascinating and lively. Gradually, the sense of teleology seems to have come in when we find that the concept *Rita* not only connotes a mechanical principle but a moral idea also. Thus in the concept of *Rita* we find both the principles; the causal and moral are amalgamated.

When we pass on to the Upanishads we find that a great discovery has been made about man and the whole universe. The discovery is the oneness of the whole universe—oneness of all beings, and all entities. The germ of this concept, however, was already there in the Vedas. The most important feature in the concept of oneness is the emphasis on its nature as being essentially *chit* or consciousness. Thus the view that many forces are working and essentially spiritual in character is presented. The older idea of dualism between man and universe is replaced by a non-dualistic conception. Its culmination is found in the Vedanta of Shankara.

The Upanishads contain so many different concepts and ideas that almost all the later systems of Indian philosophy have drawn their views from them. A careful study of the different systems of Indian philosophy reveals that the concept of change has been viewed in different ways. We may mention as many as three different views with regards to *Prakriti* as the changing world. These are (1) Change as cyclic (2) Change as linear (3) Change as unreal.

Most of the systems of Indian philosophy accept the cyclic view of creation and destruction of *Prakriti. Srishti, Sthiti,* and *Pralaya* are the three phases of this world. There may be difference in regard to the nature of creation and destruction of the world, in regard to the questions whether the creator is merely an efficient cause or both, efficient as well as the material cause. The *Nyaya-Vaisheshika* the *Sankhya-yoga* and the theistic Vedanta accept the cyclic view. This view has permeated through the Puranas and has been accepted by most people of India as a part of their religious faith.

In the *Purva-Mimansa* we come across a different view of the world. This system does not accept the cyclic view of creation and destruction of the world. In this view the world is *anadi* and *ananta.* Nature is a continuous process. It gives a linear conception.

Coming to Advaita Vedanta we find that the changing world has been denied an ultimate Reality. The Advaita Vedanta gives us the concept of Reality, which is not in time. That which is not in time cannot have any change. Change and many are for it phenomenal. For all practical purposes change is real, the changing world has its *srishti, sthiti* and *pralaya* but ultimately it is unreal.

In connection with the conception of *Prakriti* or Nature we have also dealt with the problem of man's relation to Nature and his destiny. The remarkable thing that we find in the Indian systems but not in the Western systems is that Nature is not conceived as something opposed to man or apart from him.

It is not just an 'aggregate of material lumps' or a 'heap of atoms and molecules'. It is radiant with the same Light, which is the very essence of man. Whether a particular system regards Nature as real or unreal and whether it accepts the cyclic concept of creation or not, one thing is certain, that is man's life in this world is largely due to his karmas of the past life. In fact it will not be far from truth to say that the whole of Nature is a product of the totality of the *karmas* of the numberless *jīvas* living in the world. And so life in this world is an opportunity to work out the load of past *karmas.* Not only that. There is another aspect worth considering. By no orthodox system of Indian philosophy is man conceived as wholly a part of Nature, there is something in man, viz., his soul which is not governed by physical laws, there is a moral law which governs the life of man. Thus he is of Nature and beyond it. This implies two things. First, it explains the possibility of human aspiration which may be of two kinds (a) by doing virtuous deeds he can ensure to himself a happy and prosperous life in this world; (b) if, however, he feels fed up with worldly life he can also chalk out a spiritual programme of life and can pursue the course of spiritual freedom. Nature would not hinder or obstruct him in following these courses. Secondly, it explains the possibility of freedom of human soul, because, the essence of man or his soul though related to the world is not part of it. And though the soul of man is not part of the world yet life in the world undoubtedly helps him if properly pursued in getting out of it.

The conception of four *purusharthas* makes it abundantly clear that life in the world is not useless and purposeless but perfectly relevant to the two goals of life, called *Preyas* and *Shreyas.* The right way of earning and spending money, the proper way of enjoying life, and virtuous life are possible in this world and they are all helpful in man's progress towards his destiny. If the desire for pleasures requires us to lead a moral life, the experience of pain awakens in us the urge for freedom, i.e.' *mokhsha*. So the whole life of man in this world is meaningful.

If we review the different orthodox systems of Indian philosophy there seems to be four ways of looking at man and his relation to the universe. First, he is viewed as a part of Nature to the extent that he has a body, which is governed by physical laws. Secondly, it is soon discovered that man's relation to his environment or Nature is based on a moral law inasmuch as his life is governed by the law of *Karma*. There is a third stage, however, where man becomes master of Nature and no more remains a slave to it. This is the kind of power attained by yogic practice. Finally, there is the fourth stage when man not only distinguishes himself from Nature, not only develops powers to control it but discovers the great truth that the Brahman who is identified with his real soul is the only Reality and the so-called Nature is but a product of *Maya* or *Avidya*. It establishes not only the unity of man with other men and other living beings, but also with the supreme reality of the universe or Brahman. The Reality within and without is one and the same. This supreme state of man is not a matter of philosophical speculation or faith only, it is something, which can be tested, experienced and lived here and now.

1

NATURE, MAN AND GOD IN THE VEDAS

1. THE PROBLEM OF CAUSATION

Man is most concerned with his environment; the world in space and time. Hence, it is natural that when he becomes reflective, he wants to understand the nature of this world. The physical world seems to him part and parcel of his life. When he tries to understand the nature of the physical world, the questions that come up are—who has created this world; what are the constituent elements out of which it is created and how it was created? In other words, we want to know its efficient cause, the material cause, and the process of creation.

Thus the problem of causation is the primary question in the understanding of the physical world—or what we call Nature. The Vedas, as is known, are more poetic in their content than logical. Still one can trace certain important ideas regarding causation behind the poetic imaginations.

The principle of causation in the Vedas, the earliest literature of the Hindus, seems to appear in the concept of *Rita*. *Rita* represents the law, unity or rightness, underlying the orderliness we observe in the world. *Rita* literally means the 'course of things'. This conception seems to have been originally derived from the regularity of the movements of the heavenly bodies like the sun, the moon, and the stars, the alternations of day and night and of the seasons.

In the Vedas, there are no hymns addressed specifically to *Rita*, but brief references to the important concepts are found repeatedly in the hymns to Varuna (who maintains the physical order), Agni and Vishvadeva etc. The following hymn will illustrate the point:

He, the upholder of order, Varuna sits down,
among his people; he, the wise sits there to govern.[1]

Gradually, the concept of *Rita* takes a new meaning—from external physical order or uniformity of nature—it acquires the significance of a moral order. The whole world was thought to be governed by some universal principles and these were included under *Rita*. Thus the whole universe is controlled by Varuna who is not only the upholder of the physical order but also the custodian of moral order—*Ritasya gopa*—and who punishes the sinner. The following hymn is an example: —

The great lord of these sees as if he were near,
If a man thinks he is walking by stealth,
the gods know it all.[2]

He who should flee far beyond the sky, even he
would not be rid of Varuna, the king.
His spies proceed from heaven towards this world,
with a thousand eyes they look over this earth.[3]

In *Rita*, two fundamental concepts of equal importance, that of causality and that of morality, are rooted. As the principle of moral order of the world, it is the anticipation of the doctrine of Karma, one of the distinguishing features of Indian thought. Sacrifice was regarded as almost the only kind of duty, or karma. The creation of he world itself was even regarded as the fruit of sacrifice performed by the Supreme Being. So *Rita* furnishes us with the original idea of causality, which is not only a physical principle but also a moral principle. It has been said: "The principle of karman is the counterpart in the moral realm of the physical law of causality"[4].

2. THE CREATION OF THE WORLD

It was but natural that in the beginning the human mind liked to divide the universe into two regions—the Heaven and the Earth. The Heaven is above and the Earth is below. The Heaven and the Earth have been mentioned as the Father and the Mother of the world. They have also been mentioned as the twin sisters.

> The two maidens, uniting from a pair,
>   twin sisters in their parents'
>   lap, caressing the navel of the world.
> May Heaven and Earth protect us from fearful evil.[5]

> May, this, O Heaven and Earth, be
>   true, O father and mother that
>   which I here implore you.[6]

The world is not merely what is encompassed by the two regions of the Heaven and the Earth, forming an inseparable pair like Father and Mother. The Vedic poets also sing about the third world; the atmospheric region between the Heaven and the Earth. It is mentioned as the middle sky or Antariksha.

> I will proclaim the mighty deeds of Vishnu,
> of him who measured out the earthly spaces,
> who firmly propping up the higher station
> stood out in triple regions widely pacing.[7]

Alone the universe in *three divisions*
The earth and sky and all created beings.[8]

From his navel arose the middle-sky,
from his head the heaven originated,
from his feet the earth.[9]

We also find further sub-division of each of them into three.
The Vedic poets speak of the three Earths, three Heavens and
three Antarikshas.

Ruler whose mighty far-seeing
rays, pervading all three earths
have filled the three superior
realms of heaven.[10]

Three heavens there are, two Savitars
adjacent: in Yama's world is
one, the home of heroes.[11]

It is difficult to work out the theory of the five elements,
which seems to be a later development of philosophy in India,
on the basis of the three divisions of the world into Earth, Air
and Heaven. But Prof. C. Kunhan Raja suggests this division
to be equated with the Five Elements of a later stage. He observes: —

I am inclined to equate this division of the world with
'Five Elements' of a later stage in the development of
philosophy in India, the Elements being the Earth, the
Water, the Fire, the Air, and the Ether (Akasha). The
close relation of the first three of the Five Elements with
the three worlds of the Veda cannot escape the attention

of even the most causal reader of the Vedas. The references to the sound, to language and to songs and the mysteries related to them, may be equated with the fifth Element, Akasha (Ether), which, according to later philosophy, is connected with sound. There are prayers to Vayu and Vata, both meaning air. One may be tempted to connect this Vayu or Vata with the fourth Element.[12]

The question as to how this universe came into being seems to have been raised in the following statements: —

What was the place on which he gained a footing?
Where found he anything, or how, to hold by,
What time, the earth creating, Vishvakarman
All seeing, with his might disclosed the heavens?

What was the tree, what wood in sooth produced it,
from which they fashioned out the earth and heaven?
Ye thoughtful men inquire within your spirit where on
he stood when he established all things.[13]

In the earlier stage, every god was looked upon as the creator of the universe. Every god that was considered as the supreme at one time or other must necessarily have made heaven and earth. Sometimes, the world is presented as a great architectural art. In the Rigveda, God Vishnu is shown as having measured out the three worlds with his three steps:

I will proclaim the mighty of Vishnu
of him who measured out the earthly spaces;
who firmly propping up the higher station
stood out in triple regions widely pacing.[14]

Him whose three footsteps filled with mead, unfailing,

reveal his blissful joy; who has supported
alone the universe in the divisions.
the earth and sky and all created beings.[15]

There are places where gods like Vishvadevas, Indra, Agni,
Maruts, and Trastar are spoken of as having made firm the
earthly and the heavenly regions.

What was that one who in the unborn's
image hath stabilized and fixed
firm these worlds, six religions (regions).[16]

But behind the plurality of the Vedic gods, there was something real of which Agni, Indra, and Varuna, etc. were only the
forms. Max Muller observes: —

So, it was with these names of the Vedic gods. They were
all meant to express the beyond, the Invisible behind the Visible, the Infinite with the Finite, the Supernatural above the
Natural, the Divine, Omnipresent and Omnipotent.[17]

The oft-quoted lines in this connection are as follows: —

The real is one, the learned
call it by various names,
Agni, Yama and Matarishvan.[18]

Among the architects of the universe Vishvakarman,
Hiranyagarbha and the Person are important. Vishvakarman
is the maker of all. There are two hymns about him in the
available text of the Rigveda. These hymns describe the process of the formation of the world with Vishvakarman as the
active agent in giving the form to the world.

The question is raised as to which abode could he have

been in when he created the world. He has eyes all round, he
has his face turned in all directions. He, the one god, created
the Heaven and the Earth, and in so doing he blew out with
both his arms, with wings. What could have been the wood
and the timber when he constructed the Heaven and the Earth?
Wise men can ask this question as to what abode he had been
in when he created the world. What were his highest abodes,
intermediate abodes and the lowest ones? Vishvakarman is
asked to give instruction about oblations and also to perform
the sacrifice with his own body. Through oblations,
Vishvakarman expands. He is asked to perform a sacrifice with
the Heaven and the Earth.[19]

In the second poem, the different qualities of Vishvakarman
have been mentioned. He is the creator and the author of the
diversifications in the world. He sees all, knows all the worlds,
bearing the one name of the gods. The waters are spoken of as
bearing the first 'Law' where all the gods had the vision.[20]

We find some clear information regarding the formation of
the world in the hymn attributed to Hiranyagarbha. The hymn
starts with a glorification of Hiranyagarbha, as the one who
existed in the beginning at the head of all, the one lord of all
that has come into existence. The hymn contains ten verses,
and in the first nine of them there is a refrain at the end, 'To
which god may we make offerings?' he is described as sup-
porting the Heaven and the Earth, as the giver of soul and
strength, as one whose commands the gods adore, whose shadow
both immortality and death are, as the king of all that breathe
and that keep their eyes open, as the overlord of the bipeds
and the quadrupeds, as the one to whom belong the snow-clad
mountain and the oceans and the cardinal points. He made the
Heaven and the Earth firm, he established the heaven, and he
measured out the space in the atmospheric regions. The Heaven
and the Earth look upon him. The whole of immense waters

went to him, bearing pregnancy creating the Fire. The life of
gods was produced from him. He viewed the waters in his
greatness, when the waters bore dexterity, when they produced
the Sacrifice. He was the one God above all the gods.[21]

When we come to the 'Sukta', attributed to 'Purusha' as
the source of the universe, we find a significant change. In the
case of the Vishvakarman and the Hiranyagarbha, they are
only the active agents and the material cause is external. In the
'Supreme Person' we see, for the first time a monistic principle
in which the efficient and material cause got united. The description appears in a Sukta of sixteen verses. Here we find the
self-transformation of the Infinite one into the finite many.

First, there is a glorification of the 'Purusha' as having a
thousand heads, a thousand eyes and a thousand feet. He encompasses the whole world and stands out ten fingers beyond
that. It is to be noted that Purusha is not wholly one with the
world but beyond it. The idea of transcendence is suggested
by the statement that he is ten fingers beyond the cosmos. This
all is the Purusha, whatever had been and whatever will be.
He lords over immortality. Such is his greatness, and the
'Purusha' is greater than that; the whole world is just one quarter of His and the three quarters of His, the immortal, is in the
Heaven.

It is here that what is termed as Virat is said to have come
out from the 'Supreme Person'. And another person was produced out of it. This person, being born, surpassed the world
both before and behind. When this person sacrificed (*yajna*),
all the beings in the air, in the woods and in the villages were
born. The Vedas arose out of this sacrifice. The various animals like the horses and the cows and the goats and sheep
were also produced in this sacrifice. Here the entire process of
creation is spoken of as a sacrifice (*yajna*). Here a question is
raised about this Purusha that was transformed into material at

the sacrifice by the gods as to what became of his face, arms, thighs, and feet. The reply that is given is that the wise people were his face, the warriors were his arms, the thighs became the traders and out of his feet were produced the manual labourers. The moon was born out of his mind and the sun from his two eyes. Indra and Fire were born from his face and the air came out of his breath. The atmosphere was produced out of his navel, and the heaven from his head. The earth was born from his two feet and the cardinal points came out of his ears. In this sacrifice, The Spring Season became the ghee, the Summer Season became the fuel and the Autumn became the oblation. The whole world was produced in this way. This is what happened when the gods performed the sacrifice with the Purusha.

The Sukta concludes with a verse in which it is mentioned that this sacrifice performed by the gods became the first process of Law. It is also said that in this sacrifice, the demi-gods (*Sadhyas*) and the poet-sages (*Rishis*) also participated. Here we find that the threefold agencies of the gods, the demi-gods (*Sadhyas*) and the poets participate in the sacrifice. But there is no clear indication about the way in which these agencies came into being. And in so far as they participate in the sacrifice in which the 'Purusha' is the offering, they precede the appearance of the 'Purusha'. [22]

There is another idea about the formation of the world found in the Vedas. It is highly philosophical in nature but stated in a beautiful poetical language. It is called the 'Song of Creation'. The Sukta starts with a description of the state of the world prior to its appearance as a world of many and varied objects when there could be no distinction between what is and what is not. There was no atmospheric region, nor the celestial region beyond. In such a condition what is it that can cover up, and where, in whose support? There was no indication of night and day. Here we find the principle of causality, which not only traces the whole universe to a single source but also suggests what its nature may be. All opposites like being and non-being, death and life, good and evil, are viewed as developing from within and, therefore, have the possibilities of being reconcilable again in this fundamental principle. There was that one who breathed without a breath of air. Other than that there was nothing. In the beginning there was darkness hidden in darkness. All this was a sea of water with no mark or indication. On this there arose a will in the beginning, which was the first germ for the mind, the rays of light stretched across, was it below or was it above? Who then knows, who can explain, whence there arose this manifold creation? Even gods appeared only after this manifold process. Hence who knows whence that came into being? Listen, this manifold came from something, whether it created this or did not create it.[23]

In this Sukta the expression 'Tad Ekam' is very significant. It shows how the notion of a monistic principle is tending to emerge out.

3. THE PHYSICAL WORLD AND THE RELATION BETWEEN MAN AND NATURE

In the hymns of the Rigveda, we come across a sort of simple Nature worship. The mystery of the world deeply stirred the mind of the Vedic poets. The beauty and grandeur of Nature awakened their profound enthusiasm and admiration and in the striking phenomena of the heaven and the Earth they saw the manifestation of some higher powers. For them the whole world was full of these powers. The whole of Nature was alive to the poets of the Vedas and in the presence of gods the germ of 'religious morality' was quite obvious. Every act of Nature, whether of the earth or in the air, or in the highest heaven was ascribed to their agency. Max Muller observes: "When we say, it thunders, they said Indra thunders; when we say, it rains, they said *Parjanya* pours out his buckets; when we say it dawns, they said the beautiful *Ushas* appears like a dancer, displaying her splendour; when we say it grows dark, they said Surya unharnesses his steeds."[24]

A.S. Geden in his discussion of the Hindu conception of Nature states: —

> Perhaps in no other early religion is the natural element so clearly revealed or the material origin so little obscured by passing into the divine also the qualities and attributes of the various gods, being constructed, as it were, after one pattern, that of man, present little variety, and the same epithets may be and are applied to each and all.[25]

During this period, people lived an active life on the earth. They worshipped the gods; and it was a kind of force, which these gods exercised and by this their influence was felt. These gods were all-powerful; able to accomplish their demands and to do whatever they willed. Moreover, with few exceptions they were conceived as gracious and kindly disposed to listen to the petition of men who approached them in sincerity with prayer and sacrifice. They were supposed to wage continual war against the power of evil. The great warrior, God Indra, kills the dragon Vritra as a result of the worship of men on the earth, and thus he lets 'the seven rivers' flow freely. He also kills another demon, Vala and he releases the cows that are concealed behind the mountains in the caves.

> The heroic deeds of Indra shall I proclaim,
> the deeds that the thunder wielder performed first:
> He slew the dragon, freed the waters,
> slit the bowels of the hills.[26]

Petitions to the gods in the hymns are for the material prosperity in this world. Human prayers to the gods are for plenty
of provisions, good pasture-grounds, health, cows and horses,
good harvests, material wealth, physical strength, a strong family
stock, longevity, and fame and position in life.

Illustrious far and wide, may Indra
prosper us; may Pushan prosper us,
the Master of all wealth May Tarkshya
With uninjured feelings prosper us;
Brihaspati vouchsafe to us prosperity.[27]

Thou art the giver of horse, Indra,
thou art the giver of cows, the giver
of corn, the strong lord of wealth,
the old guide of man, disappointing
no desires, a friend to friends—
to him we address this song.[28]

Thou lord of wealth: and giver of
wealth, be thou wise and powerful,
drive away from us the enemies.[29]

A deity like Rudra, sometimes supposed to be creating
horror and destruction was also prayed to.

Slay us not, nor abandon us, O Rudra,
let not thy noose when thou art
angry seize us. Give us trimmed
grass and rule over the living.
Preserve us even more, ye gods, with blessings.[30]

But Rudra becomes gracious when he becomes the greatest of physicians: —

Thou very gracious god, hast a thousand
medicines, inflict no evil on our sons and progeny.[31]

Thus the material world where men lived was supposed by
them to be controlled by supernatural powers or Gods, who
were closer to men—because men thought them to be their
saviours or helpers at the time of their distress. The world was
there, but it was a place for men where life was full of uncer-
tainties and suffering due to natural calamities like floods, epidemics, and droughts. So Nature was not only generous to the
people with her crops and fruits and animals that supplied
food—she was cruel also. And it was when Nature was cruel
that men sought help from the supernatural.

But this naturalistic interpretation though obvious, is not
enough. There was also an appeal to the gods by men for 'good'
and for deliverance from sin.

Loose me from sin as from a band
that binds me: may we swell, Varuna,
thy spring of order.[32]

The view, therefore, that the Rigvedic thinkers were only
after worldly pleasure and in their petitions there is no prayer
for moral virtues is not correct. The following verse supports
the point: —

The wealthier man should give unto the needy
considering the course of life hereafter
for riches are like chariot wheels revolving;
Now to one man they come, now to another.[33]

Here, the third line of the verse prepares the background
of the Upanishadic dialogue in which Nachiketa vehemently
condemns worldly pleasures, as they are transitory.

In the Vedas, thus we find that the reality of the external world is never questioned. The idea of Rita leads us to conclude that it is an ordered whole, divided into the three realms, Earth, Atmospheric region and Heaven, each guided and illumined by its own specific deities. The idea of 'Being'—Tad Ekam—of the 'Song of Creation' shows that people believed that there was an intelligence behind the formation of this changing and moving world and 'Tad Ekam' is the only Reality called by various names, "Agni, Yama and Matarishvan."[34]

There are also allegorical and symbolic interpretations of Vedic hymns[35]. But for our purpose, the interpretation of Sayana seems to be satisfactory. But whatever may be the interpretation, it is true that man and Nature were intimately related. Nature, however, seems to be external to man though related to him. He was a child in Nature's lap and thought himself to be at her mercy. Yet it was in this world where he lived with his friends and foes, and experienced the sorrows and joys of life. Nature was indeed the cause of man's fear and suffering, yet in this world people of the Vedic time had their aesthetic experiences also. They saw the beauty and sublimity of this world and felt grateful to Nature for her supply of food and shelter.

Moreover, the concept of Rita shows that people saw uniformity in Nature, in the order of the seasons and days and nights, in the appearance of floods and rains and storms. They could not find the causal relation no doubt, but experienced an order, a system in the external world. This led them to a belief that there must be some general moral principle operating behind the external events.

Thus the relation between man and Nature became more meaningful, and Vedic poets were led to have a faith in the existence of higher supernatural powers or Gods, who controlled the universe and its events. They thought that in this universe, man and Nature were parts of a whole. The world, therefore, was dear to them, and they wanted to make their environment not only secure but also beautiful. The earliest primitive decorations and patterns found in the crudely built huts and later in the ashrams prove this fact abundantly.

REFERENCES

1. RV. 1. 25, 10 C.R.T.H. Griffith, *The Hymns of the Rigveda* (Benares, Lazarus & Co., 3rd ed., 1920-6)
2. A V. IV, 16, I
3. AV. IV, 16, 10
4. T. M P. Mahadevan in "*History of Philosophy, Eastern and Western,*" Vol. I, p. 69
5. RV. I. 185, 5 (E.I. Thomas, Vedic Hymns) (London: John Murray, 1923)
6. RV. I. 185, 11 (Thomas)
7. RV. I. 154 1 (A.A. Macdonell, *Hymns from the Rigveda,* 1923)
8. RV. I. 154, 4 (Macdonell)
9. RV. X. 90, 14 (Thomas)
10. RV. VIII. 41, 9 (Griffith, *The Hymns of the Rigveda,* 3rd ed. 1920-6)
11. RV. 1. 35. 6 (Griffith)
12. *Fundamental Problems in Indian Philosophy*, p. 118
13. RV. X. 81. 2-4 (Griffith)
14. RV. I. 154. 1 (Macdonell)
15. RV. I. 153. 4 (Macdonell)
16. RV. I. 164. 6 (Griffith)
17. The Vedas, p. 119. (First Ed. 1956, Sunil Gupta (India) Ltd., Calcutta)
18. RV. I. 164. 46 (Griffith)
19. (a) He who sat down as Hotar priest, the Rishi, one father

offering up all   things existing—He, seeking through his wish a great possession came men no earth as archetypal.

(b) What was the place whereon he took his station? What was it that supported him? How was it? Whence Vishvakarman, seeing all, producing the earth; with mighty power disclosed the heavens.

(c) He who hath eyes on all sides round about him, a mouth on all sides, arms and feet on all sides. He, the sole god, producing earth and heaven, weldeth them, with his arms as wings together.

(d) What was the tree, what wood in sooth produced it, from which they fashioned out the earth and heaven? Ye thoughtful men inquire within your spirit whereon he stood when he established all things.

(e) Thine highest, lowest, sacrificial natures, and these thy friends at sacrifice, O blessed, and come thyself, exalted to our worship.

(f) Bring thou thyself, exalted with oblation, O Vishvakarman, Earth and Heaven to worship. Let other men around as live vitally: here let us have a rich and liberal patron.

(g) Let us invoke today, to aid our labour, the lord of speech, the thought-swift Vishvakarman.

May he hear kindly all our invocations, who gives all bliss for aid, whose works are righteous. RV. X. 81, 1-7, (Griffith).

20. (a) The father of the eye, the wise in the spirit, created both these worlds submerged in fatness. Then when the eastern ends were firmly fastened, the heavens and the earth were far extended.

(b) Mighty in mind and power is Vishvakarman, maker, disposer and most lofty presence. Their offerings joy in rich juice where they value one, only one, beyond the seven rishis.

(c) Father who made us, he who, as disposer, knoweth all

races and all things existing. Even he alone, the deities, name-giver-him, other beings seek for information.

(d) To him in sacrifice they offered treasures—rishis of old, in numerous troops as singers, who, in the distant, near and lower region made ready all these things that they have existence.

(e) That which is earlier than this earth and heaven, before the Asuras and gods had being—what was the germ primeval, which the waters received where all the gods were seen together?

(f) The waters, they received that germ primeval wherein the gods were gathered all together. It rested set upon the unborn's navel, that one wherein abide all things existing.

(g) Ye will not find him who produced these creatures: another thing hath risen up among you.

Enwrapt in misty cloud, with lips that stammer, hymn-chanters wander and are discontented. RV. X. 82, 1-7 (Griffith)

21. (a) As the golden germ he arose in the beginning when born he was the one Lord of the existent. He supported the earth—and this heaven. What God with our oblation shall we worship?

(b) He who gives breath; who gives strenth, whose command all the gods wait upon, whose shadow is immortality, is death—what God with our oblation shall we worship?

(c) Who through his greatness over that which breathes and closes the eyes is only king of the world, who is the lord of two-footed and four-footed—what God with our oblation shall we worship?

(d) Whose are the snowy mountains through his greatness, whose as they say, are the ocean and the Rasa, whose are the regions, whose the arms—what God...?

(e) Through whom the mighty heaven and the earth have been fixed, through whom the sun has been established, through whom the firmament; who in the middle sky measures out the air—what God...?

(f) To whom the two realms (heaven and earth) sustained by his aid, looked up, trembling in spirit, over whom the risen sun shines—what God ...?

(g) When the great waters came, bearing all as the germ, and generating fire (Agni), then arose the one life—spirit of the Gods—what God...?

(h) Who through his greatness beheld the waters, that bore power and generated the sacrifice, who was the one God above the gods—what God...?

(i) May he not injure us, who is the generator of the earth, he of true ordinances, who produced the heaven, who produced the shining mighty waters.

(j) O Prajapati, none other than thou has encompassed all these created things. May that for which we desiring have invoked thee, be ours.

May we become lords of wealth. RV. X. 121, 1-10 (Thomas).

22. (a) Thousand headed was the Purusha, thousand eyed, thousand footed.

He embraced the earth on all sides and stood beyond the breadth of ten fingers.

(b) The Purusha is this all, that which was and which shall be. He is Lord of immortality, which he grows beyond through (sacrificial) food.

(c) Such is his greatness and still greater than that is the Purusha.

One-fourth of him is all beings. The three-fourth of him is the immortal in Heaven.

(d) Three fourth on high rose the Purusha. One fourth of him arose again here (on the earth).

Thence in all directions he spread abroad, as that which eats and that which eats not.

(e)   From him viraj was born, from viraj the Purusha.
      He when born reached beyond the earth behind as well as
      before.

(f)   When the Gods spread out the sacrifice with the Purusha
      as oblation,
      spring was its ghee, summer the fuel, autumn the oblation.

(g)   As the sacrifice on the strewn grass they besprinkled the
      Purusha, born in the beginning. With him the Gods sacri-
      ficed, the Sadhyas and the sages.

(h)   From that sacrifice completely offered was the sprinkled
      ghee collected. He made it the beasts of the air, of the
      forest and those of the village.
      From that sacrifice completely were born the Verses
      (Rigveda) and the Saman—melodies (Samaveda) (class of
      gods or celestial beings).

(i)   The metres were born from it. From it was born the sacri-
      ficial formula (Yajur Veda).

(j)   From it were born horses, and they that have to rows of
      teeth. Cattle were born from it. From it were born goats
      and sheep.

(k)   When they divided the Purusha, into how many parts did
      they arrange him? What was his mouth? What his two arms?
      What are his thighs and feet called?

(l)   The Brahmin was his mouth, his two arms were made the
      Rajanya (warrior), his two thighs the Vaisya (trader and
      agriculturist), from his feet the Sudras (servile class) was
      born.

(m)   The moon was born from his spirit (*manas*), from his eye
      was born the sun, from his mouth Indra and Agni, from his
      breath Vayu (wind) was born.

(n)   From his navel arose the middle sky, from his head the
      heaven originated, from his feet the earth, the quarters

from his ear. Thus did they fashion the worlds.

(o) Seven were his sticks that enclose (the fire), thrice seven were made the faggots. When the gods spread out the sacrifice they bound the Purusha as a victim.

(p) With the sacrifice the Gods sacrificed the sacrifice. These were the first ordinances. These great powers reached to the firmament, where are the ancient Sadhyas—the Gods"

RV. X. 90. 1-16 (Thomas)

23. (a) "Non-being then existed not, nor being:
There was no air, nor sky that is beyond it:
What was concealed? Wherein? In whose protection?
And was then deep unfathomable water?
Death then existed not nor life immortal;
of neither night nor day was any token.

(b) By its inherent force the One breathed windless.
No other thing than that beyond existed.

(c) Darkness there was at first by darkness hidden,
Without distinctive marks, this all was water.
That which, becoming, by the void was covered,
that one by force of heat, came into being.

(d) Desire entered the One in the beginning:
It was the earliest seed, of thought the product.
The sages searching in their hearts with wisdom.
Found out the bond of being in non-being.

(e) Their ray extended light across the darkness.
But was the one above or was it under?
Creative force was there and fertile power:
Below was energy, above was impulse.

(f) Who knows for certain? Who shall here declare it?
Whence was it born, and whence came this creation,
The gods were after this world's creation.
Then who can know from whence it has arisen?

(g) None knoweth whence creation has arisen;

And whether He has or has not produced it:
He who surveys it in the higher heavens
He only knows, or happy he may know not." RV. X. 129,
1-7 (Macdonell)

24. The Vedas, p. 118.
25. Encyclopaedia of Religion and Ethics, pp. 229-30.
26. RV. II, XI, 1 (S. Muir), Orig. Sans. Texts, London, 1890
27. RV. I. 89, 6 (Griffith)
28. RV. I. 53. 2, (Max Muller—'Hymn to Indra')
29. RV. II 6. 4, (Max Muller—'Hymn to Agni')
30. RV. VII. 46.4 (Griffith)
31. RV. VII. 46. 3 (Griffith)
32. RV. II. 28. 5 (Griffith)
33. RV. X. 117.5 (Macdonell).
34. RV. I. 164, 46. (Griffith).
35. By Bergaigne and by Sri Aurobindo.

2

THE UPANISHADS AND THE CONCEPT OF REALITY

1. THE NOTION OF THE 'FIRST CAUSE'

As in the Vedas so in the Upanishads we do not meet any systematic philosophic theory. The Upanishads are the records of experiences of profound thinkers and seers in the form of stories, parables, and intimate dialogues. All their teachings are not equally clear and well defined. Some are flashes of visions; some are merely hints; some are mentioned by the way; while some are often repeated and well emphasized.

There is no systematic theory of causation in the Upanishads. But in their dialogues, theories of causation have been discussed.

In the Shvetashvatara Upanishad, we come across the question in regard to the ultimate cause of everything.

What is the cause? (Is it) *Brahman*? Whence are we born? By what do we live? And on what are we established? Time, inherent nature, necessity, chance, the elements, the wombs or the person (should they) be considered as the cause? It cannot be a combination of these, because of the existence of the soul. Even the soul is powerless in respect of the cause of pleasure and pain.[1]

Then, the same Upanishad continues: —

He is the beginning, the source of the causes, which unite
(the soul with the body). He is to be seen as beyond the
three kinds of time (past, and future), and as without
parts having worshipped first that adorable God who has
many forms, the origin of all being, who abides in one's
thoughts.[2]

In the Upanishads, cause is also taken in the sense of the
ground. A series of examples can be quoted in this respect.
Shvetaketu Aruneya's father asked his son when he returned
having studied all the Vedas, thinking himself well read, whether
he learnt "By which the un-hearable becomes heard, the
unperceivable becomes perceived, the unknowable becomes
known."[3]

Similarly, the Taittiriya Upanishad says, 'that verily, from
which these beings are born, that by which, when born they
live, that into which, when departing, they enter, that seek to
know. That is *Brahman*.'[4]

In the Chhandogya Upanishad, we find that the substratum of the world, or the first cause is Being. 'In the beginning,
there was Being alone, one without a second.'[5]

2. THE CREATION OF THE PHYSICAL WORLD

It is natural that the human mind when it becomes reflective,
wants to know the ultimate substance from which this world is
created. In the Upanishads, various ideas are to be found as to
the nature of this ultimate substance. These may be conve-
niently grouped under three classes: (1) Those views according to which the ultimate substance is water, fire, air, space or
the life principle—the *prana*; (2) The second view accepts Be-

ing or Non-Being as the ultimate source of this world; (3) The third view is that there is a creator of the world who is a person. Over and above these three classes, there is also the notion of emanation from the Atman.

(i) Water as the Ultimate Substance:

The Brihadaranyaka tells us that water was the source of all things whatsoever: "In the beginning, verily, the Water alone existed; from the Waters was born *Satya* or Truth."[6]

(ii) Fire:

In the Upanishads, we do not find fire as the origin of all things explicitly mentioned. A passage in the Kathopanishad tells us that fire having entered the universe, assumed all forms.[7] The Chhandogya tells us that fire was the first to come out of the Being, and from fire came water and from water the earth.[8] At the time of dissolution, the earth goes back to water, the water to fire and the fire to the Being. Thus though Being is the ultimate source, Fire is accepted as the first to be born of Being.

(iii) Air:

Raikva holds the theory of air as the final absorbent of things and probably also as the origin of these things. In the Chhandogyopanishad Raikva observes: "When fire is extinguished, it goes to the air, when the sun sets, it goes to the air, when the moon sets, it goes to the air, when the waters dry up, they go to the air. Thus verily Air is the final absorbent of all things whatsoever."[9]

Here it is suggested that air is the ultimate substance to which everything finally goes and, therefore, is the origin also of all things.

(iv) Space:

In the Chhandogya Upanishad it has been stated by P. Javali: "All these beings emerge from space and are finally absorbed in space; space is verily, greater than any of these things; space is the final habitat."[10] In the same Upanishad another passage says: "Space is really higher than fire. In space, are both the sun and the moon, the lightening and the stars. It is by space that man is able to call...In space and after space are all things born. Meditate upon space as the highest reality."[11]

(v) Prana:

Prana constitutes the life of every living thing. It is the life-principle. It is the cosmic vital principle. In the Chhandogya it is said: "It is into Prana that all these beings enter and it is and form Prana that they originally spring."[12] Again "Prana is verily the final absorbent, for when sleeps his speech is reduced into Prana, his eye, and his ear and his mind are all absorbed in Prana. It is Prana which is the final absorbent of all these things."[13] The supremacy of Prana has been pointed out by Sanatkumara to Narada. The Chhandogya thus says that "Just as all the spokes of a wheel are centred in its navel, similarly all these beings and in fact, everything that exists is centred in Prana."[14] Kaushitaki says that, "Prana is the ultimate Reality, the mind being its messenger, the eye the protector, the ear the informant, and the speech the tire-woman. To this Prana as the ultimate Reality, all these beings make offerings, without Prana having ever sought them."[15] The above statements show that Prana has been thought to be not the ultimate source of everything but is the basic principle on account of which human personality functions.

(vi) Being or Not-Being—as the Beginning of Creation:

In the Chhandogya Upanishad we find the idea that in the beginning, being alone existed. This Being wanted to be many and there came out fire, from fire, water and from water, earth.[16] These three, fire, water and earth seemed to be the three ultimates which exist in all things having name and form.[17] The sun for example is a form, a name. What really exist in the sun are the three colours of fire (red), water (white) and earth (black).[18]

Here what exactly is the nature of this primeval Being is very difficult to understand. It seems it is just a metaphysical entity without a name and form. How out of this indeterminate something—the three original material causes of the world came out is not clear. It only suggests that it is to avoid the problem of the first cause that this idea of the primeval Being was entertained. The indefinable one was at the Beginning. But when the Upanishad suggests that this Being thought 'let me be many, let me create'[19], we are led to accept that Being is personalized—and acts like a creator God, though His nature is inexplicable.

There are other statements in the Upanishads where we find that in the beginning there was Not-Being. For example in the Taittiriya Upanishad it has been stated 'in the beginning there existed only Not-Being. From it Being was born.'[20] Here again what exactly is meant by this Not-Being is not easy to understand. But it is an attempt to go beyond anything definite, even Being as the ultimate. Not-Being is just void, which has also been referred to as the ocean of Night in the Rigvedic Nasadiya Sukta and as Death in the Brihadaranyaka Upanishad.[21] In the Nasadiya Sukta this ultimate has been said to be beyond both Being and Not-Being. Thus the ultimate source—or the First Cause—is unmatchable and as such is not even referred to as Being or Not-Being. That is beyond all relations.

(vii) The Ultimate Creator—a Person:

According to this view there was only a Creator in the beginning. He wanted to create and there arose two principles one subtle and the other gross—one may be said as material, the other spiritual. Thus in the Prashnopanishad we find that at the beginning of creation, the creator had a desire to create and, for that he practiced penance. Then he created a pair namely Rayi and Prana, a gross and a subtle principle with the desire of creating all existence whatsoever from them. The moon is matter, he says, while the sun is spirit. It was in this way that the creator was able to create all the dual existence whatsoever in the world.[22] In a similar spirit does the Taittiriyopanishad tells us that

> ...the creator at the beginning of things practiced pen-
> ance and having practiced penance created all things
> that exist; and having created them entered into them,
> became himself both the manifest and the un-manifest,
> the defined and the undefined, the supported and the
> unsupported, the conscious and the unconscious, the true
> and the false.[23]

(viii) The Notion of Emanation:

The Taittiriyopanishad tells us: "From the Atman, first came out space, from space air, from air fire, from fire water and from water earth."[24] Here we find the five different Elements, which came out progressively one after another from the primeval Atman. This suggests something like emanation. The Atman "created" space, and from space comes out air, and so on. At the time of dissolution, the earth goes back to water, water to fire, fire to air, air to space and space to the eternal atman. This passage of the Taittiriya is very significant. For the first time we have a definite enumeration of the five different elements. Secondly, Atman does not create the universe out of an external '*upadana*', but that the universe is rather an emanation of the Atman. It is both the material and the efficient cause of the world. The world then is the gradual modification of the Atman. The Chhandogya Upanishad says that, "by knowing the clay, all that is made of clay becomes known. The modification is only a name arising from speech; the truth is that it is only clay."[25] In the Upanishads the Atman is identified with *Brahman*. The Taittriya says that *Brahman* is the cause of the creation, sustenation and destruction of the universe.[26] In the Kena Upanishad we find that *Brahman* is referred to as the prime mover of all things: By whom impelled soars forth the mind projected? By whom enjoined goes forth the earliest breathing?... That which is the hearing of the ear, the thought of the mind.[27]

The manifestation of the world out of Brahman is like the ejection of the cobweb out of a spider.[28]

3. THE PHYSICAL WORLD AND THE RELATION BETWEEN MAN AND NATURE

In the Upanishads as it has been shown that there is an ultimate Tattva from which gradually the world has been evolved and though it is true that the Upanishadic thinkers' main pursuit is the search after the One, the Brahman, the ultimate Reality, they are not oblivious of the many, the world, the phenomena. And it is also true that though the Upanishadic think-

ers have given explanations for the creation, evolution or emanation of the world, their main interest was rather metaphysical than cosmological. In a sense the thinkers of the Upanishads
were more realistic and practical because they were concerned
with one of the vital problems of life—the problem of suffering.
Suffering or '*dukha*' is inevitable in life. It is not merely the
suffering because of the want of material comforts or because
of social maladjustment. Suffering has been taken in the wid-
est sense including suffering of man at the mental plane as
well. A search was for the absolute cessation of suffering. Man
may suffer amidst plenty; the most powerful may suffer if no-
body loves him. Thus the suffering on the human level is subtle
and complex and it is almost impossible to remain free from
suffering and enjoy permanent happiness.

Thus the desire for liberation or '*mukti*' in the beginning
was *dukha-mukti*, a merely practical demand of the human
soul. We may say, therefore, during this period of Indian philosophy the Upanishadic enquiry originated as a practical demand, a man's encounter with his life in the world. In India,
therefore, philosophy did not begin in wonder, but it began
because of a necessity, which the realistic human mind in India felt.

And this did not come as a sudden flash of imagination;
the discovery of the Upanishadic truth was the result of deep
analysis and profound experiences of life as lived. The
Upanishadic thinkers saw that human desire is the most dynamic aspect of his inner life and though it leads to painful
consequences it cannot be easily controlled. Desire is not an
abstract idea. When a man desires he desires for something.
Every desire has a concrete reference to some particular object. Desire, therefore, forces the '*Jivatman*' to go forward and
get his object of a desire and here begins the confrontation
with the world and consequent misery. This desire shows that

the man who desires something feels himself incomplete without it. But after getting the object of his desire he cannot remain forever happy and peaceful; no sooner his one desire is satisfied another originates. This point has been very lucidly brought out in the Kathopanishad where the God of Death grants all worldly pleasures to Nachiketa.[29] He refuses outright to be imprisoned in these chains: "Ephemeral things: that which is a mortal's, O End-maker, even the vigour of all the powers, they wear away, even a whole life is slight indeed. Thine be the vehicles: Thine be the dance and song."[30] This shows that man always feels himself incomplete and limited, and he wants something more for his completion and fulfillment. This again proves that man always wants to transcend his finitude but the continuous procession of desires makes him also conscious that all these objects, which he is hankering after cannot give what he really wants.

But why this is so? Why is all that even after getting the object of his desire he is not satisfied permanently? The experience of life has taught man that the object of his desire after achieving it does not remain an object of his desire because it has lost its charm and novelty. It has become old and hackneyed. Thus to put it in another way the Upanishadic mind thought that if there is something which does not change, but which remains for ever interesting and new after-realising that man may be for ever happy. This is well elucidated in the Katha while explaining the nature of two different paths—the path of the good, i.e., *Sreyas*, and the path of the pleasant, i.e., *Preyas*.[31] Thus an analysis began. Each object of the world, the dearest and nearest, the most beautiful and the most pleasant was considered and seriously evaluated but nothing proved to be permanent or everlasting. In other words the Upanishadic thinkers discovered that there was nothing in the external world, which did not change.

Then the search began within the inner world of man. The modes of sensuous experiences, the fleeting passions and emotions, the uncertain sentiments and moods, all proved to be just passing events. But at last they discovered that there is something within this inner world of man, the very core or center of his personality or being, which remains unchanging. That is why a man takes himself as identical, the same person from birth to death; though factually he changes physically, mentally and in every sense, as he grows older and older. The three-year-old baby, from the common-sense standpoint and for all practical purposes is not the same person when he is a twelve-year old by studying in a school. And this boy certainly changes physically and intellectually when he becomes a student in a university. Yet he never doubts that he is not the same person throughout. How is this so? How in spite of the continuous changes a man retains his identity? How does he know that all the events of his life are events of his life? He is as it were experiencing throughout, the objects of his experience are changing but he as an experient remains the same. This indicates that there is an unchanging principle at the center of man's subjectivity amidst the changing modes of the world as objects. This is the point so dramatically discussed in a dialogue between Prajapati and Indra, narrated in the Chhandogya.[32]

The Upanishadic philosopher discovers finally something, which is unchanging and remains forever new. Everything in the world may lose its interest and charm, may become old, but he himself remains for ever the same.[33] The Upanishadic seers have named this innermost subject as Atman. If a man realizes Atman he realizes something, which is eternally the same, which will never become old. Here, therefore, is a clue to a culmination of all desires. The *Mundaka* tells us that all his desires come to an end, when he attains the fulfillment of the highest desire, namely the realization of the Atman.[34] The

Shveta maintains that having realized the Atman, he finds eternal happiness everywhere.[35] Here is, therefore, a possibility that no desire world emerge again. This is indeed the greatest discovery through psychological analysis by the Upanishadic philosophers. The self is to be known not as an object, but it is to be experienced as the fundamental *Tattva*. How these experiences are to be attained has been explained by the later systems of Indian thought by various methods.

In the Vedas, if we accept the naturalistic interpretation as suggested by Sayanacharya and the western scholars, man's position with relation to the world was of utter dependence and he was at the mercy of the mighty powers of Nature or the deities. For getting rid of suffering, man used to pray and ask for the blessings of gods to be relieved of his distress. Later on, as the concept of the Rita developed into the idea of a cosmic moral power (so much so that performing the rituals and sacrifices as laid down in the scriptures) the deities were considered to be under the obligation of fulfilling the demands of man.

But as experiences became more extensive, man came to realize that all his prayers were not heard by the gods and goddesses, nor his performing the rituals and sacrifices with utmost care would secure certainty of his freedom from the miseries in life. In spite of prayers and sacrifices, there were famines, epidemics, floods, earthquakes and battles. As a natural consequence, the intelligent and more reflective section of the people tried to search for a new solution. Through the Aranyaka to the Upanishads, we find the progress of the search and the ultimate solution—know thyself—'*Atmanam viddhi*' for *Dukha-mukti*.

Here, therefore, emerges a new concept, which was no more in the Vedas. In the Vedas, man depended on the mercy of Nature but in the Upanishads man depends on his own ability and effort. The Upanishads have given man dignity and confidence for going beyond Nature.

Not only this, man discovers now the true nature of his relation with the universe. He is part and parcel of this universe, [36] yet he cannot be considered as an ordinary object like other objects. He has discovered the core of his subjectivity and finds through direct experiences '*tattvas*' of different manifestations of Reality that in the subtlest form he is one with the Reality. In his search for true subject, he is to penetrate beyond the five sheaths (*Koshas*), i.e. *annamaya, paranamaya, manomaya, vijnanamaya*, and even *anandamaya*, the sheath of bliss. The true subject or Atman—the Reality in man and *Brahman*—the Reality in the universe, are one and the same. Here is an equation, which is complete, and the same. Here is an equation, which is complete, **Brahman = Atman**. This is the chief point of Upanishadic teaching and is expressed in the 'great sayings' (*mahavakyas*) like '*Tat tvamasi*'[37] and '*Aham brahmasmi*'[38]. Deussen rightly observes: "It was here that for the first time, the original thinkers of the Upanishads to their immortal honour, found it when they recognized our Atman, our inmost individual being as the *Brahman*, the inmost being of universal nature and all her phenomena."[39] He understands now the true nature of relation between the One and the Many, between unity and diversity. He now understands that he is both *Anu* and *Virat*, the microcosm and the macrocosm. This is indeed the greatest discovery the man has ever made.

REFERENCES

[1]　Shveta Upa. 1. 1-2. (The Principal Upanishads by Dr. Radhakrishnan)

[2.]　Shveta Upa, VI. 5 (Radhakrishnan)

[3.]　Chhand. Upa. VI. 1-3 (Radhakrishnan)

[4.]　Tait. Upa III. I. I.

[5.]　Chhand. Upa. VI. I. I.

6. Brihad. Upa. V. 5. 1.
7. Katha Upa. II. 5.
8. Chhand. Upa. I. 9. I.
9. Chhand. Upa. IV. 3. 1-2.
10. Chhand. Upa. 1. 9. 1.
11. Chhand,. Upa. VII. 12. 1.
12. Chhand. Upa. 1. 2. 5.
13. Chhand. Upa. IV. 3. 3.
14. Chhand. Upa. VII. 15. 1.
15. Kaust Upa. II. 1.
16. Chh. Upa. VI. 2. 104.
17. Chh. Upa. VI. 3, 2-3.
18. Chh. Upa. VI. 4. 1-4.
19. Chh. Upa. VI. 2. 1-4.
20. Taitt. Upa. II. 7.
21. Brihad. Upa. 1-2. 1-2.
22. Prashna Upa. 1. 3-13.
23. Taitt. Upa. II. 6.
24. Taitt. Upa. II. 1.
25. Chhand. Upa. VI. 1. 4.
26. Taitt. Upa. III. 1. 1.
27. Kena. Upa. I. 1-3.
28. Brihad. Upa. II. 1. 20.
29. Katha Upa. 1-25.
30. Katha Upa. 1-26.
31. Katha Upa. 1.2. 1-2.
32. Chh. Upa. VIII. 7. 12.
33. Brihad. Upa. III. 2.2.
35. Shveta Upa. VI. 12.
36. Brihad. Upa. III. 2. 13.
37. Chh. Upa. VI. 8. 7.
38. Brihad. Upa. I. 4. 10.
39. *Philosophy of the Upanishàds*, P. 40.

3

NYAYA-VAISHESHIKA ATOMISM AND THE STATUS OF JIVATMAN

1. THEORY OF CAUSALITY

The Two systems of Indian Philosophy—the Nyaya and the Vaisheshika though independent in their origin are closely allied in their common sense and realistic outlook. So far as the physical world is concerned, the theory of the Nyaya is the same as that of the Vaisheshika. The Vaisheshika theory, however, has given a more detailed explanation, and the Nyaya has accepted it. As it is known later on these two systems have actually been synthesized as in the works like Tarka-sangraha and Karikavaei. The spirit of synthesis was already there in the *Vatsyayana bhashya* but formally this synthesis appeared in the works like Saptapadarthi in the tenth century. Though there are differences in regard to many aspects of the two systems, concerned, their theory is the same.

The common sense and realistic view regarding creation must be based on the concept of causation. It will be convenient for us to begin how the Nyaya-Vaisheshika explains causation.

In this system a cause and realistic view regarding creation must be based on the concept of causation. It will be convenient for us to begin by considering how the Nyaya-Vaisheshika explains causation.

In this system a cause is defined as an invariable (*niyata*) unconditional (*ananyatha siddha*) antecedent of an event.[1] There are three important points in this definition, and these may be stated as follows: (i) The cause is an antecedent to the effect, the cause precedes the effect (*Purvabhavitam*). (ii) The antecedence of the cause is invariable and it must invariably precede the effect (*Niyatapurvabhavitam*). (iii) Its unconditionality or necessity, it must unconditionally precede the effect (*Ananyathasiddha*). We examine the implications of these points in the following lines: —

The Naiyayika does not agree with those who maintain that the cause is only a logical prius of the effect. The word 'antecedent' clearly resolves causal relation into one of time.

Again the word 'antecedent' implies the numerical difference arises only where there are two distinct facts. The effect, itself in a different form, but a creation *de novo*. Although a cause is necessarily an antecedent but an antecedent is not a cause. An invariable antecedent alone can be a cause. A vehicle carrying the clay of which a pot is made, is an antecedent to the pot, but not a cause, for the clay may be brought either by the ass of the potter or by his servant. So the vehicle is not a cause because its antecedence to the pot is accidental and not invariable. A causal antecedent is invariable in the sense that it never fails to be an antecedent.

But the invariable antecedence of cause does not necessarily lead to the effect. Clay is the invariable antecedent of the pot but it cannot be held that where there is clay there is a pot. It may be held that clay alone is not the cause of a pot, but clay together with accessories, such as a potter and his stick, etc.

To exclude such causal antecedents, which are not invariable, the Naiyayika has to refer his definition by adding the attribute ananyathasiddha. He thus insists that the cause must be necessary to the occurrence of the effect. To determine the necessary cause of an event for the production of the effect the main task is to eliminate all antecedents, which are irrelevant and superfluous. Such antecedents are of many kinds. Vishvanatha mentions five types of anyathasiddha[2]. These are the following: —

First, the qualities of a cause are mere accidental antecedents. The colour of a potter's staff is not the cause of a pot. Secondly, the cause of a cause or a remote cause is not taken to be a cause. The potter's father is not the cause of a pot. Thirdly, the co-effects of a cause are themselves not causally related. The sound produced by the potter's staff is not the cause of a pot, though it may invariably precede the pot. Night and day are not causally related. Fourthly, eternal substances like space etc., are not unconditional antecedents as cause. Fifthly, unnecessary things like the potter's ass etc., are not unconditional antecedents. Though the potter's ass may be invariably present when the potter is making a pot, it is not the cause of a pot. A cause must be unconditional and necessary antecedent.

The Nyaya-vaisheshika system distinguishes three kinds of causes, viz. (i) the *Samavayi karana* (material cause), (ii) the non-material cause (*asamavayi karana*), and (iii) *Nimitta karana* (accessory cause).

The Samavayi karana is defined as that in which the effect abides by the relation of inherence.[3] The threads are the Samavayi karana of the cloth since as components (*avayava*) of the cloth, they are not only responsible for its production but also constitute the substratum in which it subsists by inherence.

The Samavayi karana is necessarily a substance, for an effect can inhere in a substance alone[4]. The material cause may have for its effects a substance or a quality or an action. The threads, for instance, are held to be the material cause not only of the cloth, that is made out of them, but also of their own colour and of their dropping down from the hand of a careless weaver.

The asamavayi karana is that which inheres in the material cause and helps the production of the effect[5]. It is of two kinds accordingly as the nature of its relation to the material cause varies. One kind of non-material cause is related to the material cause of its effect directly by means of inherence, as when the conjunction of the yarn is held to be the non-material cause of the cloth.

A rather complex relation indirectly connects the second kind of asamavayi karana with the material cause. It arises from its inherence in that in which the latter also inheres. An example of this kind is the colour of the yarn, which is held to be the asamavayi karana of the colour of the cloth. The colour of the cloth inheres in its own material cause, viz., the cloth, the cloth in its turn inheres in the yarn, and so also does the colour of the yarn.

The *nimitta karana* is different from the two kinds of causes mentioned above.[6] It is neither the sustaining locus of an effect nor anything bound up with the existence of the effect through the medium of that locus—which both are the characteristics of the material and non-material causes respectively. The *nimitta karana* is a purely extrinsic factor, though indispensable to the production of the effect. The weaver, his apparatus, his operation or any other factor necessary for the production of a piece of cloth, is the accessory cause of the cloth. According to *uddyotkara* the *nimitta karana* is the principle karana[7]. It is as Keshava Mishra says, the *cause par excelence*.[8]

Does the causation imply manifestation (*avirbhava*) or origination (*arambha*)? In other words, is the effect a preexisting thing appearing in a developed form or is it a new creation? Nyaya-vaisheshika adopts the latter position. According to it the effect is a thing, which comes into beginning negating its previous non-existence. This is *asatkaryavada*, the doctrine that the effect does not exist before its production.

The Naiyayika holds that the interpretation of production as manifestation does not stand scrutiny. The manifestation is apparently a contingent fact: so the question arises: Is the manifest pre-existent or not? If pre-existent, it means that there is no necessity for any causal operation to bring manifestation into existence. So when the effect exists in its cause, its manifestation is also present. But this means that the effect exists in its cause in a manifested form and does not stand in need of the causal operation for its manifestation. It cannot be contended that the pre-existent manifestation was in an un-manifested state before the operation for such a contention would necessitate the postulation of an infinite series of manifestations. If, however, the manifestation is pre-nonexistent we have to assume that it is created by the operation of the cause.

To all these criticisms, the Samkhya may of course reply by saying that the questions raised about manifestation may be raised about origination too. Is the origination of a pre-nonexistent effect pre-existent or not? On the first alternative the causal operation becomes unnecessary; on the second, an infinite regress is inevitable.

The Naiyayika, however, asserts that the difficulty does not arise, since origination is, according to him, not something that is produced. Origination of a positive effect (*bhava karya*), which alone can have a material cause—is really a case of the inherence of the effect in its material cause, or a case of the inherence of the universal existence in the effect. When a pot is said to come into existence, what is meant is that the pot comes to inhere in the material, clay, of which it is composed, or that existence comes to inhere in a pre-non-existent pot. And since the relation of inherence is an eternal fact, origination as a form of inherence precludes the necessity of another origination. Causation as origination, thus, involves no logical absurdity. The effect is neither merely an actualized potentiality of the cause nor is it merely the cause with a changed form. Cause and effect, therefore, are not identical in their essence, they are different; in fact, cause would not be cause if it did not produce something new or different.

We shall examine the Samkhya view and along with it discuss the grounds on which the Naiyayika disapprove of the view.

The Samkhya argues that a non-existent (*asat*) effect cannot by any means be brought into existence. No amount of technical skill can turn red into yellow. The effect therefore, should be supposed to pre-exist in some form or other.

The Naiyayika objects that the Samkhya makes no distinction between what is an absolute non-entity and what is merely pre-nonexistent. An absolute non-entity like a hare's horn is, by its very nature, non-existent for all time and is therefore un-producible. An effect, such as jar produced by a potter, is, on the contrary, non-existent only so long as it is not produced. So it is characterized by both non-existence and existence—non-existence before the necessary causal operation and existence after that operation until destruction. Such a position does not involve the law of contradiction since the contradictory properties—non-existence and existence—characterize the effect successively and not simultaneously.[9] A question arises: If the effect does not exist before its production, how can the property of non-existence be predicated of it at that time? To this the Naiyayika replies that when the property is non-existent, the effect can possess it only by not existing, for nothing can be both non-existent and existent at the same time.[10]

Then a fiction like the hare's horn can never be produced. But the Naiyayika replies that fiction is not produced, not because it is non-existent but because there is no cause of it. That alone is produced which has a cause. It is, however, not suggested that anything that is non-existent can be produced, or that non-existence by itself is a condition of production.[11]

Then Samkhya argues that there is a necessary relation between cause and effect. To deny this relation is to say that anything may produce anything. A definite cause produces a definite effect—because of a necessary relation between the two. And since no relation is possible in the absence of either of the *relata*, the things connected as cause and effect must exist together.

The Naiyayika observes that the fact that there is a necessary connection between cause and effect does not prove that the two terms exist together. No doubt, there is such a connection, but it is not true that such a connection is impossible without the contemporaneity of the effect with the cause. The peculiar efficiency of a class of things to produce a particular class of effect is established on the evidence of their agreement in presence and absence (*anvayavyatireka*).

The Samkhya advances another argument to prove the pre-existence of the effect. According to it, the cause and the effect are identical in nature and so when the cause exists, the effect cannot be non-existent. The Naiyayika, however, thinks the arguments to prove the identity of cause and effect are not only unconvincing but also fallacious. We never feel that a pot is the same thing as a lump of clay. They differ in their structure and configuration; they produce different results and serve different ends; they occur at different times and are expressed in different terms.[12]

We may make the following observations. Generally it is believed that according to both the Samkhya and the Nyaya-vaisheshika an effect like cloth is produced out of its cause, i.e., the threads, and that the only difference between the two theories is that while according to the Samkhya an effect is existent before its manifestation, according to the Nyaya-vaisheshika, it is non-existent. It is seldom realized that even according to the Samkhya a cloth as such does not exist before its manifestation; only its essence or substance-stuff exists in the form of threads. According to the Nyaya-vaisheshika theory, the non-existence of an effect before origination—implies that its essence or substance stuff also did not exist before. As it is observed: "A cloth according to the Nyaya-vaisheshika is not produced out of the threads, but in the threads."[13]

The new entity, viz., the effect cloth, appears in the form of a whole (*avayavin*) made up of the 'parts' (*avayavas*, i.e., threads). As the emergent effect is a new entity, it follows that it was altogether non-existent before. The essence or substance-stuff, which constitutes the effect—did not exist before its origination. The new emergent—whole—is not a mere aggregate (*samudaya*) of parts but quite different from them; it is a new entity, which has emerged as a result of the connections of parts. The effect, the 'whole' (cloth) resides in its cause, i.e., the parts (threads) by inherent relation. It is obvious here that according to the Nyaya-vaisheshika theory, the material cause and the effect are always, in the form of 'parts' and the 'whole', and the whole necessarily resides in its cause (the parts) by relation of inherence. Thus the effect is produced in the form of an *avayavin* in the parts, which are the material cause. The cause (threads) continues to exist even after the origination of the effect (cloth). In other words, the cloth is not produced out of the threads, but in the threads. The threads do not impart their essence to the cloth for the simple reason that the threads continue to exist intact side by side with the cloth. The threads are the cause of the cloth in the sense that they are the condition precedent to the origination of the cloth. It is said: —

The position is similar to the Buddhist theory of *Pratiyasamutpada* in so far as according to both of them a cause does not transfer its own essence to its effect. The only difference is that while according to the Buddhist theory, the preceding cause—moment is totally annihilated before the origination of its effect, according to the Nyaya-vaisheshika theory the cause contains its existence and holds its effect in itself.[14]

The Samkhya maintains that a cause changes into the state of its effect, but the essence of the cause and the effect is identical. For instance, when a gold vessel is broken and changed into a different form, the change occurs only in the form of gold (*bhava*) but not in the substance (*dravya*) gold.15 thus the Samkhya theory of change of the form without any change in the essence-stuff of the cause, inevitably leads to the Vedantic theory of *vivartavada*. If the threads and the cloth are essentially identical, the change from the threads to the cloth must be held to be unreal.

It is argued: "The Nyaya-vaisheshika has created a world in which there is constant birth but no death so far as the cause and effect series is concerned. New children (effects) are born but the parents (causes) never die. For example, when a jar is produced from the atoms through the process of *dvy-anuka*, *try-anuka*, etc., there accumulate a series of substances—atoms, *dvy-anuka*, *try-anuka*, parts and further parts of the jar and finally the jar—where a previous cause has given birth to a new entity without itself being destroyed. This is repugnant to common sense. Now, in order to avoid this, if we were told to hold that the cause disappears when its effect is produced, we arrive at the full-fledged Buddhist doctrine that a cause disappears *in toto* without leaving any residue or without imparting any essence to its effect and there arises in its place an altogether new entity, i.e., the effect. It would thus, appear that the Buddhist theory of causation is merely the logical culmination of the Nyaya-vaisheshika theory."[16] It was here that Shamkara remarked that the Vaisheshika is a semi-nihilist (*ardha-vainashika*) in comparison with the Buddhist who is a full nihilist (*Sarva-vainasika*).[17] Vachaspati Mishra observes:—

The Vaisheshikas are semi-nihilists because while they accept as eternal the five substances, ether, time, space, soul and manas and the categories—*samanya, vishesha,* and *samavaya,* and also some qualities, they hold that the destruction of other objects (effects) comes about without the continuity of its cause—stuff (*Nirvayavinasa*), Hence, they are seminihilists.[18]

From the above arguments and counter arguments it is found that neither the Nyaya-vaisheshika nor Samkhya-yoga are convinced by the opponents' arguments; but each continues to hold its own views and thus we have two doctrines of causation, *Satkaryavada* and *asatkaryavada.*

The above theories of causation we propose to analyse here further and evaluate the merits of the arguments.

According to the Nyaya-vaisheshika, the effect is not in the cause as effect, that is to say if cause and effect are symbolically represented as 'A' and 'B', according to Samkhya-yoga 'B' is in 'A' before it emerges as 'B' (i.e. of course potentially) the Nyaya-vaisheshika will say that if 'B' was in 'A' then it was not 'A' but 'A'+'B'. If it is suggested that 'B' exists in 'A' not as 'B' but as 'A' then the cause is merely 'A' and cannot be said that 'B' exists in 'A' even potentially. From the common sense standpoint, which the *Satkaryavada* holds butter exists in the milk potentially. But this potential state of butter and actual butter are not the same. *Gaudapada* in his *Mandukya-karika* has analysed admirably the two positions of the

Satkaryavada and *asatkaryavada* suggesting that while one emphasises *necessity*, the other emphasises *novelty*. Both these aspects are mixed up in the idea of the cause-effect relation. Let us consider the problem from another angle. Every substance has matter and form. No substance is mere matter or mere form. Butter as a substance, therefore, if we take the often-quoted illustration, has matter and form. According to the Samkhya-yoga view, the matter of butter exists in the milk before it is produced as butter and common sense certainly approves it. According to the Nyaya-vaisheshika on the other hand, the form of butter does not exist in the milk. This also common sense approves. Therefore, the substance of the whole argument is that the matter of butter exists in the milk and the form of butter does not exist in the milk as its cause. Therefore, if somebody asserts that butter exists in the milk as its cause he really means the matter of butter whereas if somebody asserts that butter does not exist in the milk as its cause he means the form of butter. Therefore, both assertions are only half-truths. They are not so contradictory as they appear to be. It is only the question of a particular standpoint from which the event is explained.

2. ATOMISM AND THE PROCESS OF CREATION

According to the Vaisheshika, there are six categories of reality, viz., substance (*dravya*), quality (*guna*), action (*karma*), universal (*samanya*), particular (*vishesha*) and inherence (*samavaya*).[19] Kanada and Prashastapada mention only these six positive categories which are believed to cover the entire sphere of reality, including the subject and the object of thought. A seventh category viz., negation (*abhava*) has been added by the later exponents of the school.[20] Gautam in his Nyaya Sutra proposes a scheme of sixteen categories,[21] but on subtle scrutiny, it is established that he accepts the general metaphysical position of the Vaisheshika. As a matter of fact, eminent writers of the Nyaya school are found to have clearly expressed their approval of the Vaisheshika ontological scheme and the Vaisheshika principle of classifying and labeling the reals[22] while the Vaisheshika is mainly a study of reality itself in its various aspects, the Nyaya is a *pramanashastra*, an investigation into the problem of knowledge in its relation to reality.[23]

According to Prashastapada, the categories under which all reals are included are characterized by isness (*astitva*), namability (*abhidhevatva*) and knowability (*jneyatva*).[24] These reals exist as distinct categories and they also have the character of being knowable and expressible which means that they are real ontological categories and not intellectual constructs.

Shridhara explains 'isness' (*astitva*) as the distinctive character or nature (*Svarupa*) of a thing.[25] The real must possess a self-being, i.e., a distinctive self-identity, without which it would neither be what it is, nor different from what it is not. We have examined 'isness' as one of the criteria of reality. Still there are two more criteria, viz., knowability (*jnevatva*) and namability (*abhidheyatva*) to be examined. It is the nature of the real that by relating itself to and acting upon the human mind it produces therein the knowledge of itself. We may say that a real is whatever is knowable (*jneya*). Thus a real having its own self identity 'isness' also implies that it is a given fact, i.e., it can be an object of knowledge (*jnanayogya*). This is the second criterion of knowability. The third one, viz., namability logically follows from the second one for naming or verbal expression is nothing but thought externalized. The two later criteria of knowability and namability as a matter of fact do not add anything new to the concept of 'isness' but they rather bring out explicitly something that was implicit in the latter. So by the criterion of 'isness' we find that the Vaisheshika philosopher tries to emphasize that the real is what it is and not what we imagine of.

The Nyaya-vaisheshika realist conceives the universe as comprising an infinite number of independent substantive reals—the substances. Kanada defines substance as that which possesses qualities and actions, and is an inherent cause.[26] Substance has been conceived in this definition as the substratum (*asraya*) of qualities and actions. Here we find that something is presented to our mind through its qualities, which inhere in a substance.

According to Shridhara, substance apparently means more than merely something, which has qualities. It means, above something that is felt as self-subsisting, something that exists in its own right[27]. While qualities and actions exist and are intelligible, only in relation to substances, the latter is felt to exist independently of any foreign reference.

Kanada enumerates three distinct characteristics (*lakshana*) of substances, viz., substance is that which possesses action and qualities and is the inherent cause.[28] Here we examine the first characteristic, viz., action or motion. Motion, of course, need not be actual in all cases; even the mere possibility of motion in a thing entitles it to be classed as substance. But motion whether actual or potential, is always finite and limited in space and time (*murtatva*) and it cannot belong to ubiquitous substances like akasha, and time, etc., which are incapable of changing their position. The Nyaya-vaisheshika thinkers tried to defend Kanada by interpreting motion differently but ultimately they failed. It is clearly acknowledged that substance cannot be defined by means of motion as such. All that can be said is that whatever is mobile is necessarily substance, but no logical definition can be derived from this.

Kanada's second lakshana[29] is that substance possesses qualities. According to the Vaisheshika theory substance is the inherent cause (*samavayikarana*) of its qualities, and as the cause is the antecedent to the effect, the substance will be antecedent to its qualities and remain quality-less at the moment of its origination.

To avoid this difficulty the definition of substance as the substratum of quality has been interpreted by Vallabha, the author of *Nyayalilavati* to imply that substance is that which is never the substratum of the absolute non-existence (*atyantabhava*) of quality or such.[30]

The third *lakshana* of substance as proposed by Kanada is material cause (*Samavayikarana*). It is an established fact that a quality or an action can never be an inherent cause of anything, as by its very definition an inherent cause is that in which the effect directly inheres. An effect, be it substance, quality or action, must have a substratum to inhere in and this substratum is invariably a substance. Now it may be asked: "What is the effect that can be universally referred to substance as its inherent cause? It cannot be a specific quality like colour or sound because substance like time or space has no specific quality and so the definition would not extend to them. For this reason conjunction (*Samyoga*) or disjunction (*vibhaga*) has been suggested to be the effect which can be affiliated to all substances irrespectively.[31] Even eternal and ubiquitous substances must come into the relation of conjunction with or disjunction from another substance, conjunction and disjunction being qualities must have a substratum in which they can inhere as their cause and their inherent cause is substance. So the definition of substance as the inherent cause of conjunction or disjunction is complete and does not exclude any substance out of its scope.

Kanada enumerates nine different types of substance. They are the following: earth (*Prthivi*), water (*ap*), fire (*tejas*), air (*vayu*), ether (*akasha*), time (*kala*), space (*dic*), soul (*atma*) and mind (*manas*).[32] Here the first five are what are regarded as the ultimate elements (*bhutani*), time and space are quasi-material substances and the last two viz., mind and the soul stand for non-material reality.

The Nyaya-vaisheshika tries to explain the physical order of the world in terms of the five physical substances—earth, water, fire, air, and akasha. Every bhuta has some specific quality perceptible to an external sense.[33] Kanada defines earth in the following way: Earth possesses colour, taste, smell and touch.[34] Smell is established in earth.[35] Gautam observes: Smell, taste, colour, touch and sound are objects of the senses and qualities of the earth etc.[36] Water is described: "Waters possess colour, taste and touch and are fluid and viscid."[37] And then, "coldness is the special characteristic of water."[38] Fire is said to be: "Fire possesses colour and touch."[39] The special quality of fire is: "Hotness (is the characteristic) of fire."[40] Air is described as: "Air possesses touch."[41] Kanada gives so many arguments to prove the substance-ness of Ether: "These characteristics are not found in Ether."[42] "By the method of exhaustion (sound) is the mark of Ether."[43] (Ether is one), because there is no difference in sound which is its mark and because there exists no other distinguishing mark.[44]

The four bhutas, earth, water, fire and air are obviously material in character. Because they necessarily possess some of the important characteristics by means of which matter is ordinarily defined, for instance, such characteristics are size, shape, mobility, etc. These bhutas have been treated by the Nyaya-vaisheshika system as ultimate material principles, which are neither transmutable into one another nor reducible to a common ground. According to it each of them is fundamental and homogeneous kind of matter, characterized by its own specific quality. The four bhutas really represent four distinct types of concrete sense stimuli, earth, therefore, does not simply differ from water as a solid differs from a liquid but as fundamentally as odour differs from taste. In our perceptual experience of the external world, it is these specific qualities that come first and we know the substances as the objective fields or abiding grounds of these qualities. It has been rather attempted to differentiate these substances on the basis of the reactions of our sense to them. And this is exactly what the Nyaya-vaisheshika philosophers have done. As a matter of fact they were unable to adopt any other more satisfactory principle of differentiation than this, because they had to depend mostly upon the evidence of their senses for acquainting themselves with the facts of the external world.

It is common knowledge that a gross thing is produced by a combination of finer constituents. Hence we face three possibilities: First, the process of division may be endless. Secondly, the process of division may reach a point where no further division is possible because nothing is left to be divided. The ultimate nature of all things is absolutely void. Thirdly, the division may come to a definite point, which refuses to be further divided.[45]

The first alternative is ruled out because it is found to fail to render an account of the infinite variety of sizes possessed by sensible things. If a whole is divisible into parts and these parts into further parts and so on ad-infinitum. There will be no final unit of a determinate size and in the absence of such a unit there will be no logical basis for explaining different sizes.

The second alternative, viz., the essential void-ness of these is also ruled out because the process of division cannot be pursued to infinity as we have just examined. If the division is a finite process, it must come to a halt, either on the discovery of positive indivisible reals, which are always parts and never wholes or on the discovery that there is a nothing at the core. The latter hypothesis is untenable, because it involves a series of contradictions. Division is possible only if there is a thing to be divided. We find that the third alternative which holds that each material object is composed of a finite number of indivisible particles has thus to be accepted as the only possible explanation of its constitution.

Nyaya-vaisheshika, therefore, accepts there must be ultimate constituents, which they call Paramanus, which are the constituents of the objects of the world. Gautam defines atom: "An atom is that which is not capable of being divided."[46] Kanada observes: "The effect is the mark (of the existence) of the ultimate atoms."[47] So the Nyaya-vaisheshika system postulates the atom as the ultimate constituent of the material world. The Nyaya-vaisheshika thus proposes to explain the nature of the physical world with the help of their concept of Paramanu. The question arises: What is the process by which atoms contribute to the formation of gross bodies? The position of Nyaya-vaisheshika philosopher is that two *paramanus* combine to form a dyad (*dvanuka*) and three such dyads are the constituents of a triad (*tryanuka*), which is the smallest form of a gross body visible to the naked eye. Between atom and triad there is an intermediate entity called the dyad which takes a direct part in the formation of a triad.[48]

A question arises: What role does the dyad play in the formation of the gross bodies? Atoms cannot directly produce the gross bodies because in that case it would be absolutely unrecognizable. Moreover, if a gross body were to result from the combination of invisible atoms, the destruction of the body would imply its immediate disappearance because of the invisibility of its parts, i.e., atoms. The position is this that the disintegration of a gross body is gradual and takes place through a series of smaller and smaller bodies until we reach at the bottom the minimal gross body viz., the triad.[49] Thus the triad represents the first stage of perception of any gross body.

Now the question is: Do the atoms directly combine to produce a triad or is there any intermediate factor (viz., dyad) necessary? The Nyaya-vaisheshika position is that two atoms unite to form a dyad and three such dyads produce a triad. The atomic magnitude is held to be devoid of causal efficiency[50] that is why when two paramanus combine to produce a Dvayanuka (dyad) the dyad is not necessarily greater in magnitude than the paramanu.[51] Similarly the dyad also has no efficiency to produce something of a greater magnitude than itelf.[52]

Thus according to the Nyaya-vaisheshika we have magnitude only at the stage of the triad. But, there must be some explanation as to wherefrom this triad gets its magnitude if not from the *paramanu* or *dvayanuka*. The cause of gross magnitude (*mahattva*) in a triad of a substance is, according to the Vaisheshika philosopher, either the gross magnitude of its formative cause (*karana mahattva*) or the looseness of their conjunctions (*karana-pracaya*), or the plurality of their number (*karana bahuttva*).[53] The verification of the first alternative is found in the difference of size between two pieces of cloth when they are produced from the same number of threads woven together with the same degree of closeness. That one piece of cloth is of greater length than the other, is due to the greater length of the threads. The second alternative is verified by the increase in size of one piece of cloth over another when both of them are made up of threads that are equal in number and length. This can be due only to the threads being conjoined more loosely in the larger piece of cloth. The truth of the third alternative is verified by the fact that one piece of cloth is found to be larger than another even when both of them are produced from threads which are of the same length and which are woven with the same degree of closeness. The larger size of one of the two pieces of cloth is to be accounted for by the greater number of its threads.[54]

Atoms as well as dyads are both devoid of gross magnitude and incapable of loose conjunction, it is not possible to explain the production of grossness in a triad on the basis of the two alternatives. Naturally, it is the third alternative, which provides the necessary explanation. In other words, the Vaisheshika philosopher sets down the gross magnitude of a triad to the causal influence of the plurality of its constituents. To be more precise, it is maintained that the number of dyads that constitute a triad is three and the gross magnitude of the resulting triad is held to be due to the plurality of its formative cause and not to their magnitude.[55]

Hence we find that the magnitude of a dyad does not fare any better than that of an atom so far as it's bearing upon the formation of gross bodies is concerned. It is the number that is supposed to contribute to the production of gross magnitude. Here a question arises: Why is this causal efficiency denied to atoms? If the plurality of dyads can produce gross bodies, why not the plurality of *paramanus*? What is the logical necessity of a dyad? The Vaisheshika system offers a number of arguments in support of the dyad. It is argued that a substance of gross magnitude can be produced only from a plurality of substances, which are themselves products. If a single eternal substance like an atom were supposed to be independently productive, the condition for production would be perpetually present, and production would never cease. Moreover, such a supposition would make the product indestructible. So the dyads, which are the first produced substances and which have been shown to be devoid of gross magnitude, should be held to be directly productive of gross bodies.[56]

The existence of atoms has been already proved. If atoms exist and move, naturally they combine together. If they combine, it will necessarily result in a product. And this product cannot have greater magnitude than that of atoms on account

of the law mentioned above, it must be assigned a place between an atom on the one hand and a triad on the other.[57] This
is the reason why a dyad has been accepted.

Akasha:

Akasha is enumerated as the fifth substance in the Vaisheshika
philosophy. Akasha is believed to be a ubiquitous (*vibhu*) and
eternal substance (*Nitya*). It is one and is not susceptible to
division (*akhanda*). The only function of Akasha on the
Vaisheshika view is to afford a substantial basis for the phenomenon of sound.

There is only one Akasha so that it is by its very nature a
unique particular. According to Kanada and Prashastapada,
the oneness of Akasha is proved by the fact that sound cannot
be explained without the concept of Akasha as its ground.[58]
Akasha is an all-pervading (*vibhu*) substance. Its ubiquity follows from the consideration that there is no place, where sound
cannot be produced. In other words, it is possible for sound to
be produced anywhere because Akasha, the only originating
and sustaining ground of sound, is present everywhere.[59] From
the unity and ubiquity of Akasha its eternality follows.[60]

Time:

Time is held in the Nyaya-vaisheshika system as a unique all
pervading and eternal substance. It possesses no specific physical quality like colour and thus cannot be the object of perception. To the question, what is the source of our knowledge that
time exists, Kanada observes: Posterior in respect of that which
is prior, simultaneous, slow, and quick—such (cognitions) are
the marks of Time.[61]

Here first of all we shall try to examine the implications of
our notions of priority (*paratva*) and posteriority (*aparatva*).

The Vaisheshika tries to explain the notion of priority and posteriority independently of reference to time. According to him, priority or posteriority is a quality, which every generated substance possesses by virtue of its relation to a relatively large or small number of revolutions of the sun. In other words, when we say that an individual 'A' is prior to another 'B' it is equally true to say that 'B' is posterior to 'A', we really mean that 'A' is a contemporary of 'B' and has been connected with a larger number of solar revolutions than 'B'.[62] The fact is that solar motion is a well-known phenomenon of Nature and is found to be spontaneously presented as a qualifying element wherever we perceive an individual as prior or posterior to another.

But how can 'A' be connected at all with solar motion and be qualified by it? No direct connection through the relation of inherence is possible between them as the motion of the sun inheres in the sun and, as such, is connected with it alone. Nor can there be a relation of conjunction between 'A' and the revolving sun, which are widely separated from finite substances. But the notion of priority or posteriority as we have already seen implies a connection between 'A' and solar motion. As direct connection is out of the question, the two terms should be supposed to be related only indirectly through something forming the connecting link. This something according to the Vaisheshika must be a substance, which alone can be in conjunction both with the individual and with the sun in which its motion inheres. And this special substance is given the name of time.[63] Likewise; the concepts of simultaneity and succession and of quickness and slowness are the logical grounds for the influence of time.

Time is also presupposed in the operation of the causal principle. Causation is possible only in the case of an event which is contingent, i.e., which comes into being after having been previously non-existent. If there were no time, there could be no happening and things would either merely exist or not exist at all. Causality, thus, is found to be inexplicable without reference to time.[64]

The notion of time is also derived from our experience of change. Material bodies, whether inorganic or organic, are found to pass through successive states and modifications. And this can be explained only on the supposition that it is time that makes a difference to the bodies and helps their development or decay.

Absolute time is maintained by the Nyaya-vaisheshika realist to be an infinite ever-present continuant, which is not affected by the variations of time determinations. The plurality of time determination is relative but not unreal.

Space (*dic*):

Kanada tells us that it is because of space that, of two simultaneously existing bodies, one is perceived as in front of or behind another. "That which gives to such (cognitions and usages) as this (is remote) from this" (the same is) the mark of space.[65] Space, in other words, is that which sets up certain positional relations among co-existent bodies. It is substance and it is infinite and continuous[66] space is all-pervading.[67]

According to Prashastapada, and other classical writers, our perception of directions as east, and west, etc., is another independent proof of the existence of space.[68]

The qualities of space, as those of time are infinite extension, numerical unity, separateness, conjunction and disjunction.[69] Space is eternal since it is an in-composite substance and does not depend on anything for its existence.[70] Space is thus marked by absolute continuity (*akhandatva*). There can be no gaps in it. When we speak of discrete portions of space we actually do not speak about space as it really is, but deal with it in an artificial manner for achieving some theoretic or practical end. There is only one space. It is wrong to suppose that corresponding to our ideas of directions as east, west, south, and north, etc., there are different spaces. If akasha is the special inherent cause of sound, space (like time) is the common locative cause of both sound and cognition and all other products.[71]

We have seen above how the Nyaya-vaisheshika accepts the elementary atoms of earth, water, fire, and air, and the absolute *Akasha, Kala,* and *Dic* are the ultimate constituents of the physical world. But the universe is not only the physical world but it includes *manas* and *Atman.*

The Nyaya-vaisheshika then explains the creation of the universe. Here this system accepts the existence of God as creator though in the sense of an architect, that is to say the ultimate constituents both material and non-material are there already existing and God only helps the designing of the universe with these materials. The Nyaya-vaisheshika describes the process of creation accepting a teleological concept. The universe is created with a purpose. The purpose is to provide an environment for the ignorant and suffering souls to work out their liberation.

The most important point about this Nyaya-Vaisheshika cosmology is that it is cyclic. There is Srishti and Pralaya and again a new Srishti and Pralaya—this rotation goes on. Thus before a new creation the ultimate physical constituents are there and also the souls with their respective *adrishtas.* The motive for the creator God is to make a world where these souls, according to the consequences of their karma, can fulfil their destinies.

In the following paragraphs we shall examine the process of creation: —

It is held that after pralaya there is a period of cosmic rest. The accumulative *adrishtas* of the *jivas* then come to operate through the Divine Will for the creation of beings and objects suited to their needs for the purpose of reaping the fruits of

their past deeds. Through the help of these *adrishtas* conjunctions are produced between the *Atman* and *paramanus*. These
conjunctions produce motion in the ultimate particles of the
air, which then join together so as to form *dvyanuka*, *trasrenu*,
and consequently, the final air, which remains vibrating in the
sky. Thus the creation begins with the creation of Air
(*Mahanvayu*). Air possesses continuous and strong vibration;
because (i) it is the first product, (ii) there is intense velocity in
it, and (iii) no other substance which would have put obstacles
in its way, has been, as yet produced.[72] This *mahanvayu*, which
is a kind of a substratum produces heaviness in it and under-
goes a process of condensation and water is produced, from
the watery *paramanus* through the usual process.[73] After this
further condensation takes place and from the *paramanus* of
earth is produced the big earth, which exists in a solid form.
After the production of earth, in that very reservoir of water, a
being overpowered by anything else remains luminous. In this
way, the four *mahabhutas* are produced one after the other.

This being done, the *paramanus* of fire and earth are combined by the divine will to produce the cosmic egg, Brahmanda.
From this Brahmanda comes out by the Divine Will the
chaturmukha Brahma who is endowed with the infinite power
and wisdom to work out the details of creation. It is this *Brahma*
who creates the living beings. Being endowed with intellect,
dispassion and other extraordinary powers, and also, knowing
the time of the fructification of the past deeds of beings, *Brahma*
begins to create, First, there are mental productions, such as
Prajapatis, *Manus*, several groups of *devas*, *rishis* and *pitris*
and next, out of his mouth, arms, thighs and feet are produced
the four *varnas*, Brahmana, Kshatriya, Vaishya, and Shudra
respectively and also other living beings of all grades, high and
low. Having produced these, *Brahma* associates them with
adequate degree of *dharma*, *jnana*, *vairagya* and *aisvarya*
according to their past deeds. He also adds to them the proper

degree of *adharma, ajnana* and *anaisvarya* and the result of these namely, pleasure, pain, and the rest.[74]

In this process of creation, we find, therefore, the *jivatmanas* are placed in the environments, which they deserve according to the merits and demerits of their actions done in their previous existence. Human actions are very complex and the consequences produced are complicated because of both moral and immoral tendencies that induce them to do whatever they desire. Therefore, the characteristics of the environment must necessarily be as varied as these of their actions. The result, therefore, is that we have a world of infinite varieties and complexities. The idea behind cosmology is that no other agency can create such a complex world to accommodate all the consequences of all actions of all the souls that belong to this world except God.

3. THE STATUS OF PHYSICAL WORLD AND ITS RELATION TO MAN

Neither Kanada nor Prashastapada felt any need to prove the existence of the external world, although later Vaisheshika writers found it necessary to do so in order to combat the idealistic arguments denying such existence, particularly those of the Buddhist idealists. Common sense never doubts the reality of the external world. Whatever we experience must have an external existence. The guiding principle of the Nyaya-vaisheshika realism is that sense experience is the sole criterion of our acceptance of the reality of external objects.[75] The Nyaya-vaisheshika Realism is based on the analysis of the common experience of all mankind, which accepts the reality of the external world as made of many realities—atoms, individual souls, minds, and God, existing external to one another in space, time and akasha.

Common experience reveals that the world consists of infinite objects, which are called substances (*dravyas*). These substances are full of properties (*gunas*) so they are in the relation of the container and the contained (*adhardheyabhava*) and therefore the two cannot be identical. Essentially they are different. For instance, in the case of the experience of a white cow, the white colour is experienced as a property, which resides in the substratum cow, and therefore, whiteness and cowness are different in essence. The realistic structure is rooted in the essential differentiations between the substratum and its properties (*dharma-dharmi-bheda*).[76] All the categories accepted by the Nyaya-vaisheshika follow as corollaries from this very principle.

Substratum (*dharmin*) is always in the form of a substance (*aravya*). But the properties (*dharmas*) residing in a substratum are of various kinds. Some like colour etc., appear stationary. They are called qualities (*guna*) others are temporary in nature, for example the motion of the body. They are called movements (*karma*) of the innumerable objects of our experience, some are so similar that they are designated by a common noun and there must be something common to all individuals. That common element was termed as universal (*Samanya* or *Jati*). Each and everything of the world has its own speciality and particularity, which differentiates it from others. It was termed as *vishesha*. Of the five categories, so far mentioned, the last four are of the nature of the properties (*dharmas*) and are only found to be residing in the substratum (*dharmin*), which is the first category i.e., substances. Although the properties (*dharmas*) are in essence different from *dravyas*, they cannot exist as separate from or independent of a *dravya*. Therefore, the relation between the former and the latter cannot be an ordinary one, called conjunction (*Samyoga*). A sixth category, therefore, in the form of special relation called *Samavaya* was assumed. To these six categories originally accepted by the system, a seventh one namely *abhava* (nonexistence) was added later on.

The Nyaya-vaisheshika theory of causation also rests on the same basic principle, the differentiation between properties and their substratum (*dharma-dharmi-bheda*). An effect-like cloth, which is experienced as produced in its cause, viz., threads, is like a property of the threads, which are its substrata. A substratum and its properties being different in essence, according to the above-mentioned principle, the Nyaya-vaisheshika school, true to its principle declared that the essence of cloth was different from that of threads. Thus the principle of differentiation between properties and their substrata (*dharma-dharmi-bheda*) is the corner stone of the Nyaya-vaisheshika realism.

But could the Nyaya-vaisheshika adhere to the last to the principle that every cognition must have its counterpart in the external world? No, for example, in a case of recognition (*pratyabhijna*) where something does not exist as an outside reality, enters into our experience. In the example, he is the same Devadatta whom I saw at Varanasi, the past condition of Devadatta being at Varanasi is not present before my eyes, there is no reality-like Devadatta's being at Varanasi existent now, yet it does enter our cognition.

Then the acceptance of the *Svarupa-Sambandha* by which *abhava* (non-existence) resides in an external object is not an external reality but only a mental one.

Then the cognition of duality (*dvita*), which has no corresponding reality at the time of cognition, goes reverse to the principle of the Nyaya-vaisheshika. Shridhara himself declares: "There is nothing extraordinary in the production of an object by knowledge. It is well known that pleasure, etc., are produced by knowledge."[77]

Kanada gives the following marks of self. The ascending life-breath, the descending life-breath, the closing of the eye-lids, the opening of the eye-lids, life, the movement of the mind, and the affections of the other senses and also pleasure, pain, desire, aversion and volition are marks of the existence of the self.[78] Likewise Gautam holds: "Desire, aversion, volition, pleasure, pain, and intelligence are the marks of self."[79] Kanada mentions the plurality of souls: "Plurality of selves is proved by status."[80] The peculiar feature of the system is that it makes *jnana* or knowledge an attribute of the self and that too not an essential but only an adventitious one. Consciousness arises when the soul is in contact with the mind, the sense organs and the external objects. The self thus differs from matter only in that is may become conscious and not that itself is sentient in nature.

The system treats mind as a substance. Kanada describes the mark of mind: "The appearance and non-appearance of knowledge. On contact of the self with the senses and the objects or the marks (of the existence) of the mind."[81] Each self has its own *manas*, which is merely an instrument of knowing and is therefore, as inert as any other sense. Kanada observes: "From the non-simultaneity of volitions, and from the non-simultaneity of cognitions (it follows that there is only) one (mind) (in each organism).[82] So man is *Atman* combined with *manas* and sense organs.

Kanada himself does not refer to God. His aphorism—the authority of the Veda is due to his (or their) word[83] has been interpreted by the commentators in the sense that the Veda is the world of God. All the great commentators of the Nyaya-vaisheshika system including Prashastapada, Shridhara and Udayana are theistic and some of them have given arguments to prove the existence of God.

Undoubtedly Nyaya-vaisheshika advocates realism, pluralism, and atomism, but its atomism is not purely materialistic or mechanistic while giving a philosophy of atomism it does not ignore the moral nature of the world. All finite physical objects are created out of four kinds of atoms in the forms of dyads, triads, and other larger compounds arising out of them no doubt, but though the world is a physical system, the life and destiny of all individual selves are governed by the moral law of Karma. The creation of the world is explained in the light of the unseen moral principle (*adrishta*)[84], of individual souls and serves the moral dispensations.

When we critically evaluate, we find that the Nyaya-vaisheshika system is not a synthetic philosophy. It is mere commonsense explanation of the world. The system gives us a mere catalogue of categories without succeeding in synthesizing them. Through inherence it tried to synthesize the different categories but inherence itself proved to be quite shaky.[85]

The system holds that *Atman* is a substance, which is unintelligent in itself and becomes intelligent when it comes into the contact of mind (*manas*). The *Atman* is treated just like an object: And likewise it is regarded as innumerable, each having a peculiarity of its own. In this system the fate of the individual souls is not satisfactory. They have been reduced to the status of material objects.

In no way is the fate of God better. He is not even the creator of the world. He is a mere architect; innumerable atoms and innumerable selves are co-eternal with Him and therefore limit Him. He is simply a supervisor. And even as a supervisor He has to depend on the law of Karma for the creation of the world. He has simply to exert His Divine Will so that atoms may become dynamic according to the nature of the *adrishta* of the individual selves.

From the idea of different substances as mentioned in the Nyaya-vaisheshika system, we get the concept of man or *jivatman,* which is not very definite. *Jivatman* is a living and thinking being where the material, atom as his physical body, mind or *manas*, and also a substance called *Atman* by the system exist together as a unit. But it is clear that the concept

of *Atman* for the Nyaya-vaisheshika is not purely a spiritual
entity and therefore consciousness becomes an accidental quality of the self. The Nyaya-vaisheshika philosopher is not conscious of difficulty in regard to the concept of *Atman* based on
the *adhara-adheya sambandha* or substance-quality relation.
The *Atman* of the Nyaya-vaisheshika, therefore, is really the
jivatman, that is to say it is the man endowed with his sensuous
organs, the mind, though the Nyaya-vaisheshika has brought
in cognition or *jnana* as a higher type of quality than what is
possessed by the *manas* but that has not given us a true picture
of the Atman as a purely spiritual entity.

It appears, therefore, that the common sense realistic approach of the system does not allow it to consider the true
nature of man as a qualitatively different something above
Nature. The commonsense attitude keeps the man bound up
with the physical world. However, the Nyaya-vaisheshika philosopher might have tried his concept of self—that is the *jivatman*
or man remains part and parcel of this world, and not a higher
spiritual entity.

But this concept, which is positively oriented, has made
man highly responsible for working out his destiny. Man is to
work out his destiny remaining a part of Nature, and passing
through the pleasures and pains of life, he must realize his
goal.

But what is his goal? According to the Nyaya-vaisheshika
the goal or the highest end to be realized by man is a state
where there is no trace of suffering. It is the absolute cessation
of suffering—*atyantika duhkha-nivritti.*[86] This highest end as
explained by Madhavacharya[87] therefore implies that the liberation or *mukti* of man is coming out of his cycle of birth and
death. Like all other systems, it accepts ignorance or *mithya
jnana* as the cause of suffering. This *mithya jnana* is removed
when man acquires *tattva-jnana*. With the acquiring of *tattva-
jnana*, *dosha* or the conditions of false knowledge are destroyed,

and this destroys *pravritti* or mind's tendencies to be associated with the objects of pleasure, when there is no more desire in the mind after the *pravritti-laya*, there is no birth any more. And now the self attains the state in which there is no suffering at all. This according to Nyaya-vaisheshika is the realisation of *Nihshreyas* or *apavarga*.

The description of the highest end realized after *mukti* as explained above does not give us anything positive about the nature of the highest goal. It is a fact, no doubt, thus man is always confronted with *duhkha* or suffering in this life. It is also a fact that his life is essentially a life of struggle between *pravritti* and *nivritti*. The picture of struggling man in this world as suggested by the Nyaya-vaisheshika is, therefore, not a very happy one. The man wants to get rid of this world of suffering but he is not in a position to know anything of his future status. Merely getting out of this cycle of birth and death and therefore the suffering belonging to this world is definitely a negative approach. Moreover, the self after realising the *nihshreyas* does not have an existence of pure consciousness the characteristic of Spirit; but rather the self exists without any consciousness at all. Not that it has a life of peace and bliss but its life is an inert existence without any characteristic at all. The highest end is not the state of a higher type of immediate experience, but rather it is a state of no experience. In the Samkhya-yoga the self in the *mukta* state has a passive existence no doubt, he is a *drashta* who exists in his *svarupa*. But this *svarupa* is *sadaprakashasvarupa*—consciousness as such. The Nyaya-vaisheshika concept of the highest end is obviously far inferior to that of the Samkhya-yoga.

It seems, though, the Nyaya-vaisheshika has accepted a teleological view of Nature with its concept of *adrishta*, yet the relationship between man and Nature remains rather mechanical. The Nyaya-vaisheshika asks the *jivatman* to come out of the bondage due to Nature, but does not provide for him any

better place where he should live after coming out of his bondage. The assumption here is that outside this Nature or beyond
this physical world the selves may live somewhere and somehow without suffering. The *mukti*, therefore, provides no charm
for the man who is suffering in this world. For him it is only
just to get out of this world—the concept, which is very similar
to a man who being unable to face a troublesome situation in
life seeks the path of suicide. The only difference is that as the
mind is to be made desire-less this going out of the world is not
to come back again.

Again the Nyaya-vaisheshika has not provided for man
anything, which can satisfy his emotional religious urge. The
divine will functions mechanically and it does not come down
to this world with his grace to relieve man in distress. To the
question, why a man should worship God, the Nyaya-vaisheshika
answer is because He is the creator, maintainer and destroyer
of the universe; because He is the moral governor of the world—
the *karmaphaladata*. But Nyaya-vaisheshika never tries to establish a relation between man and God.

The Nyaya system is so much engaged with *pramana* that
it has not been able to think deeply about the *prameya*. The
vaisheshika was so much conscious of its atoms that it could
not give a relevant picture of Nature, which evolves and plays
its role for man who has his struggle with the situations and
events that happen in Nature. Nature in the Nyaya-vaisheshika
is just a *samghata* of different types of atoms, the *adrishta*, and
divine will. The products of Nature or the events and situations
that occur in Nature are moulded according to the nature of
atoms and the nature of *adrishta*, which is due to man's Karma.
God acts like an external agent only to switch on and switch
off. Man is left to depend on his own effort. It does not satisfy
us that by knowing the *padarthas* whether sixteen or seven
men can have *tattva-jnana*. Thus the concept of Nature and
man's relation with her is an incoherent picture and not at all

satisfactory to build any type of philosophy of humanism, in which man's rational and emotional aspirations may be satisfied. The Nyaya-vaisheshika system, therefore, fails to supply a satisfactory philosophy of life.

REFERENCES

1. Ananyathasiddha niyata Purvabhavitam Karanatvam TBH p. 28; also BHP. Verse 15
2. BHP, verses 19-22
3. TBH, p. 28
4. VS, X. ii. 1
5. NK, p. 101
6. TBH, p. 31
7. Asadharana karanatvat pradhanam, pradhanyat ca sadhakatamatvena, bhidhyate NV. 1.1.1. p.8
8. Prakrishtam karanam TBG. p. 28
9. NK. P. 144
10. NK. P. 144
11. Na ted asattvan na kriyate kintu karanabhavat, na ca'sattvam utpatter hetur apitu sato, 'nutpatter asad utpadyate, N.V, IV 1.50. p. 49
12. NV. IV. 1. 49, p. 493, NK. p. 144
13. D.N. Shastri, *Critique of Indian Realism*, p. 237
14. D.N. Shastri, *Critique of Indian Realism*, pp. 241-42
15. Bhavanyathatvam bhavati na dravyanyathatvam-vyasabhasya on yogasutra—III. 13
16. D.N. Shastri, *Critique of Indian Realism*, p. 245
17. S.B. II. II. 18
18. Bhamiti. II. II. 18
19. VS. 1. 1. 4
20. NK. p. 7
21. NS. 1. 1. 1
22. SM. p. 41
23. Nyaya-vaisheshika Metaphysics p. 4 (S. Bhaduri)

24. PPBH. p. 16
25. *Yasya Vastuno yat svarupam tad eva tasya' sritvam*, NK. P. 16
26. US. 1. 1. 15
27. *Svapradhanyapratitir eva dravyatvapratitih*, NK p. 13
28. VS. 1. 1. 15
29. *Gunashraya dravyam*, NLV. P. 752
30. NLVP. 753
31. NLV. pp. 94&99
32. VS. 1. 1. 5
33. PPBH. P. 22
34. VS. 2. 1. 1
35. VS. 2. 2. 2
36. NS. 1. 1. 14
37. VS. 2. 1. 2
38. VS. 2. 2. 5
39. VS. 2. 1. 3
40. VS. 2. 2. 4
41. VS. 2. 1. 5
43. VS. 2. 1. 27
44. VS. 2. 1. 30
45. NV. IV. II. 15, p. 51
46. NS. 4. 2. 17
47. VS. 4. 1. 2
48. NK. P. 32
49. NK. P. 32
50. NK. P. 157
51. NK. P. 137
52. NK. P. 135
53. PPBH. P. 131
54. VKT. II. II. 11. p. 504
55. PPBH. P. 131. NK. P. 135
56. NK. P. 32
57. NK. P. 32

58. VS. II. I. 30, PPBH. P. 58
59. NK. P. 62
60. VS. II. I. 28
61. VS. II. II. 6. PPBH. P. 63
62. KV. Pp. 114
63. KV. Pp. 115-16
64. VS. p. 65
65. VS II. II. 10
66. VS. II. II. 11
67. VS. VII. I, 24
68. PPBH. P. 66, NLV. PP. 218-29
69. PPBH. P. 67
70. Vup. II. II. II
71. NLV. PP. 307-08
72. KV. P. 94
73. KV. P. 94
74. PPBH. PP. 48-9
75. *Samvid evahi bhagavati Vastupagame nah sharanam.* NVT. P. 506
76. *Dharmas ca dharmino vastuto bhidhyae.* NVT. P. 506
77. *Jnanad orthasyotpada iti nalakikam idam. Sukhadinam tasmad utpatti-darshanat.* NK. P. 116
78. VS. III. II. 4
79. NS. 1. 1. 10
80. VS. III. II. 20 and 21
81. VS. III. II. 1
82. VS. III. II. 3
83. VS. I. I. 3. (*Tadvachanadamnayasya pramanyam*)
84. VS. V. II. 2
85. SBS. II. II. 13
86. NS. I. 1. 2. (*Tadatyantavimoksh apavargah*)
87. NS. I. 1. 2, also quoted by Madhavacharya in his *Sarvadarshanasamgrah-akshapada—32*

4

EVOLUTION OF THE WORLD IN THE SAMKHYA PHILOSOPHY

A

1. A SYSTEMATIC ACCOUNT OF THE EMPIRICAL WORLD

Change has a tremendous influence on human mind. It gives the human mind not only an idea of a sequence leading to an idea of time, but also makes him conscious of the many and the variety of things and situations, which he meets in his day-to-day existence. When man becomes reflective and begins to philosophize, he tries to understand these changing things and events of the world and tries to discover an underlying principle to explain its nature. The first question, which arises naturally in the human mind, is whether there is anything, which does not change.

But the world as man experiences is full of changes in regard to its constituents, and there is nothing which remains eternally the same, yet if man cannot find the unchanging eternal in this world as a fact, he assumes such an eternal entity, and hypothetically puts it side by side with this world of change as a co-existent.

This is what a Samkhya-yoga philosopher had in mind when he thought about *Purusha* and *Prakriti*, the conscious and the non-conscious or the spiritual and the non-spiritual as the two ultimate eternal principles. He then gives us a very systematic explanation about the significance of man and his universe. Here we find for the first time in the ancient Indian philosophical thought a kind of cosmic evolution from the subtle to the gross. This system, says B.N. Seal, "possesses a unique interest in the history of thought as embodying the earliest clear and comprehensive account of the process of cosmic evolution."[1] And what was of decisive importance about it was the conception of matter in eternal motion as Stcherbatsky puts it,

> ...the idea of an eternal matter, which is never at rest, always evolving from one form into another, is a very strong point of the system, and it does credit to the philosophers of that school that they at so early a date in the history of human thought, so clearly formulated the idea of an eternal matter which is never at rest.[2]

Here also we find an explanation and analysis of the nature of man, his relation with this empirical world and the nature and fulfillment of his destiny.

2. THE CHANGING AND THE CHANGELESS AS TWO ETERNAL PRINCIPLES

Thus, the Samkhya-yoga begins with a dualistic conception. The ultimate Reality is explained in terms of these two ultimate principles, the Conscious Spirit and the Non-conscious Nature. This non-conscious entity is called '*Prakriti*', which has neither beginning nor end. It is a dynamic principle but this dynamism has two phases—the first phase is the un-manifested potentiality. It is a kind of equilibrium (*Samyavastha*), which is unstable in character. In this phase *Prakriti* remains apparently static on account of the three forces acting against one another, neutralizing as it were without any movement: the concept of *Prakriti* as thought by the Samkhya-yoga is a unique point. The whole philosophy of Samkhya-yoga would have been explained with *Purushas* and three gunas—*Sattva*, *Rajas*, and *Tamas*. *Prakriti* is not a new entity but the three gunas existing together,[3] without yet a definite character as Sattva or Rajas or Tamas, like an eternal possibility ready to be actualized at any moment. That is why this existence is called an un-manifested state or *Avyakta*.

Prakriti becomes *vyakta* and evolution begins. This means that the *Avyakta*, which was timeless and dimensionless manifests through time and dimensions. In this evolution there is no dualism between a world of matter and another world of mind as is generally found in the western philosophy of the modern period. The manifestation or evolution is from the subtle to the gross, from a kind of universal Intellect becoming more and more individualized, finally emerging as gross material elements. Thus what is called matter is only the crudest expression of universal Intellect. And Intellect is only a subtle stage of matter. It is rightly observed: "This matter embraces not only the human body, but all our mental states as well; they are given a materialistic origin and essence."[4] The whole world from the universal Intellect to the *panchbhuta*, therefore, can be called empirical in a wider sense of the term. In western philosophy, the empirical is restricted to that which is known by the senses. Hence *Prakriti* is not merely a material principle but it also includes mind.

The implication of the above concept of an evolution from the subtle to the gross in a descending order of magnitude is, therefore, this that within this framework of the evolution of *Prakriti* we cannot have Spirit—pure consciousness anywhere. The necessary corollary is to discover that pure consciousness. We must reach it outside the realm of *Prakriti* though the search is to be made through *Prakriti*. This has tremendous significance because this is the key principle that explains the nature of human destiny from the Indian standpoint.

The unchanging principle, the pure consciousness, is, therefore, accepted as the other eternal Principle by the Samkhya-yoga philosopher. But here he suddenly becomes realistic and considers this eternal principle not as one but as many. They are called *Purushas* or Selves that is eternal, free, beyond qualities and of the nature of pure consciousness.

3. EVOLUTION AS THE KEY PRINCIPLE UNDERLYING NATURE

The most important feature in the Samkhya-yoga philosophy is its emphasis on the changing aspect of reality. This changing aspect of reality has not been merely mentioned by the founder of the Samkhya-yoga system but he has made this principle of becoming an ultimate *Tattva*. In the Samkhya-yoga system, the changing reality has been taken to be an independent reality though opposed to the spiritual entity; and also though this changing *Prakriti* is an environment serving as a bondage to the Spirit.

Thus, though *Prakriti* has been accepted as an eternal independent reality, it is still something, which the Spirit must conquer when it is in bondage by being involved in *Prakriti* and loosing its freedom. It seems that the Samkhya-yoga system, even though it accepts *Prakriti* as an independent reality, it still gives it an inferior status from the standpoint of the highest end of man. This changing world including matter life-mind is, therefore, a place, which the *Purusha* is always trying to come out of. Matter, life, and mind are like the covering sheaths of the Spirit, which have taken away his freedom by entangling him in the cycle of birth and death. The journey of a soul in bondage is from one life to another underlying *Trividhi dukham.* To realize a state of absolute cessation of suffering—*Atyantika duhkha nivritti*, becomes therefore, the fulfillment of human destiny.[5] teleology has, therefore, two kinds of significance in the philosophy of Samkhya-yoga. The existence of this world has a purpose. It serves like an environment where the soul is to work out its destiny. It realises its true state. The second significance is the purpose of realising the highest end or liberation. Thus, there is the purpose as the highest end to be realised. This is the purpose with respect to the end, whereas there is the purpose that there must be *Prakriti,* which is the purpose as the means. The idea of Samkhya-yoga is that the changing world of matter, life, and mind inevitably exists and *Purushas* are naturally entangled in it. Thus, though the world is the place of bondage, it is naturally there for the *Purusha* or Spirit.[6] It is true that the highest end to be realised is the real state of the free and eternal *Purusha* yet in the Samkhya system we find an elaborate and systematic explanation and technique of realising that end. In fact, the method of realisation has become more important. This only proves that this world of plurality has been taken by the Samkhya-yoga philosophers very seriously, and their analysis, method, and experiments have become intensely realistic.

In the order to conquer *Prakriti* and to come out of the clutches of allurements it is necessary that we must understand and know her nature. Thus, in Samkhya-yoga the knowledge of *Prakriti* is not limited to observation of facts by the senses or understanding the causal principle by the mind, but it is the experiencing directly the twenty-four principles—*Chatur vinsati-Tattvam.* The experience is *Tattva-Sakshatkara.* Thus, to understand this changing *Prakriti*, it is not enough to know it from outside but to know it through entering into its fundamental nature, that is, the manifestation of *Prakriti* from the subtle to the gross. This inner aspect of evolution is not a fact in the western sense of the term but is a Tattva to be directly acquainted with. So in the Samkhya system one who aspires for *Mukti* must know directly this subtle manifestation of *Prakriti.* Here one is to understand the key-principle of evolution not as an external change but an internal transformation of one Tattva into another. It is the understanding of this inner transformation of Tattvas, which is the basis of evolution, which we find in the Samkhya philosophy. Therefore, the principle of evolution in this philosophy has a deeper significance than what we find in the western philosophical systems.

4. CAUSALITY-SATKARYAVADA, THE BASIS OF EVOLUTION OF NATURE

Instead of any flight into mystic imagination, the method of approach in this system is quite rationalistic. As the Karika says, the cause of the world is to be inferred from the nature of the effect.[7] Accordingly, an effort is made to understand the nature of causality and make it the starting point of philosophy. This theory of causality known as Satkaryavada takes a common sense realistic standpoint and tries to show that something cannot come out of nothing.

According to Kapila: "There cannot be the production of something out of nothing (*navastuno vastu siddhi*); that which is not, cannot be developed into that which is. The production of what does not already exist (potentially) is impossible like a horn on a man; because there must of necessity be a material out of which a product is developed, and because everything cannot occur everywhere at all times; and because anything possible must be produced from something competent to produce it."[8] Besides, Kapila supports the Satkaryavada in his several aphorisms.[9]

This theory is formulated by Ishvarakrishna as follows: — "The effect subsists (even prior to the operation of the cause) since what is non-existent cannot be brought into existence by the operation of a cause, since there is recourse to the (appropriate) material cause, since there is no production of all (by all), since the potent (cause) effects only that of which it is capable, and since (that effect) is non-different from the cause."[10] That the effect must pre-exist in the cause may be

seen, it is held by Samkhya from the following arguments: —
(1) The non-existent cannot be the object of any activity. What
is non-existent can never be made existent. Even a thousand
craftsmen can never turn blue into yellow or extract oil from
sand. Hence the effect X requires an antecedent YX, such that
X is already to be found in its cause YX, for: —"It would be
useless to grind the sesame for oil, unless the oil existed in
it..."[11] (2) The product is not different from the material out of
which it is produced. It is also seen that one, who wishes to
produce a particular effect seeks the appropriate material cause;
e.g., the water pot is made of clay, while cloth is made of yarn.
(3) If the effect does not pre-exist in the cause, then it is possible for anything to come out of anything: — "For before production there is no difference between cause and effect."[12] In
the words of Prof. S.N. Dasgupta, that the cause and effect are
the undeveloped and developed states of the same substance
is called the doctrine of Satkaryavada.[13] (4) The causal efficiency belongs to that which has necessary potency. It is seen
that particular effects are produced only by particular causes,
because of the varying potencies of the latter. A particular potency cannot create any effect whatsoever but only that of which
it is capable. (5) Finally, the effect is non-different from the
cause. The effect, cloth, is non-different from the threads since
they would he neither separated nor brought together if they
were different; they could be conjoined as a pool and a tree on
its banks, or disjoined like the Himalayas and the Vindhyas.

It is rightly observed: —

All causation depends upon (energy) what possesses ex-
tensity and quantum. Energy does work; it overcomes
resistance. Potential energy is the energy of motion in
imperceptible form. Every moment of existence requires
a disturbance of the original (primordial) equilibrium by
means of a preponderance of energy, inertia, or essence

(the principle and stuff of consciousness). The particular
real (*guna*) that is predominant in any phenomenon produces a positive effect as and when energy predominates
and motion results, while the other two (inertia and essence) remain potential...In any material system at rest
the Mass...is latent, the energy latent and the conscious
manifestation sub latent.[14]

According to this system, there are three kinds of cause,
material, efficient, and final. The material cause enters into
the effect and is contained in it, while the efficient cause is
external to the effect. To get the oil from the sesame seed, it is
necessary to press the seed. This activity of pressing is the
efficient cause. The effect is potentially in the cause but must
be actualised through the agency of the efficient cause which
acts by means of concomitant conditions, place (*desa*), time
(*kala*), form of the thing (*akara*)[15]. The final cause points to
something outside the sphere of *Prakriti*, it being either *bhoga*
or *apavarga*.

The worldly experience (*bhoga*) or release (*apavarga*) both
have reference to the self.[16] The Samkhya teleology is most
important; for in its absence there would be no progressive
movement in *Prakriti*. —"The organs (external and internal)
discharge their respective function, prompted by mutual im-
pulsion; the goal of the spirit is alone the cause; by nothing else
is any instrument actuated."[17]

There are two kinds of effects: —simple manifestation, and
reproduction. An example of simple manifestation is to be seen
in getting cream from milk; an example of reproduction is the
changing of gold into some products, such as an ear-ring.[18]

The Samkhya-yoga theory of causality may be elucidated
in terms of scientific concepts. The doctrine of the conserva-
tion of energy and the transformation of energy is already hinted
at by Prof. B. N. Seal. The gunas are neither created nor destroyed, hence the totality of energy (gunas) remains constant.

Growth and decay are only changes of collocation, from potential to actual or from actual to potential. The total energy remains the same even while the world is in process.

This has been lucidly expressed by Prof. B. N. Seal: —

The sum of effects exists in the sum of causes in a potential (or un-evolved form). The grouping...alone changes, and this brings on the manifestation of the latent powers of the gunas, but without creation of anything new. What is called the (material) cause or sum of material causes is only the power, which is efficient in the production, or rather the vehicle of the power. This power is the unmanifested (or potential) form of the energy set free in the effect...the manifestation of an effect is only its passage from potentiality to actuality, a stadium in the process of evolution from possible (future) existence to actual (present) existence.[19]

Here we find that the distinction between the causal and the effectual condition is one of non-manifestation and manifestation of the effect. All the different arguments advanced by Samkhya-yoga are logical corollaries of the fundamental proposition that the cause and effect are identical in substance. But what is the implication of the concept of identity in this system is not very clear. It is rightly observed: —

How does the advocate of Samkhya himself conceive of the identity? He holds that the world is born out of what is itself unborn, that the cause of the evolved is the unevolved. What is the identity between the alleged cause and effect? The *Pradhana* should itself be conceived to be born, or the world must be said to be unborn; the former complies with the Samkhya, while the latter is palpably absurd. Nor is it possible to adopt a middle position, stressing each in turn, any more than it is pos-

sible to cook one half of a hen and to keep the other half
for laying eggs.[20]

5. PRAKRITI AND ITS EVOLUTION

Prakriti as the ultimate causal ground and prius of the whole
flux of phenomenal order is the logical corollary of the Samkhya
theory of causality. The manifold phenomena are seen to originate, to perish, to occupy limited space, to move, to be dependent for subsistence. Now these must have their causes. But
this causal link logically cannot go far; so a first cause is conceived. And this first cause in the Samkhya-yoga system is
termed as *Prakriti.* Ishvarakrishna argues for the existence of
Prakriti on the following grounds: —

> The un-evolved exists as the cause of the diverse (as seen)
> from the finitude, and homogeneous nature (of the lat-
> ter), from its functioning through energy, and from there
> being the respect of the variegated world both the emer-
> gence of effect from cause as also their merger; it (the
> un-evolved) functions in respect of the three constituents
> both (individually) and in their combination, being modi-
> fied like water, by the specific nature abiding in the re-
> spective constituents.[21]

These arguments may be arranged as follows: —(1) All
individual things in the world are limited, dependent and finite. So the finite as finite cannot be the source of the universe.
(2) All worldly things possess certain common characteristics
from which they all issue. (3) Evolution implies a principle,
which cannot be equated with any one of its stages. The activity, which generates evolution, must be inherent in the world
cause. (4) The effect differs from the cause and hence the
limited effect cannot be regarded as its cause. The effect is the
explicit and the cause is the implicit state of the same process.

(5) The unity of the universe points to a single cause. The effects of this ceaseless modification are, however, diverse. This diversity is due to varying relations of the respective constituents. Kapila holds: —"Since root has no root, the root (of all) is rootless."[22] Likewise in so many other aphorisms he establishes *Prakriti* as the ultimate cause of the physical world.[23]

The products of *Prakriti* are caused, dependent, relative, many and temporary as they are subject to production and destruction. But *Prakriti* is uncaused, independent, absolute, one and eternal, being beyond production and destruction. In the words of Ishvarakrishna: "The evolved is caused, non-eternal, non-pervasive, mobile, manifold, dependent, mergent, conjunct, and heteronomous, the un-evolved is the reverse (of all these)."[24]

Ishvarakrishna maintains that *Prakriti* is subtle, so it can only be inferred: —"The non-perception of that (Primal Nature) is due to its subtlety, not to its non-existence, since it is perceived in its effects; the great one (i.e., the intellect) and the rest are its effects (which are) both like and unlike (their cause)—Nature."[25] Kapila also maintains that *Prakriti* is subtle and that it is inferred.[26]

Prakriti is though a material principle, not matter pure and simple.[27] It gives rise not only to the five elements of the material universe but also to the psychical. Dr. Radhakrishnan observes: — "The Samkhya arrives at the conception not from the side of science, but from that of metaphysics."[28]

Prakriti is said to be the unity of the three gunas held in equilibrium.[29] They are termed as Sattva, Rajas and Tamas.[30] They are the essence of *Prakriti* and in that way of all the phenomena.[31] The gunas are not perceived, but are inferred from their effects. The nature and functions of the gunas are described by Ishvarakrishna as follows: —

The constituents are of the nature of pleasure, pain and indifference; they serve to illumine, to actuate and to restrain each of these functions through suppression, cooperation, transformation and intimate intercourse with and by the rest. Sattva is considered to be buoyant and illuminating, Rajas to be stimulating and mobile, Tamas alone is heavy and enveloping; their functioning for the goal (of the spirit) is like (the action of) a lamp.[32]

Because of the expression "gunas" (literally meaning qualities) there is a likelihood of confusion of attributes as contrasted with substance. But in this system, gunas should not be confused with the attributes of a substance rather they themselves are the constituents of the substance, i.e., Primal Nature. Hence it is that they are rendered here as "constituents" not as "attributes".

The nature and functions mentioned in the twelfth verse are to be understood in the order in which the constituents are mentioned in the next Karika, i.e., in the order, Sattva, Rajas, and Tamas. Sattva (goodness) is of the nature of pleasure; Rajas (Passion) is of the nature of pain; Tamas (darkness) is of the nature of indifference. Sattva serves to illumine, Rajas to actuate and Tamas to restrain. These results follow not from any individual guna, but from co-operative activity. Illumination results through Sattva as actuated by Rajas and not restrained by Tamas. It is not Sattva alone that is active in enlightenment, but Sattva as dominating Rajas and Tamas. Similarly, the other two dominate each in turn, with corresponding variations in the result. Each is the cause of transformation in the rest, hence no external cause is needed to account for their changes and not being caused from without, and they are not liable to destruction either. They are intimately conjoined in their activity; each is the consort of the other as it were. In the words of the Devi-Bhagavat, III, 8, "Sattva is the consort of Rajas; Rajas is the consort of Sattva; both these two Sattva and Rajas are the consorts of Tamas. The consort of both Sattva and Rajas is said to be Tamas. The original conjunction or separation of these has never been perceived."[33]

Lightness of things, upward movement of the burning fire or the blowing across of the wind is due to Sattva elements. Tamas weighs down things and renders them inactive. Both of these are energized and stimulated by Rajas.

It is said that these three constituents of Primal Nature co-operate for the *summum bonum* of the spirit. It is illustrated through the analogy of a lamp. The wick, the oil, and the flame are substances of opposite nature and yet they cooperate in the lamp in giving light. The combination of the three constituents of Primal Nature is of the same kind. The co-existence of the three constituents is observed even in every day experience, as seen from an example well known in the exposition of the Samkhya: — "As wife is beautiful, young, and well-endowed with all the qualities of head and heart that are requisite in the ideal wife. These constitute the Sattva element in her, because of that she causes A, her husband, to rejoice. She is, however, the cause of jealousy in her co-wives B and C and despair to a neighbour D who has not had the good fortune to be married to her. Jealousy is Rajas and despair is Tamas; they are due to the elements of Rajas and Tamas in A's wife, these becoming active only in respect of the co-wives or the neighbour, as the case may be."[34]

The gunas are said to be ever-changing. They cannot remain static even for a moment. Even in the state of dissolution, *Prakriti* is supposed to maintain its dynamic character; only then, instead of producing unlike forms, it produces itself (*Sajatiyaparinama*) so that perpetual motion is a fundamental postulate of the system so far as the physical world is concerned[35]. The gunas are always uniting separating and uniting again.[36]

Nature appears to science as dark ways and only accidentally lighting upon order and development. But Samkhya evolution embraces an everlasting purpose. Ishvarakrishna observes: —"The association of the two, which is like that of a lame man and blind one, is for the purpose of Primal Nature being contemplated (as such) by the spirit, and for the release of the spirit (from threefold misery) from this (association) creation proceeds."[37] The evolution is teleological. Ishvarakrishna gives so many illustrations: "This creation, from intellect down to the gross elements, is brought about by Primal Nature, to the end of the release of each spirit; (this is done) for another's benefit, as if it were for her own (benefit). As non-intelligent milk functions for the nourishment of the calf, even so does Primal Nature function for the liberation of the spirit. Just as (in the world (one undertakes action in order to be rid of desire (by satisfying it), even so does the un-evolved function for the release of the Spirit—She who endowed with the constituents (Sattva etc.) helps in manifold ways the spirit, that being without the constituents, does nor require her, functions for the benefit of the latter, without any benefit (to herself)[38]. Kapila maintains the teleological evolution.[39] Thus the whole evolution unnecessarily tends towards the realization of the purpose of the *purusha*. Prof. Hiriyanna observes: "Evolution is here regarded as teleological; but as *Prakriti* is by hypothesis not sentient, we cannot take it wholly so. We may characterize it as quasi-teleological, however hard it may be to understand that term."[40] While Prof. Hiriyanna gives some concession to the teleology of the Samkhya, Prof. S.S. Suryanarayana Sastri outright challenges it: —"The initiation and direction of evolution by a purely non-intelligent material principle would thus seem to be unacceptable in theory and without any legitimate analogue in practice."[41]

The Samkhya conception of evolution has certain special features. First, it is based on an assumption of the indestructibility of matter and the persistence of force. It is actually deduced from its causal theory, i.e., Satkaryavada. It is contended that the difference between *Prakriti* and its evolutes is similarly one between an indefinite incoherent homogeneity and a definite coherent heterogeneity. In the words of Dr. B.N. Seal: —

> The process of evolution consists in the development of differentiated (*Vaishamya*) within the undifferentiated (*Samyavastha*) of the determinate (*Vishesha*) within the indeterminate (*Avishesha*) of the coherent (*Yutasiddha*). The order of succession is neither from parts to whole nor from a whole to the parts, but ever from a relatively less differentiated, less determinate, less coherent whole to a relatively more differentiated, more determinate, more coherent whole.[42]

Just as the varieties of biological evolution are explained solely by the life-urge and not by determination from without the diversity among the evolutes of *Prakriti* is explicable solely by differences of stress among the three constituents of *Prakriti.* And lastly, as the life force is present in all its evolutes, undiminished by the putting forth of one or more forms, even so the energy of *Prakriti* is present in all its evolutes.

But here the agreement ceases and we have to admit that there are important points of difference between the biological evolution and the evolution of the Samkhya, which is a metaphysical theory. These differences are well summarized by Dr. T.M.P. Mahadevan when he says that Samkhya evolution is not like biological theories of evolution particularly Darwinian for the following reasons: — (1) *Prakriti* does not evolve like the forms of life that biological evolution speaks about, since it is unlike anything discussed in the biological theory (e.g., the amoeba, etc.); (2) *Prakriti* can scarcely struggle and evolve in any environment, since it itself is the environment; (3) in comparing the evolutes of Samkhya with those in the biological theory, there appears to be no greater coherence in the latter evolutes of Samkhya, whereas there does appear to be in the Darwinian scheme.

Secondly, evolution is conceived as cyclic or periodical. That is, there are periods of evolution and dissolution alternating so that it is not a process of continuous progress in one direction only.[43]

Thirdly, evolution is here regarded as teleological, though it is logically not consistent, a fact we have already examined.

Lastly, even if the evolution as teleological, however, is conceded, it has reference to the individual and not to the species. Its aim is securing *bhoga* for the individual or his *apavarga*.

In the state of dissolution, the three gunas of *Prakriti*, though perpetually active are in perfect equilibrium. This equilibrium is disturbed at the beginning of the period of evolution. The initial stimulus for this alteration, according to yoga comes from God.[44] According to the Samkhya on the other hand, which acknowledges no such Supreme Being, the stimulus comes from the mere presence (*Saniddhy-matra*)[45] of the *purusha*. This influence is illustrated by a magnet attracting iron. This is a point, which is rigorously defended by the system but this is far from satisfactory.

Now we shall examine the evolutionary process of the system. In the following *Karikas* Ishvarakrishna enumerates the twenty-three evolutes of *Prakriti*: "From Primal Nature proceeds the great one (intellect), thence individuation, thence the aggregate of the sixteen and from five out of these sixteen, the five gross elements."[46] The sixteen includes the eleven *indriyas* (i.e., the five organs of cognition, the five organs of action and the mind) and the five subtle elements, (*tanmatras*). These five subtle elements, in turn, produce the gross elements. Next Ishvarakrishna illustrates the nature of the first product of Primal Nature: "Intellect is a determinative virtue, wisdom, nonattachment, and the possession of lordly powers constitute its *Sattvika* form (i.e., of its nature when *Tamas*, darkness preponderates).[47] Kapila also says that the first evolute is the great one—*Mahat* or Intellect.[48] *Mahat* being the evolute of Primal Nature is material, though subtle, and that is why, it is capable of reflecting clearly the *Purusha,* which is consciousness. From *Mahat* comes the *Ahamkara*. Ishvarakrishna tells the nature of *Ahamkara*: "Individuation is conceit in the ego. There from, creation proceeds in two ways, as the eleven-fold aggregate and as the fivefold subtle elements."[49] Ishvarakrishna continuing further observes: "From that form of individuation (which is known as) *Vaikrita* proceeds the eleven-fold aggregate (of indriyas) characterized by *Sattva*; the subtle elements (proceed) from (that form known as) *Bhutadi*: it is of the nature of *Tamas* (darkness); both (proceed) from (that form of individuation known as) *Taijasa*."[50] *Ahamkara* is a single principle, it gives rise to different kinds of evolutes according to the domination of *Sattva* or *Tamas*. In either case, a certain degree of domination of *Rajas* is essential otherwise there can be no activity. When *Sattva* predominates the eleven organs appear. When *Tamas* predominates the five subtle elements (*tanmatras*) appear. A certain degree of domination of *Rajas* is essential for the origination of the *Sattvika* and *Tamas* evolutes. If *Sattva* and *Tamas* are to be regarded as the material causes of these evolutes *Rajas* may be regarded as their moving cause.

The ten organs of sense and action are next enumerated by Ishvarakrishna: "Eye, ear, nose, tongue and skin are called organs of cognition; voice, hands, feet, and the organs of excretion and generation are said to be the organs of action."[51]

The nature of mind (*manas*) is described in the following *Karika*: "Among these the mind (*manas*) is of the nature of both (organs cognitive and active); it is explicative; it is also an *indriya* because of the community of nature (with other *indriyas*); from specific modifications of the constituents proceed diversity (as do) differences of external form."[52]

Intellect, individuation and mind constitute the internal organs (*antahkarana*) as compared with the ten *indriyas* (other than mind) (*manas*), which are external organs. The three constituents of internal organ (*antahkarana*) represent the three psychological aspects of knowing, willing, and feeling.

In the following *Karika* Ishvarakrishna describes the activities done by the external organs and the internal organs: — "The internal organ is of three kinds: the external (organs) which make known objects to (those) three, are tenfold; the external (organ functions) in the present; an internal (organ functions) in the present; an internal organ (functions in respect of all) three times."[53]

This is the epistemological aspect of this system. The external senses are the channels whereby enters the material whereon the inner organs work. An external sense functions only in the present time while an internal sense functions all the three times.

Next Ishvarakrishna enumerates the five subtle essences which are called *Tanmatras*: —"The subtle elements are non-specific, from those five (proceed) the five gross elements; these are known as specific, (being variously) tranquil, terrific, and delusive."[54]

The subtle elements are not cognizable by our limited faculties; their distinction thus not being perceived by us, they are non-specific. The gross elements, however, are perceived as distinct, being possessed of different qualities. From the essence of sound arises the element of ether. From the essence of touch combined with the essence of sound arises the element of air. From the subtle essence of colour combined with those of sound and touch arises the element of fire. From the essence of taste combined with those of sound, touch and colour arises the element of water. And lastly, from the essence of smell combined with those of sound, touch colour and taste arises the element of earth.

There are three stages in the development of matter.

1) The primordial infinitesimal units of inertia on which Energy does its work;
2) The atomic unit—potentials having energy, following the impregnation of inert units of inertia; and,
3) The different classes of infra-atoms the minute divisions of which gross matter is capable, that which are themselves complex *Tanmatric* systems.[55]

The first stage is composed of homogeneous units of inertia (having mass), which are uncreated and eternal. These units are called *bhutadi* to which is added potential energy (*Rajas*). The third stage is made up of *tanmatras* that possess physical properties such as penetrability, power of impact, heat and cohesive and viscous attraction. It is observed: —"The difference between *tanmatra* and *bhuta* is a difference of subtle and as opposed to gross matter subtle matter is beyond the ken of our senses, while gross matter is what makes up the world of objects and perception."[56]

Now we shall try to examine the nature of space, time and motion in this system.

Vijnanabhikshu in his commentary of Samkhya-Sutra maintains: —"The bondage of man is not cause by time, because (if that were the case) there could be no such separation as that of liberated and un-liberated; because time, which applies to everything and is eternal, is at all times associated with all men (and must, therefore, bring all into bondage if any)."[57] Vijnanabhikshu maintains *Prakriti* itself as eternal, infinite space and time. It becomes quite clear by the following comments on Samkhya Sutra: —"The space and time which are eternal (and absolute) being the source of the Ether, are really sorts of qualities of Nature, therefore, it is consistent that space and time should be all-pervading. But the space and time, which are limited arise from the Ether, through the conjunction of this or that limiting object."[58]

Limited space and time are Ether itself particularized. In this system space and time are not substances. Events stand in relation to time and space. We cannot perceive the infinite time or infinite space.

Vachaspati asks why Samkhya does not recognize time as an independent category? "Even if we do recognize it, as Naiyayikas do we have to look to something other than time itself? It would be simpler to recognize and deal with these defining conditions instead of postulating a superfluous entity called time."[59] That is to say, there are times, but no time; and the times like spaces are the products of *akasha*, i.e. cosmic ether.

Vyasa observes: —"As an atom is substance in which minuteness reaches its limit, so a moment is a division of time in which minuteness reaches its limit or a moment is that much of time which an atom takes in leaving the position in space that it occupies and in reaching the next point. The succession of moments is the non-cessation of the flow thereof. The moments and their collections do not fall into a collection of actual things. The *muhurta*, the day and night, are all aggregates of mental conceptions. This time, which is not a substantive reality in itself, but is only a mental concept, and which comes into the mind as piece of verbal knowledge only appears to people whose minds are given to outgoing activities; as if it were an objective reality."[60]

Thus we find that in this system absolute space and time are the forms of *Prakriti* itself. So far as relative space and time are concerned they are mental conceptions. And so far as the problem of motion is concerned, it is inherent in *Prakriti* itself. *Rajas,* which is one of the constituents of *Prakriti* is the principle of motion. *Prakriti* by its very nature is mobile. Thus *Prakriti* is the very form of absolute space and time and it is by its nature mobile.

Evolution is the play of these twenty-four principles, which together with the *Purusha,* who is a mere spectator and outside the play of evolution[61], are the twenty-five categories of Samkhya. Out of these twenty-five categories: "Primal Nature is not an evolute, the seven beginning with the great one (the intellect) are both evolvents and evolutes; sixteen (the five organs of sense, the five of action, the mind and the five gross elements) are only evolutes, the spirit is neither evolvent nor evolute."[62] Yoga adds one more category, i.e., that of Ishvara.

Samkhya-yoga seems to have presented the first theory of evolution. It has been rightly said: —

"Here probably do we get the first comprehensive and consistent theory of evolution. The world was hammered into shape out of refractory materials by a perfect architect. It developed naturally and even necessarily by well-marked stages out of primordial elements and is developing still but without any intervention from outside. Such is the view of the Samkhya and it is one to which evolutionists of every shade give their assent."[63]

B

1. MAN AS THE UNCHANGING PLUS THE CHANGING

The concept of man has profound meaning in Indian philosophy, particularly in the Samkhya-yoga. Man is generally referred to, as *Jivatman.*[64] He is *Jiva* and *atman* both that is, the non-spiritual as well as spiritual. Man is *Purusha* in bondage or *Purusha* entangled in *Prakriti.* Vijnanabhikshu says *purusha* with *ahamkara* is the *jiva* (man) and not *purusha* itself.[65] Thus the non-spiritual aspect of man has been analysed and explained in minute detail and with utmost care. Here emerges the concept of the "*Linga Sarira*"[66] in the Samkhya-yoga.

It is interesting to note that when the Samkhya system enumerates the characteristics of the *Purusha*, sometimes it takes *Purusha* as pure consciousness or spirit[67] and sometimes as *jivatman*.[68] At one place it takes *purusha* as *nitya suddha*, *buddha*, and *mukta*—pure spirit but when it brings in the concept of *bhokta*, where explaining the nature of *purusha* it unconsciously confuses with the *jivatman*. *Bhoga* losses it's meaning unless *purusha* is with *buddhi*. It is possible to give a new meaning of *bhokta* from the standpoint of Samkhya-yoga. For example, one may suggest that this *bhoga* is a kind of objectless experience, a kind of pure subjectivity or Experience as such. But considering the whole system as such and also the arguments put forward by Samkhya-yoga for the existence of many *purushas*[69] such a meaning is not tenable. To accept such a meaning will logically lead to the Advaita Vedanta position. The emphasis, both on Spirit and Nature by Samkhya-yoga definitely suggests that the system is essentially concerned with *jivatman* more than the pure *Atman*. The aspiration for liberation (*Kaivalya*), the gradual and continuous struggle against the forces of *Prakriti*, the concept of a peculiarly significant teleology based on *Purusha-Prakriti*—cooperation—all these point to the fact that it is man as he is with his *indriyas* though he aspires for transcending his individuality.

The Upanishadic discovery that man is a finite-infinite being is re-echoed in the Samkhya-yoga in a different way. That man is a finite is experienced by man through his dissatisfaction with the limited capacities for enjoyment. He wants to extend his enjoyment up to the infinite dimensions. The significance pointed out by the Upanishads as we have already stated is that it is the consciousness of his finiteness that makes man aspire for transcending finite-hood. This means again that the pure Spirit wants to regain its original status. In the Samkhya-yoga the concept of *purusha* has been taken sometimes as finite sometimes as infinite because of this.

Thus, in the Samkhya-yoga, we find a philosophical explanation (given by the Samkhya) and concrete experiences leading to the discovery of the one through the many (given by the yoga).

The status of man in the universe, therefore, becomes unique in this philosophy, in spite of the vacillation we find in the arguments regarding the nature and status of the *purusha* given in the Samkhya-yoga philosophy. Man according to this system is Spirit entangled in Nature. This is because the system is neither satisfied with the *purusha* or Spirit nor with *Prakriti*; it wants both because it finds in man both of these co-existing. The Samkhya-yoga only tries to provide a rational explanation of how these two co-existing principles function together in man's life.

2. MAN'S STRUGGLE WITH PRAKRITI TO REGAIN HIS FREEDOM

The Samkhya-yoga accepts the *purusha* as a *bhokta*. We shall rather accept the *jivatman* or man as a *bhokta*. It is found that though man wants *bhoga*, he is never satisfied with whatever extent of enjoyment he gets. The enjoyment reaches the saturation point and the experience of further enjoyment becomes impossible, so here man discovers the paradox, which becomes the inevitable consequence of his *bhoga*. Therefore, we must find out a method by which we can get rid of such consequences. In other words, man wants the status of pure enjoyment. In the *yoganusasana* we find a method that helps man going from one experience to another qualitatively different[70].

If the evolution of *Prakriti* is the coming down of the Primal *Avyakta* into the grosser *Vyakta* entities the *Yoganusasana* is the going up from these grosser manifestations to the most subtle stages of these manifestations and finally to know that *Avyakta* source. When the knowledge of the *Avyakta* source

Prakriti is realized man comes out of his bondage due to *Prakriti* and regains his original spiritual status.[71]

The most dominant feature of man's inner life is his *chitta-vritti*. After *Prana* or the vital force this *chitta-vritti* is the most predominant in controlling the human behaviours and making him responsible for the consequences of such actions. This *chitta-vritti* is descending force of *Prakriti* taking man always towards the sensuous contact with the external objects and inducing him to create a world of images and concepts that further force him to have more contacts with the objects. This *bahirmukhata*, which is natural with the human mind, is responsible for creating his bondage more enduring.

Hence, Samkhya-yoga teaches us to be cautious in regard to this naturalistic force and prescribes the control of the *chitta-vrtti*.[72]

Not merely controlling the *chitta-vrtti* but the method is to make whole mind functionless—the cessation of *vritti*. When the mind is absolutely calm, a qualitatively new type of experience begins. So long as mind is functioning such experiences do not appear. Thus the man is asked by the yoga system to turn inward to become *antarmukhi*.[73] the idea is to go with the mind and then to go beyond it. Hence it begins with concentration or focusing the scattered psychic energies to a particular point and then to make this point gradually disappearing. Thus, a new world of over-mental knowledge begins here. And the man gradually ascending from the direct knowledge of one *tattva* to the next higher one gradually moves forward towards the *Avyaka Prakriti*. When he has realised the 24th *Tattva*, he realises *vivekakhyati*[74] and comes out of his bondage.

Thus, in the Samkhya-theory and yoga-practice we get a picture of a man struggling against Nature. But this struggle has created a lot of misunderstanding and misinterpretation in the history of Indian thought, and culture. The struggle is not a struggle for acceptance or rejection of Nature or the world. In the western culture, the concept of evolution—of adaptation or lately of life-affirmation—is based on the acceptance of the world through struggle. In Indian culture, we find in some quarters the emphasis is rather on rejection of the world after the struggle. But we think that a truer interpretation would be the struggle of man against *Prakriti* is neither accepting nor rejecting her. 'Man struggles against the world' is not to accept it or to reject it but to conquer it with a purpose. This victory over Nature is not, as the western thinkers have suggested, to improve it with its own forces and equipments and utilize it for more material comforts of man. But the Indian ideal underlying this concept of *Prakriti-jaya* is not for furthering the sensuous enjoyments and comforts of life, but we should conquer Nature in order to mould it and control it so that it may help us in realizing our true spiritual status. In other words, this conquering of Nature is not to float away comfortably with its downward stream, but it is swimming against the naturalistic descending manifestations and trying to reach the higher and subtler stages of *Prakriti-Parinama*. The Indian standpoint, therefore, is neither life-affirmation nor life-denial, but it is to have the direct experience of that which makes this vital force and psychic force possible and meaningful.

C

1. NATURE AS A BLIND FORCE

Man becomes conscious of his own limitations when he finds out to his utter despair that in spite of his thousand promises and vows he becomes a victim to the allurements of the sensuous experience. Retardation and rethinking are not new in his life yet he finds himself utterly incapable of withstanding the forces of *Prakriti*. Thus man when he becomes reflective, that is when he begins to philosophise he feels that though he does not like it, he is dragged sometimes against his own conscience by these worldly forces. This is because man suffers from the absence of that knowledge which can give him strength to fight against these forces and instead of becoming a servant of *Prakriti*, —can become a master of it. This means that the ignorant man is behaving like a manifested entity of the blind *Prakriti*. Though there are moments when he feels that he is not one like the many other things of the world yet his total behaviour compels him to act as if he is one of them. This ignorant attitude of man or cosmic blind force[75] working universally is perhaps what has been called Maya in other systems of Indian Philosophy. The pleasure principle as the western thinkers suggest is a universal principle for a man in bondage. The mind is always associated with the *indriyas* and *indriyas* are always moving forward to meet the object of desire. This is the allurement of the world, which makes man ultimately entangled in it. In fact, there is no problem for a man if he is satisfied with his world. But as it is found everywhere in the world man is not satisfied with his world, and his search for more satisfaction has only made him abnormal—deserving psychotherapy as the so-called advanced western world statistically proves. The fact, therefore, remains that man is certainly being controlled by the blind forces of *Prakriti* but he cannot accept it to be his destiny. This is what the Samkhya-yoga has shown.

2. NATURE OF HUMAN DESTINY

But what is human destiny? It has already been stated that man's destiny is to realize his true status as a spiritual entity.[76] This is the demand of the human soul itself. There are occasions when the human soul is not satisfied with what he gets from Nature even though it is pleasurable. The soul as it were turns away from these commonplace things for which people generally hanker. This brings a kind of *vairagya* and the man tries to get at the more basic reality, because everything in Nature for him is meaningless and superficial. This is the awakening of the soul. This awakening proves that the human destiny is not to affirm life with its fullness but it rather proves that man must transcend this affirmation of life for his affirmation of Spirit. Mere affirmation of life cannot stand by itself and that is why Indian thinkers have said *bhumaiva sukham*—nothing less than the infinite can give us eternal happiness. Spirit alone is that infinite ultimate as suggested by the Indian philosophers. Thus the human destiny is as the Samkhya-yoga suggests, to live the life through only to discover the Reality, which is still more basic than even *buddhi, ahamkara* and mind. Human destiny is a journey of progressive realisation; it is a gradual discovery of the deeper and subtler manifestations of the ultimate Reality. This is the human destiny.

REFERENCES

1. Positive Sciences of Ancient Hindus, p. 2
2. Buddhist Logic, 1-18
3. S.P.S. 1. 61
4. Stcherbatsky, T. Buddhist Logic, 1-8. Mahat of Buddhi is translated as Intellect but it is not to be understood in the western sense of Intellect. Here in the Samkhya Intellect is not a conscious principle but an organ of conscious principle
5. Samkhya Karika, 1
6. S.K. 21
7. S.K. 8
8. Samkhya Pravachana Sutra—1-78. (Trans. By M. William, Indian Wisdom, pp. 89-90)
9. Ibid, 1-115-18, 121
10. Samkhya Karika—9. (Edited and Trans. By S.S. Suryanarayana Sastri).

11. S.K. 9. Gaudapada Bhashya.
12. S.K. p. 38
13. History of India, Phil. Vol. I, p. 257.
14. B.N. Seal, The Positive Science, p. 5.
15. S. Radhakrishnan, *Indian Phil.* Vol. II, p. 258
16. S.K. 21
17. S.K. 31 (S.S.S.)
18. S. Radhakrishnan, *Indian Phil.* Vol. II. P. 258
19. The Positive Sciences, p. 13
20. S. Suryanarayana Sastri—S.K. IIXVIII-XIX
21. S.K. 15-16 (Trans. & Edited by S.S.S.)
22. S.P.S. 1-67
23. S.S. 1-69, 74, 78, 5-35
24. S.K. 10 (S.S.S.)
25. Ibid. 8
26. S.S. 1-19, 10
27. S.K. 11
28. Indian Philosophy, Vol. II, p. 262
29. S.K. 11, 16
30. S.K. 13
31. S.S. (Kapila) 5. 39
32. S.K. 12-13 (S.S.S.)
33. As quoted by S.S.S. in S.K. p. 38
34. S.S. Suryanarayana Sastri in S.K. p. 41
35. S.T.K. Sta. 5
36. Yoga-var. IV, 13, 14
37. S.K. 21 (S.S.S.)
38. S.K. 56, 57, 58, 60 (S.S.S.)
39. S.P.S. 2-11, 59
40. *Outlines of Indian Phil.*, p. 273
41. S.K.P. XIV (S.S.S.)
42. Samkhya Phil., Lecture delivered in the Graduate School of Madras University, Oct. 23, 1951
43. Outlines of Indian Phil. Hiriyanna, p. 273
44. Bhoja Vritti on. Y.S. 1. 24

45. S.P. 13.1.96
46. S.K. 22 (S.S.S.)
47. S.K. 23 (S.S.S.)
48. S.S. 1. 71
49. S.K. 24 (S.S.S.)
50. S.K. 25 (S.S.S.)
51. S.K. 26 (S.S.S.)
52. S.K. 27 (S.S.S.)
53. S.K. 33 (S.S.S.)
54. S.K. 38 (S.S.S.)
55. Seal, Positive Sciences, p, 22
56. Naturalistic Tradition, p. 207
57. S.P. B. 1-12
58. S.P.B. 2-12
59. Samkhyatattva Kumudi, 33 (S.S.S. 73)
60. Yoga-Vritti, 3-51
61. S.K. 19
62. S.K. 3 (S.S.S.)
63. I. Ghose—"Samkhya and Modern Thought", p. 68
64. Vijnanabhiksu, *Samkhya Pravaena Bhasya*—VI. 63
65. Ibid
66. S.K. 40
67. S.K. 19
68. S.K. 18
69. S.K. 18
70. *Patanjala Yogadarsana*—2-28. 29
71. *Patanjala Yogadarsana*—2-28
72. *Patanjala Yogadarsana*—1-2
73. P.Y.D. 4-26 and *Bhoja Vritti* on it
74. Ibid. 2-28
75. S.K. 1
76. P.Y.D. 1-3

5

DHARMA, HEAVEN AND HUMAN RESPON-SIBILITY IN THE PURVA-MIMAMSA

1. THE WORLD AND ITS CONSTITUENTS

The Purva-Mimamsa also gives us a realistic and pluralistic view of the world. The ultimate constituents of the world are the eternal entities, combining and disintegrating accordingly as objects are formed and destroyed. About the conception of causality there is a difference of opinion among the writers. For example, Prabhakara accepts *arambhavada* like the Nyaya-vaisheshika, whereas Kumarila accepts the *Satkaryavada* like the Samkhya-yoga.[1] About the creation of the world, the Purva-Mimamsa-*Sutrakara* Jaimini and its *bhashyakara* Shabara have not said anything clearly. It is only from the later commentators like Prabhakara and Kumarila that we get some ideas about the Mimamsa view.

Prabhakara denies the creation of the universe even though he admits that the universe is made up of component parts and as such it ought to have a beginning and an end in time—yet he maintains that there is no reason for believing that the universe as a whole has had a beginning at a particular time. In this connection he denies the existence of any extramundane supervisor of the operation of *Dharma-Adharma*, as maintained by the Naiyayikas. He holds that because the *Dharma-Adharma* of the body—which itself is the product of *dharma-adharma* must always belong to the same intelligent being to whom the body itself belongs; any other being, howsoever intelligent, can never have any knowledge of *Dharma-Adharma* of another being, however, the idea of extra-mundane supervisor is meaningless. He examines the nature of supervisor: (a) This 'Supervision' cannot be of the nature of contact or conjunction, because *Dharma-Adharma* are qualities and hence not capable of conjunction which is possible for substances only. (b) Supervision cannot be the nature of Inherence, as the *Dharma-Adharma* inhering in the other souls cannot inhere in God. Except these two possible relationships there is no other kind of relation possible. In ordinary cases agents like carpenters etc., the supervision consists in their contact with the tools and instruments, which again are brought into contact with the woodpieces upon which the carpenter works. This is not possible in case of God. The action bringing about the creation of the universe cannot be held to lie in Atoms, which operate under the will of God. Because in all our experiences we never come across any such supervision as would be implied in such a process. All supervision is done in fact by the soul over that body alone, which is en-souled by virtue of the soul's *Dharma-Adharma*. And the atoms cannot form the body of God. The Naiyayika generally puts forward the argument in proof of the creator God as follows: —"The Body of man must have a supervisor because it is itself non-intelligent." To this the counter argument is given—that God cannot be such a Supervisor, because He cannot have any motive in exercising his supervision. The Naiyayika gives the analogy of the carpenter supervising the making of wooden articles and this carpenter is a corporeal being—the same analogy necessitates the supervising God also to be a corporeal Being. But we know that no corporeal Being can exercise an effective and intelligent con-

trol over such subtle things as atoms, *Dharma-Adharma*. Even
if He did exercise such control, He Himself being a corporeal
Being would need another supervisor and so on *ad infinitum*.
Thus the supervision is impossible and it is a never-ending
process.[2]

According to Kumarila, the world is a reality. It is always
in a state of dynamic movement. There was never a time when
world was not, there will never come a time when the world
will cease to be. When the world is there and was ever there
and will continue to be there forever, the dynamic nature of
the world must also be an eternal fact. There can be no creation of the world and there cannot either be some agent for
the supervision and control of the function of the world. This
aspect of world has been well analysed by Kumarila in his sec.
16, *Sambandhakshepa—parithara* of *Slokavartika.*

Kumarila refutes creation. At a time when all this (earth,
and water etc.) did not exist what could have been the condition of the universe? As for Prajapati himself what could be his
position and form?[3] Again Kumarila questions in what manner
do we believe the world to have had a beginning in time? If it
is held that it is brought about by a desire on the part of
Prajapati, then if Prajapati is held to be without a material
body, how could he have any desire towards creation.[4] And if
He had a body, then this body could not have been created by
Himself; then we would have to postulate another creator and
so on *ad infinitum*.[5] How is it that He should have a desire to
create a world, which is to be fraught with all sorts of imperfec-
tions? For at that time he did not have any guiding principles,
in the shape of the virtue (or sin) etc., of the living being themselves. Nor can any creator create anything in the absence of
means and instruments.[6] His chain of arguments goes on. Lastly,
he concludes that there is no basis for the assumption that
there is creation and evolution of the world consisting of birth
and destruction of all things.[7]

In the same manner Kumarila refutes dissolution on the ground that there is no proof for it. He maintains that as for a *pralaya* in the form of universal destruction we find no proof for admitting it. Nor could such an action (of destruction) on the part of Prajapati serve any useful purpose.[8] Shabara's only indication with regard to the categories of the world is under Sutra 10.3.44, where kinds of things are mentioned: *Dravya* (Substance), *Guna* (Quality), *Karma* (Action) and *Avayava* (Constituent part).

According to Prabhakara there are the following categories—Substance: —Quality, Action, Community, *Paratantrata*, *Shakti*, and Similarity. Prefacing the proof of Similarity, as a distinct category he says it cannot come under any of the well-known categories—Substance, Quality Action, Community, *Paratantrata*, and ultimate Particularity, which are precisely the six categories of the Vaisheshika system. With regard to the last one, ultimate Particularity he holds that "People learned in this science do not accept any such category."[9] From this it becomes obvious that Prabhakara admits the five categories of the Vaisheshika system, and he posits 'Similarity' in place of ultimate Particularity of the Vaisheshika system.

According to Prakaranapanchika, it is quite clear that Prabhakara has full agreement with the Vaisheshika system with regard to the number of substances. Like the Vaisheshika system he admits nine substances: Earth, Water, Fire, Air, *Akasha*, Time, Space, *Atman*, and *Manas*. *Tamas* and Sound, two more substances accepted by Kumarila are rejected by Prabhakara.

Of the substances, Earth, Water, Fire, and Air are perceptible by both organs visual and tactile. *Akasha* and the rest are not regarded as perceptible.[10] *Akasha* is only inferred as the substratum of sound. *Atman* and *Manas* are admitted as substances under the chapter *Tattvaloka*.

Earth, Water, and Fire are of large dimensions and having colours are perceptible by the senses of touch and vision. Air being devoid of colour is perceptible by touch alone.

Qualities enumerated are in all sixteen. They have no philosophical importance.

Action is also supposed to be one of the perceptible categories. But it is not so. When a thing moves, what actually we see is not the moving of the thing, but only the various conjunctions and disjunctions of things in a space. Action subsists entirely in the active thing, while conjunction and disjunction subsists in space. Therefore, action cannot be held to be perceptible, it can only be inferred.

Community is the same as the universal of the Vaisheshika system.

Paratantrata, which appears to be the same as subsistence or Inherence. Inherence is not eternal because it subsists in perishable things also. It cannot be even regarded one. It is as many as there are things in the world.

As regards *Shakti, Prakaranapanchika* holds: —Everything in the world is found to be possessed of some sort of *Shakti*, potency, it cannot be perceived, but it can be inferred, for instance, fire is always seen to bring about a certain effect, in the shape of burning but some fires, when under the influence of certain incantations fail to bring about that effect. From this we are led on to conclude that in all things there is something, which enables them to produce their effects, being deprived of which they are unable to do so. This imperceptible thing is named as *shakti*—potency.[11] In eternal things it is eternal but in transitory things it is transitory.

About 'Similarity' Prakaranapanchika provides the following account. It is something entirely different from substance and the other categories as is proved by the fact that it enters into our consciousness exactly in the same manner as any category and our consciousness is the sole criterion regarding the existence of things. This 'Similarity' cannot be regarded as a 'Substance' because it is found in quality and action also and no substance is known to subsist in the latter though we speak of similar colour, similar action and so forth. It cannot be put under the category, community, because it does not form the basis of any comprehensive conception. It cannot be classed under inherence, because it is a relation. As regards the Vaisheshika category of Vishesha, it is only the quality of separateness, which differentiates the ultimate substances in the shape of atoms. It is contrary to similarity. For these reasons it must be regarded as a separate category.[12]

A comparatively recent work, the *Sarvashiddhantarahasya* supplies one more category—Number. But *Prakaranapanchika* does not accept it as a separate category. It speaks of Number as a Quality.[13]

According to Kumarila all categories are classed under two heads—*Bhava* and *Abhava* (positive and negative).

Kumarila's conception of *Abhava* is like that of the Vaisheshika system. It is of four kinds—prior negation, utter destruction, absolute negation and mutual negation.

Under the positive head, there are four categories, viz., substance, quality, action and community.

With regard to Substance, they are eleven—earth, water, fire, air, *akasha*, time, space, soul, mind, darkness and sound.

Qualities are thirteen. Actions are five like those of the Vaisheshika system—*Utkshepana, Avakshepana, Akunchana, Prasarana,* and *Gamana.*

With regard to Community they are two—higher and lower. *Shakti* and *Sadrishya* are included under 'Substance'.

Similarity is denied. The *Shastradipika* observes: —Similarity cannot be a distinct category by itself, if it were so we could not account for the varying degrees of similarity between things and things. Nor is there any reason for regarding it as a category; in fact, it consists only in the presence in one thing of character and conditions present in another.[14] Samavaya is also denied.[15]

From the above, we thus get a picture of the world, which is made up of some eternal substances, which combine to produce different objects of the world which are subject to change and destruction. The world as a whole has neither beginning nor end. Thus the Mimamsa philosopher does not need a creator of this world. Even a moral agent guiding and distributing the merits and demerits of the *Jivatman* is not needed. Yet the Mimamsa philosopher does hot accept a world, which is governed by the mechanical laws. The world is no doubt governed by moral laws but the source of morality is not God. For the Mimamsaka the sources of morality are the statements of the Vedas, which are impersonal. Thus there are certain eternal moral principles, which become concrete and meaningful through the Vedic injunctions.

The Mimamsa philosopher accepts the eternal *Shabda* in the form of Vedic statements. Thus to have a complete picture of the whole universe, we are to accept on the one hand certain eternal substances as the constituents of the physical world, on the other the eternal sound another principle to provide man with moral values. It is not very clear how the eternal *Shabda* is ontologically related to other constituents of the world. The *apaurusheya Shabda*, therefore, serves as a moral force that guides this world. In religion God is said to be a source of moral values. The Mimamsa system does not accept God but at the same time it cannot deny morality. Thus a Mimamsa philosopher though he does not accept a moral governor, he cannot deny a moral government—though without a governor. But this value-principle seems to have been taken as if from nowhere and placed side by side with the world of facts.

2. THE STATUS OF THE PHYSICAL WORLD

Mimamsa lays stress upon the reality of the external world.
This is the cardinal point, which it tries to establish.

Shabara in his *Bhasya* first postulates Purvapaksha—a position held by the Yogachara Buddhist. All cognition is baseless—i.e., without a real substratum in the external world as is
clear from the case of dream-cognition. In the case of dreams,
the Yogachara Buddhist holds, cognition has no real objective
substratum. Waking cognition being a cognition also can have
no real objective substratum. It is true, he holds, that the cognition that one has in the waking stage is perfectly definite and
determinate. But the same may be said of dream-cognition
also, which is quite definite and determinate till the time of
waking. If it is argued that the dream-cognition becomes
sublated, rejected as false as soon as the man wakes up. But
from the fact of both being of the nature of cognition, it is
presumed that the waking cognition also will, in due course of
time, become sublated and rejected.[16]

Shabara refutes this idealistic position. Falsity of dream-
cognition is not inferred because it is cognition. Its falsity is
because of some other reasons, for instance, that it is sublated
on waking by cognition to the contrary. A dream appears, as a
matter of fact, when one is only half asleep, when mind is not
quite alert. It is this sleepiness that is the cause of the falsity of
dream-cognition and as in the waking stage there is no sleepiness, mind is quite alert, there is no meaning in declaring this
cognition as false. The possibility of some defects even in the
waking stage is not ruled out, but this sort of defect is sooner or
later detected.

Again the Yogachara Buddhist objects: —As a matter of
fact cognition is an empty void, i.e., devoid of any foundation
in the external world; because no difference is perceived in

form between the cognition and its object; what is apprehended by the senses is only the cognition. It is concluded that there is no form or shape of any object apart from that cognition itself.[17]

Shabara answers this objection as follows: —Cognition has no form. It is only the external object that has a form and is actually apprehended as existing in external space. The object of the sense-cognition is not another cognition but an object. It is only when the object is cognised that the person comes to cognise the cognition. The existence of the cognition is only inferred from the fact of the object having been cognised. Thus there can be no simultaneity between the cognition of the object and the cognition of that cognition, i.e., the cognition can never be regarded as the objective of sense perception.

Even if there is identity in form between the cognition and the object of this cognition, it is the cognition that should have to be denied separate existence, not the object, which is actually perceived. As a matter of fact, however, the two are not identical. Shabara cites an example, whenever a cloth is perceived; it is only when the threads composing the cloth are there, this establishes a necessary connection between the cognition and its object in the shape of cloth whose existence therefore cannot be denied. If there were no such necessary connection between the cognition and the object cognised, it might be possible to have the cognition of cloth when the object before the eye is the jar. Thus Shabara concludes that the cognition has a real substratum in the external world.

According to Prabhakara in his *Brihati* there is no reference to the extreme nihilism in the *Bkashya* when it speaks of *Shunya*—void, all that it means is that the cognition is void, i.e., devoid of all external background.

Prabhakara also in his *Brihati* postulates the idealistic position of the Yogachara Buddhist in order to criticise and reject it: —"There is no real object in the external world; whenever we have the cognition of things, like the wall, for instance, it is baseless being due entirely to the Vasana, predisposition present in the mind of the cogniser."[18]

Prabhakara criticises this view. He points out that in finding out the cause of certain effects a cause is assumed which accounts for the appearance of the effect. In the case of dreams and other cognitions, the cognition that appears clearly manifests external things. This effect in the form of cognitions can be only explained on the basis of the real existence of the external things. The right view is that it is the external thing, which is the cause, the basis, of the said cognition. Without an external basis no cognition is ever apprehended. For these reasons, the perception brought about by the senses cannot be due merely to the predisposition present in the mind of the observer. On the basis of this predisposition some dreams may certainly be accounted for due to the thoughts and anxieties in the mind of the man when going to sleep, but it is not so in all cases. In no case it is so in our waking cognition, which is perfectly well defined. With regard to wrong cognition of the things or illusion what happens is that there is no cognition of the distinction between the things and some kind of memory not that the thing cognised has no existence in the external world.

The Yogachara idealist maintains: —Cognition is the property of the soul, or of the mind or of consciousness itself. What is meant is that *Samvit* (perception) is actually perceived, if it were not perceived then there could be no perception of things at all, and yet what is formless cannot be perceived. There is only one form, in the shape of what is perceived, e.g., a particular colour; this is the form therefore which must belong to the perceptions; this *Samvit* (perception) is not in the form of the soul, or of the mind as these two exist even without the cognition; hence perception (*Samvit*) cannot be identified with the soul or mind. It is only right to identify it with consciousness (*jnana*) so that what is perceived is only the *Samvit*, objective ideation, not any external object in the shape of sound and the rest.

But Prabhakara criticizes the above argument. The *Samvit* (perception) and the object both are perceived, not consciousness, though the form perceived is one only, yet the perception is not the entity involved, because both perception as well as the object are equally manifested in every act of perception. Though the *Samvit* (perception) by itself is formless yet it is perceptible, because the form in which it appears is only that of the resultant of the act of perception; and this resultant does not stand in need of another form. The *jnana* is to be taken as the direct cause of the said *Samvit*, which could not come about without cause. To the question what is *jnana*, the answer is that it is the cause leading to the effect in the form of the said perception. This effect, in the form of perception must have a cause, the permanent souls cannot be that cause for if it is so, then the perception also would have to be eternal; but the cognition that is inferred is a fleeting one; and when this cognition is inferred as the cause of perception or objective ideation, it is so only in the form of external things. Thus all cognition must be based upon real objects.

The next argument of the Yogachara Buddhist is that if a Blue object for example is what is perceived, how about the perception itself? Is it perceived or not? If it is not perceived, its existence should not be admitted.[19]

Prabhakara's answer to this question is that perception is certainly perceived but it is perceived as perception not as a perceptible object, i.e., the perception is perceived by itself not as the object of another perception, even without being an object, it manifests itself; it is not necessary that everything that is perceived should be perceived as an object. When, therefore, the term perceptible is applied to perception, it is only in the sense of its being perceived directly by itself, not in the sense of its forming the object of sensuous cognition. The said perception cannot be regarded as unperceived. Because it is on the basis of perception itself being perceptible that things perceived are regarded as such. This perception, however, leads on to cognition (*jnana*), which is purely inferred as the cause of the said perception or objective ideation. The inference is this, this perception is an effect, it must therefore, have a cause, this cause is the *jnana* (cognition). As a matter of fact, all men are cognisant of this twofold form—one the effect in the form of the *Samvit* and the other the cause, in the form of the *jnana*—cognition. Thus apart from the *Samvit*, there is the cognition and also the object. Thus Prabhakara concludes that entire cognitive phenomenon is based upon real objects in the external world and not upon Vasanas—predisposition.

To establish the reality of the External World Kumarila has devoted two chapters of his *Shlokavartika*. In 202 verses of *Niralambanavada* he first postulates the different possible positions of the Yogachara school of Buddhism then he refutes them. Then in 263 verses of *Shunyavada* he examines the positions held by *Shunyavada* thinkers of Buddhism and then refutes them also.

Kumarila argues in the *Niralambanavada* section that the needs of the situation cannot be met by postulating the illusory reality of things because what is real cannot be illusory and what is illusory cannot be real.[20] Then again he asserts that there cannot be two kinds of reality. It must be admitted, he says, that which does not exist, and that which really exists is real while all else is unreal and therefore, there can be no assumption of two kinds of reality.[21]

From the 17th to the 27th verses of the *Niralambanavada* Kumarila states the *Purvapaksha* argument—the position held by the Buddhist Yogachara who holds the cognition, idea, *Vijnana* without a real substratum in the external world. In the remaining verses Kumarila shows that the reasoning set forth by the Yogachara Buddhist is entirely fallacious and cannot be upheld on logical grounds.

Kumarila points out that if it be said that in the cognition of an object like a pillar, there can be no external object as the pillar. This is in conflict with an experienced fact. Further if there is no real difference between what is good and what is bad, if there be no difference between teacher and disciples, as facts of the external world there can be no real instruction by the teacher to the disciples regarding the nature of what is good. A denial of the external reality of the objects that has been instructed as what is good would result in a direct contradiction of the teaching of Buddhists in their philosophy of Idealism, denying the reality of the external world because it refutes the doctrines of their own Teacher. If there is no difference between a cognition of a pillar outside and the dream about a pillar then Buddha and his teaching are not different from dreams. Kumarila lays much stress on this point while refuting the philosophical doctrines of the Buddhists and he also shows that they are opposed to their own religion.

Kumarila has made a deep logical analysis of Buddhist idealistic positions. If it held that the ideas involved in all arguments are devoid of any externally real object that would result in a universal negation and if it is held that some of the ideas involved in the argumentation have reality in the case of the object comprehended in the argument, then the whole argument falls to the ground.

Are there distinctions like "being in bondage" and "being liberated" if both are ideas? Here again there would be contradiction with the religion of Buddha where prescriptions are made for liberation from this world, which is supposed to be a bondage. It will be contradictory if it is held that the denial of external reality in the case of ideas has application only in the case of ideas regarding concrete objects like a pillar and not to abstract ideas like good and bad, bondage and liberation. Dream experience is contradicted by waking experience and is rejected. But a pillar of waking experience cannot be contradicted by another experience. Kumarila argues that the Buddhist idealist may hold that even the experiences of the waking stage are contradicted by the Yogic experience. Kumarila does not deny the Yogic vision. But he holds that hardly one is found to develop such vision in this life; and in case, if, however, anyone attains the Yogic vision we do not know what happens to him. Even if it is admitted the experiences of the Yogic vision go against the idealistic doctrine of the unreality of the objects in experience. From the point of view of reason also, Yogic vision must have some external reality in so far as they are experiences like our own waking experiences, which have some external background. The Buddhist idealist may argue that in the case of waking experiences there is a possibility of some counter factors which at times invalidate them as is in the experience of a mirage. Kumarila does not refuse to admit such factors in our waking experiences. False cognition, as in a dream are invalidated through correct cognitions of the waking condition. Even in the cases of waking cognitions there may be some invalidations. In the same way, there is no impossibility of Yogic cognition too being invalid sometimes. Therefore, the Yogic cognition does not bring any new thing, which was not previously admitted. Thus, we have to hold the position that there are external realities and that a cognition would be valid only if it is based on such external realities and false if there is no such basis.

Further, Kumarila argues in his *Niralambanavada* that dream cognition is not absolutely false. In all instances of dream there is an external reality as the basis, the relations may be different in dream from those of the waking conditions. No dream is possible without some previous experience of a real external object. It may be during the present life, it may be in the past life, they appear in dreams as related to another time and another place and under different circumstances. In the same way, all sorts of erroneous cognitions like that of continuous circle when a firebrand is whirled or like that of a notion of cities in the clouds or of water in a desert. Even in the case of a "hare's horn" there is a reality. Separately, hare is real, as well as horn, only their combination is unreal and not the objective material itself. The main positive argument that Kumarila has put forward in support of the reality of things is this: "Because in opposition to all the alternatives (open to you) we would bring this counter argument—cognitions have real substrata, in the external world and this notion (of cognition having a real substratum) is correct because it is a notion free from contradiction—like the notion of the falsity of dream cognition, cognitions have real substratum in the external world."[22]

Kumarila concludes this chapter by saying that the followers of the teachings of the Buddha are not faithful to him. Buddha taught the Dharma or the moral order, his mission was only to see that people do not much indulge in the worldly charms. There is a difference between indifference to the world and denial of the world. Buddha taught the former, while his disciples interpreted it as the latter. As a matter of fact this denial of the reality of external objects following upon the assumption of such an "Impression—(theory) which is incorrect and devoid of reason—was declared by the Buddha, with the sole object of alienating the affections of men from such world objects and somehow or other some people (the so-called followers of the Buddha) fell into a mistake and accepted it to its extreme extent as the denial of all external substratum of cognitions."[23]

In the same strain Kumarila takes up the other view held up by the Madhyamika Buddhist who does not admit even the existence of the idea. In the first 63 Karikas of Shunyavada he analyses the different positions of the Madhyamika idealist and then in the remaining Karikas up to 263 he refutes them.

First he states Madhyamika position clearly and faithfully. In any case, all that we do is to assert the identity of the cogniser (cognition) and the cognised (object of cognition) the assumption of either externality or internality we hold to be utterly groundless[24], he refutes it. His position is that both from the subjective and the objective standpoints, there must be some concrete positive reality in the outside world as the basis for our experience. It is not so. Because you hold one and the same thing (idea) to be both the cogniser and the cognised, whereas you cannot have any instance to show that such duplicate character belongs to any simple object, Kumarila holds that duality of existence is an established fact. In any case, the duality of existence (in the shape of comprehension and the comprehended) has been established and such being the case you may make use of whatever words you like, and we have, and we have got nothing to say against the world.[25] In the following Karika, Kumarila states that the external object is not identical with internal idea: It is necessary for students of philosophy to explain things exactly according to cognition met within ordinary experiences. And (in ordinary experience) the external object is never cognized to be of the same form as the internal (idea).[26] He concludes by saying: Thus then (the reality of) the external object having been established, there can be unreality of the idea (either); and for those who know the true character of both (the object and the idea) this (couple, object and idea) is really a fit object for being made the axle of the wheel of "Investigating into Duty".[27]

Thus the Mimamsa philosopher establishes the world's existence as independent of knowledge, which is a through going realistic position. They vehemently argued that there could never be a mere idea; every idea must be an idea of something. It is obvious because the objects which we perceive in a dream are not invented by the mind but they exist by their own right in the external world and must have been perceived before we can dream of them. In dreaming, there may be new relational adjustments by the mind according to its desire, but those are of the external perceived object, which the mind does not create. This is, indeed, a common sense realistic view. The world exists whether we know it or not. The world is not in our ideas but our ideas are in the world. It is because of this real world that man has to adjust his actions according to the instructions of the *Shastras*. An unconscious man is free from all ideas. And if the ideas constitute the world, the unconscious man should be considered as liberated but the unconscious man is very much in the world, he is not mukta. This proves that the world is not an idea and man has to deal with this world every moment of his life.

3. MAN AND HIS RELATION TO NATURE

Man or jivatman in the Purva Mimamsa philosophy has been considered as a unit comprising the physical, the sensuous, the psychical and also a self, which is beyond all these. Self has a peculiar status in the Purva Mimamsa as eternal and omnipresent. Jaimini is not very clear on this point. We are not sure whether Shabara was influenced by Upavarsha while explaining the nature of *Atman* in his *Bhashya* on 1.1.5. Whatever the case may be Shabara admits that the self as an eternal being is distinct from body, senses and mind all of which perish. When the Vedic text speaks of the sacrifices equipped with the sacrificial implements proceeding to heaven, it does not mean physical body by 'equipped with sacrificial imple-

ments', but soul. It is that entity which en-souls the body and
to whom the body belongs. He also infers the presence of such
an entity from the phenomena of breathing, winking of the
eyes and the like which cannot belong to the body, as they are
not found after death, though the body is there all right.

Secondly, the feelings of pleasure and pain are entirely
private; the person himself can feel while the qualities of colour
and the rest are public to each and every body. He holds that
the agent of the act of cognising, desiring and the like is said to
be soul or *Atman*.[28]

According to Prabhakara soul is of the nature of doer and
experiencer.[29] It is entirely different from the body, the sense
organs and Buddhi.[30] It is eternal.[31] It is omnipresent.[32] It is
many.[33] The cogniser is different from Buddhi.[34] The self is
the agent, the enjoyer and omnipresent but non-sentient (*jada*)
since it is different from knowledge.[35]

According to Kumarila also the self is something distinct
from the body, the sense organs and Buddhi. It is eternal.[36] It
is the real doer of action, agent of acts and the one that experiences the results and reactions.[37] It is also all-pervading.[38] It is
the soul that passes through the experience of pleasure, and
pain, etc.[39] According to Kumarila the soul is both—unconscious and conscious as Madhusudana Sarasvati in his phrase
utters: "*Jado bhodharmakashca*". It is unconscious since it is
the substratum of consciousness, and also conscious since it is
the object of self-consciousness.

Jivatman is the self limited by body, senses and mind. In
this connection, Kunhan Raja observes: —

This continuous line on which the various links of cause
and effect are united to form a chain, is what they accept
as a soul, the *Atman*. It is only an individuality without a
material form; the presentation represented by the func-

tioning of the successive bodies are joined together into
this individuality called a soul. A soul is only such a line;
the progression is only in the material bodies.[40]

After explaining the *nature* of *Atman* as something beyond
the body, senses and mind the Purva-Mimamsa philosopher
then tries to associate the concept of jivatman with the concept
of Dharma. Dharma has central significance in the Purva-
Mimamsa system and at the same time it is responsible for
bringing inconsistence into it also.

The Mimamsa Sutra of Jaimini begins with: Next, therefore, comes the enquiry into Dharma (duty).[41] Naturally the
question here arises is—what is Dharma which is to be investi-
gated and with it a secondary question arises—what is the means
whereby the right knowledge of Dharma can be obtained. The
next Sutra defines Dharma: —Dharma is that which is indi-
cated by means of the Veda as conductive to the highest good.[42]
Dharma in this context does not stand for the merit that is
obtained by the doing of a good deed, it is used in a much
wider sense of what should be done—i.e., Duty. True spiritual-
ity lies in fixing one's attention on Dharma or such acts of duty
as lead to success in the life beyond. Dharma has extra-empiri-
cal significance in this system. The same definition of dharma
also provides the answer to the second question, regarding the
means of knowing dharma. On this point the conclusion is that
the Vedic injunction is the only means of knowing Dharma,
i.e., the right knowledge is possible only through the Veda.
Here the question arises: Is the knowledge of dharma brought
about by the Vedic injunction only or also by sense perception
and the other well-known means of knowledge? As a matter of
fact sense perception is operative only in regard to such things
as are present and in contact with the sense organs. Dharma,
however, is not anything existing at present nor is it possible

for it to be in contact with any sense organs; hence, though dharma is an object of knowledge, it is incapable of being cognised through sense perception. And when it is entirely beyond the reach of sense perception, the other means of knowledge—inference, analogy and the rest, which are simply the extension of sense perception, cannot be applicable to it. So it is established that dharma can be known by the Vedic injunction only. The expressiveness of the world is not dependent upon convention as the relationship between the world and what it denotes is inborn, eternal, without beginning or end; hence the word is self-sufficient and infallible also. Here it may be concluded that (a) dharma is what is enjoined in the Veda as conductive to welfare, (b) the Veda is the only source of the knowledge of dharma, and (c) the Veda is a reliable source of knowledge.

Thus dharma has a wider connotation in this system. Dharma means duties to be performed by a man according to the Vedic injunctions. Then a man must follow these injunctions without questioning their truth or propriety as they are infallible, they must be followed. But here a question arises, who is to understand the meaning of this authority—the Vedic injunctions? So ultimately a man will have to depend on a group of men who are considered to be the authentic interpreter of those injunctions. This group will naturally, therefore, dominate society and there will be a kind of intellectual aristocracy. This may naturally lead to exploitation of the illiterate mass by a powerful group. And history has proved that such degeneration took place in the form of religious fanaticism. This is very natural because as soon as independent thinking and judgment are banished from human decisions, the human mind finally revolts against all authorities, good or bad.

Mimamsa tries to find out a link between the sacrifices performed by man and the results of these sacrifices, which would be responsible for the realization of heaven. The sacrifices themselves are transitory, some provision must be made to store their results in some form and the concept of *apurva* is a device, which serves the purpose. Mimamsa being an atheistic system, *apurva* plays a significant role, working a link between the sacrifices and their fruits. The Mimamsa Sutra of Jaimini states: — There is *Apurva* because action is enjoined.[43] Shabara in his *Bhashya* explains it: —There must be such a thing as *Apurva*—because action is enjoined—in such an injunction as desiring heaven one should perform sacrifice. If there were no such thing as *Apurva*, such an injunction would be meaningless, because the sacrifice itself is something perishable—and if it were to perish without bringing into existence something else, then the result—in the shape of heaven could never come about.

Prabhakara maintains that *Apurva* is in the act or the exertion, which produces it; and the causal potency must reside in this exertion, *Apurva* cannot be in the self, since by its very omnipresence the self is inactive.[44]

According to Kumarila, the *Apurva* is a potency in the principal action or in the agent, which did not exist prior to the performances of that action and whose existence is proved by the authority of the scriptures. In the sacrifices themselves, in the first instance, there is an incapacity to attain heaven, and in the second place, in the agent, an incapacity to attain heaven— both these incapacities are set aside by performing the sacrifice, this performance produces a potency by virtue of which heaven is achieved, and this potency is named as *Apurva*, the proof of the existence of such an *Apurva* lies in presumption, based upon the fact that without some such capacity or potency Vedic texts are wholly inexplicable. Thus *Apurva* is the connecting link between the sacrifice and its result. It is the *Apurva*, which can explain the causal relation between these two. *Apurva* is simply a force, potency, capacity set in motion by the performance of sacrifice. And this force is the direct instrument to bring about the result.

The earlier Mimamsakas believed only in *dharma* and their ideal was the attainment of heaven. Heaven is that happy state, which is entirely free from all touch of pain, and which as such, is desired by all men.[45] Happiness is not mere absence of pain. The absence of pain is purely negative. But when we feel happy we are conscious of something positive—a positive quality, as belonging to the soul.[46]

But the later Mimamsakas believe in Moksha and substitute the ideal of heaven by that of liberation (*Apavarga*). According to Shalikanath Mishra, believed to have been a direct pupil of Prabhakara, liberation consists in the total disappearance of *dharma* and *adharma*, whose operation is the cause of rebirth. It is defined as the absolute cessation of the body cause by the disappearance of all dharma and adharma.[47] Moksha is simply the natural state of man.[48] If Prabhakara believes in liberation as *Prakaranapanchikakara* maintains, he appears to be inconsistent with his own declaration to the effect that the soul is purely the actor and experiencer.[49] It means that there is no freedom for the soul from action and experience, so that there can be no liberation.

Prof. Hiriyanna rightly observes: "But in the case of the former (Prabhakara) which pursued dharma as its own end, the acceptance of new ideal means deserting its cherished principle of doing duty for its own sake, and going over completely to the side of the Bhattas."[50]

According to Kumarila: "For those who have understood the real nature of the soul, all their karma having become exhausted through experience and there being no further karmic residue left to wipe off there comes no further body, as it is only for the experiencing of the reactions of past karma that the soul is burdened with the body; the seeker for liberation should not do any such act as has been enjoined for certain purposes; but he should continue to perform the obligatory acts as the omission of these would involve sin, which would have to be expiated by painful experience through a physical body."[51]

The Mimamsa system has no need for a God, nor for gods. Man is self-contained; man is supreme. Why? Because dharma has reference only to man. It is only a human being who an carry out the entire details of the prescribed act.[52] Hence it is man alone who is entitled to perform sacrifices.

Beings lower than the human are not entitled, because they are not able to carry on the details of the sacrifice in their entirety, hence for these beings, the sacrifice cannot be a means of securing happiness.[53]

The deities are also not entitled to the performance of sacrifices, because apart from themselves, there are no other deities to whom they could offer sacrifices and there can be no offering to one's own self, in fact, such an act would be no offering at all.[54]

Nor are the sages entitled to the performance of sacrifices, because they can have no Gotra.[55]

Thus in the Mimamsa system, man has been given the most exalted position in creation. Man alone is capable of understanding the significance of the Vedic rituals and injunctions, the various sacrifices and their consequences. The Mimamsa philosopher wants to give us a moral world and it is man who alone can discover this basic principle, which governs the world. Thus unlike Nyaya-vaisheshika, here the view is less mechanical and more ethical. The dynamic nature of the world is inherent in its constituents, integration and disintegration of the elements. But side-by-side, there is a moral force that is responsible for adjusting human actions to the environment. This moral force seems to be as fundamental and eternal as the dynamism in nature. Thus in this system we find two fundamental principles, naturalistic and ethical existing together and acting on each other. There is no supreme being to control the resultant of the naturalistic and moral forces. Hence the human responsibility and man's status have become profoundly important. Man has to depend on himself to chalk out his programme for realising the goal. He is generally attracted towards complexities that bring for him suffering and unhappiness by the naturalistic forces. But his discovery of the moral principle for the Vedic injunction explained to him by the teachers help him understanding his dharma, so that he can rise above the naturalistic forces and establish himself on dharma which ultimately leads him to the status of perfect peace and happiness. This is the heaven for man according to the Mimamsakas. Heaven is not a superior Loka where man can enjoy pleasant and good things without any experience of suffering. But heaven is a status which man attains when he rises above the naturalistic demands through performing injunctions prescribed by the Vedas. In this status the Jivatman has absolute cessation of suffering, and therefore he for ever enjoys peace and happiness as a liberated soul.

But the Mimamsa system in spite of its emphasis on a kind of cosmic moral principle is not free from vacillation due to its adherence to the naturalistic principles. It is not absolutely sure as to the true nature of ultimate reality in man. The self, though the Mimamsa philosopher suggests it to be beyond the body, senses, and mind, he makes it a *karta* and *bhokta*. The concept of self is not free from a relational texture, because of its *adhara-adheya sambandha*. It is very natural because whenever we find common sense and realistic attitude towards the world, man is taken to be a part of nature. However, the philosopher may try, the naturalistic tendencies that lead to an affirmation of life dominates his thinking. Thus we find that in most cases the concept of heaven, that of absolute absence of suffering, that of eternal happiness—all these are only using a language which is born out of man's sensuous contact with nature. Heaven is a place like earth minus its trouble, anxieties and sufferings. Therefore, Mukti becomes nothing but getting out of the bondage. If the philosopher of common sense realism tries to save him from the negative concepts and tries to give something positive in regard to the realized status of the liberated soul, he becomes a victim to the naturalistic concepts, which are key words in a realistic philosophy—like Karta, Bhokta, etc. Thus, in spite of the Mimamsa philosopher's concept of heaven as a status of liberated soul, it is not free from such naturalistic images.

Man, therefore, occupies a very peculiar status. He is in nature, a part of it, yet he wants to go out of it. But though he may go out of the world of the physical world, he cannot go out of the moral world, because he is a part and parcel of this moral world so far as his true nature is concerned. The Mimamsa never asks man to go beyond good and evil, beyond *dharma* and *adharma*. For this system without *dharma* even in its essence is inconceivable. Therefore, a very pertinent question arises here what exactly is the relation between the physical and moral world according to Mimamsa? Is the relation an interdependent one? If not, can the moral dominate over the physical world? Are the two worlds, which we may call the world of facts and the world of values externally related? All such questions cannot be answered definitely from the statements, which we find in the Mimamsa philosophy. The Mimamsa philosopher has not been able to find out the true nature or ultimate reality of man. It has not been able to take up the clue supplied by the Upanishadic thinkers in regard to the nature of self. The ideas of self, free from empirical limitations have been taken by the Mimamsa writers from the other systems but have not been properly understood so as to reach a logical culmination. Thus, the system seems to be a conglomeration of ideas not neatly synthesized together to make a logically tenable system. It has in mind a social discipline, a morally regulated life free from conflicts and quarrels and also a life where religious fanaticism having supremacy of a particular god has not the possibility of interfering. All these are social ideals of secularism and peace. The Mimamsa philosophers are, therefore, very much concerned with this world.

REFERENCES

1. SV. P. 443, sl. 32-3
2. *Prakaranapanchika*, p. 137
3. SV. Sec. 16, 45
4. SV. Sec. 16, 47
5. SV. Sec. 16, 48
6. SV. Sec. 16, 49-50
7. SV. Sec. 16, 113
8. SV. Sec. 16, 68
9. *Prakaranapanchika*, p. 110
10. *Prakarna*, p. 24
11. *Prakarana*, pp. 81-2
12. *Prakarana*, p. 84
13. *Prakarana*, p. 54
14. *Shastradipika*, p. 52
15. SV. 1.1.4
16. *Shabara Bhashya*, p. 12
17. S.B.P.12
18. Brihati, p. 69
19. Brihati, p. 82 (As quoted in the *Purva Mimamsa* by G.N Jha)
20. SV. *Niralambavavada*, 6
21. SV. *Niralambavavada*, 10
22. SV. *Niralambavavada*, 79-80

23. SV. *Niralambavavada*, 202
24. SV. *Shunyavada*, 14
25. SV. *Shunyavada*, 129
26. SV. *Shunyavada*, 229
27. SV. *Shunyavada*, 263
28. Shabara, 1.1.5
29. Brihati. P. 235
30. Brihati, p. 231
31. Ibid, p. 235
32. Brihati, p. 235
33. Ibid, p. 239
34. *Prakaranapanchika*, p. 75
35. Karta bhokta, *jado vibhuriti Prabhakarah—Siddhi Bindu.*
36. SV. *Atmavada*, 7
37. Ibid, 8
38. Ibid, 20
39. Ibid, 26
40. Kunhan Raja: *Some Fundamental Problems in Indian Philosophy* p. 272
41. M.S. 1.1.1
42. Ibid, 1.1.2
43. M.S. 2.1.5
44. Ganganath Jha's *Purva Mimamsa*, pp. 259-60
45. *Prakaranapanchika*, pp. 102-103
46. *Prakaranapanchika*, p. 149
47. *Atyantikas tu dehocchedo nissesadharmadharmapariksha-yanibandhana mokshas iti siddham.* Prakarana, p. 156
48. *Svatmaspharanarupah.* Prakarana, p. 268
49. Brihati, p. 235
50. *Outlines of Indian Philosophy*, p. 332
51. SV. *Sambandhakshepaparihara*, 108-10
52. M.S. 6.1.5
53. *Shabara Bhashya*, p. 973
54. Ibid, 973
55. *Shabara Bhashya*, p. 973

6

NATURE, MAN, AND REALITY IN VEDANTA

A

1. THE EARLY ADVAITA VEDANTA OF GAUDAPADA

(i) *The Doctrine of Ajativada:* —

As it is well known, the teachings of the Upanishads have been systematized in the *Brahmasutra* of Badarayana—which is the basis of the Vedanta system of Indian philosophy. The sutras have been interpreted by the different acharyas and we have as a result two different schools—the Advaita Vedanta and the Theistic Vedanta.

Of these two Schools, the Advaita Vedanta is earlier. The Advaita thought starts so far as it is historically recorded with Gaudapada. It is difficult to say whether Gaudapada drew his inspiration from the *Sutras* of Badarayana His *Karika* on the Mandukya Upanishad gives us his views, which are the earliest record of the Advaita thought. His *Mandukya Karika* is also known by the names of Gaudapada or *Gaudapadiya Karika* and *Agamashastra*. The Karika shows that he was much influenced by the Upanishadic thoughts, and his writings are full of terms and phrases, which are abundantly found in the Upanishads. His rejection of causation, *ajativada*, his concept of the world as mere illusion—are significant and are of profound importance for the Advaita Vedanta.

The *Agamashastra* of Gaudapada is the 'grammar' of the Advaita Vedanta. *Ajativada*, the theory of non-origination is the central thesis of Gaudapada. It states two doctrines. First, the *Atman* is *aja*. Secondly, causation is a myth and this culminates into *mayavada*. First we will examine his denunciation of causation. The main arguments against causation are the following.

(i) Nothing is born out of itself or out of another or out of both. A jar cannot produce itself, nor can it be produced out of a piece of cloth nor out of both.

(ii) But it may be asked: Is not a pot produced from clay? Is not a son born to parents? Gaudapada maintains that this is undoubtedly what is perceived. But he adds that it does not stand to reason. Nothing is in fact produced whether it be existent, non-existent or both.[2] If a thing is existent it cannot be produced for it is already there. Nor is the second view true, because the non-existent by its very nature cannot be produced. Nor can the third be accepted i.e., if a thing is both existent and non-existent, it involves a contradiction.

(iii) Causation is a myth. Why? (a) The non-existent cannot have the non-existent for its cause, as the horns of a hare cannot be the cause of the castle-in-the-air; (b) nor can the existent have the non-existent for its cause, as the horns of a hare cannot be the cause of a jar; (c) the existent cannot be the effect of the existent, because the existent already exists; if it exists already it does not need a cause as a chair cannot be the cause of a jar; (d) again the existent cannot be the effect of the non-existent for that which does not exist cannot produce anything.[3] With regard to causality we find only these four types of relations none of which is, however, possible. Hence causality is regarded as a pure myth by the enlightened.

Having refuted the concept of causality and showing it to be a bundle of contradictions, Gaudapada now examines the different theories of causation in the Indian philosophy.

The theories examined by Gaudapada are the *Satkaryavada* of the *Samkhya-yoga*, the *Asatkaryavada* of the Nyaya-vaisheshika, and the *pratityasamutpada* of the *Sarvasativada* and the Yogachara schools of Buddhism. We shall first examine his criticism of *Satkaryavada* and *asatkaryavada*.

The *Samkhya-yoga* holds that *jati* (origination) belongs to a thing, which is already existent in its cause. The Nyaya-vaisheshika holds that it belongs to a thing, which is non-existent in its cause.[4] In this way they maintain contradictory views and one criticizes the other. And their mutual criticism itself proves the *ajativada*.[5]

To that which is unborn, the disputants attribute birth. But what is unborn must be immortal. To say that unborn is born is to attribute mortality.[6] How is it possible? The immortal cannot become mortal, nor the mortal immortal, for it is impossible for a thing to change its nature.[7]

Satkaryavada maintains the non-difference of cause and effect. It is possible in two ways. Either the cause is identical with the effect, or the effect is identical with the cause. If the cause is identical with the effect, then since the effect is born, the cause also must be said to be born. The primal cause *Prakriti* should be subject to birth and the Samkhya cannot maintain it as *aja* and *nitya*. If the other alternative, viz., that the effect is identical with the cause is adopted, then as the cause is *aja*, so the effect also would be *aja*. And if it is *aja*, it cannot be produced, and if it cannot be produced, it ceases to be the effect; it is a self-contradiction.[8]

Further there is no illustration, which could prove the premise of the *Asatkaryavada*, i.e., that from what is unborn a thing is produced. Indeed, in the absence of illustration no inference is possible.[9]

Here we find that the *Satkaryavada* emphasizes the notion of cause in causation while the *asatkaryavada* that of effect; using Kantian terminology we may say that the former tries to maintain the necessary connection between cause and effect without any novelty in the effect and thus retains causation with only one term, viz., cause; the latter, on the other hand, is keen to maintain the novelty of the effect without any necessary connection between cause and effect and thus maintains causation with only one term, viz., effect. But causation involves a relation between two terms, i.e., cause and effect, and hence it becomes meaningless, if one of them is missing. To maintain causality with only one term, cause or effect, is absurd. The notion of causality, which tries to combine the novelty of the effect with the necessary connection between cause and effect, has inherent difficulty. Gaudapada notices that both *Satkaryavada* and *asatkaryavada* refute causality in their own way.

The *pratityasamutpada* of the Buddhists is treated in the same manner by Gaudapada. It believes in the dependent interconnected or combined origination (*Samutpada*) of some elements with regard to other elements.[10]

It holds the relation of simultaneity between cause (*hetu*) and effect (*phala*) and takes the series of causes and effects to be anadi. Gaudapada analyses it and shows its inconsistencies. First of all, if the effect is the cause of the cause and vice versa, how can cause and effect be beginningless.[11] The interdependence of cause and effect and their beginningless-ness are contradictory. Secondly, the view that the effect is the cause of the cause and vice versa would assert causation like the birth of the father from the son.[12] There should be some definite order between cause and effect. But the order of cause and effect cannot be determined. If it is simultaneity, it is no causation for it obtains between the two horns of an animal as well.[13] If the effect is prior to cause, the order of succession is unjustifiably reversed. Finally, if the cause is prior to the effect, it is non-existent. And a non-existent cause like the sky-flower cannot produce any effect. The three possible orders of the sequence, i.e., simultaneity of cause and effect, priority of cause to effect and posteriority of cause to effect are thus ruled out.[14] Their absolute ignorance of the order of cause and effect brings into relief the theory of non-origination.[15] Gaudapada's criticism as stated above has been considered by the earlier scholars like Stcherbatsky as directed against *Pratityasamutpada* doctrine of *Sarvastivada* Buddhism. But a recent scholar Dr. T.M.P. Mahadevan has suggested that Gaudapada's criticism is rather against the Purva Mimamsa doctrine, namely the cause and effect are reciprocally dependent. "Merit (*dharma*) and demerit (*adharma*) are responsible for producing the body; and the body in its turn occasions merit and demerit. The chain of causes and effects is without beginning, each alternating with the other, like the seed and the sprout."[16]

Gaudapada criticizes Pratityasamutpada from a different angle also. The Buddhist realist admits a plurality of separate elements, which are classified into the elements of matter and of mind. Stcherbatsky observes, it ties together the four fundamental and the secondary elements of matter "*bhuta* and *bhautika*" on the one hand, and "consciousness and mental phenomena (*chitta* and *chaitta*)"[17] on the other. Buddhist realist (*Sarvastivadin*) maintains the dependent origination together of objects and impressions (elements of matter and mind respectively).

But Buddhist idealists do not find any difference between object and impressions. In their opinion objects like jars etc. have themselves no cause and they are hence not the cause of impressions.[18] The idealists thus deny the dependent origination of objects on the one hand and of objects and impressions on the other. They, however, maintain the causal relation among impressions. Some of them, nevertheless, maintain that the mind relates itself neither to an object nor to its impression for the object is unreal and its impressions are not different from it.[19] So neither the mind nor that which is known to it is originated. Those who see its origination see the footmarks of birds in sky.[20]

Buddhist Idealism reduces all reality to the mind and the mental (the knower and the known). It provisionally relates the two by dependent origination but finally rejects it as impossible and accepts the theory of non-origination.[21]

As long as there is the least faith in causality, cause and effect will continue to operate. But if that faith be destroyed by dialectic, cause and effect are nowhere.[22]

The above arguments of Gaudapada refuting causality show that though common sense does not find any absurdity or contradiction in the relation of cause and effect, a logical analysis proves otherwise. The common sense notion of causality is based on our concept of time so that cause for all practical purposes must be an antecedent to the effect. But if time is analysed to be a mere idea without any reality, the notion of causality becomes meaningless. Gaudapada's analysis shows that there is an inherent limitation of the mind when it tries to explain causality dialectically. The mind is in the habit of taking cause and effect as entities. An entity has a definite spatio-temporal structure without which it cannot have a referential value for the mind, that is to say mind cannot refer to it. If a spatio-temporal structure is taken out all entities come under one Reality where there are no distinguishable parts. This is certainly something, which transcends mind's field of knowledge. In that experience beyond mind plurality is lost and therefore, cause and effect have no independent existence of their own, thus nothing is born, nothing is destroyed. This is what Gaudapada's *ajativada* teaches.

(ii) *Refutation of Cosmology*: —

There are different theories of creation; some of them have been examined by Gaudapada. In the first *prakarna* Gaudapada states that a distinction should be made between the *parmartha chintakas*, i.e., those who proclaim the supreme truth of non-creation and the *srishtichintakas* who take creation to be real. The various theories of *Srishtichintakas* are enumerated by Gaudapada in the following order: —

(i)   The first maintains creation as the expression of *Ishvara's* lordly power.

(ii) The second view is that creation is similar to dream (*Svapnasvarupa*).

(iii) The third theory is that creation is like a magical show.

(iv) There are some who hold that creation is the mere will of God.

(v)   According to some, creation proceeds from time.

(vi) Some believe that the creation is for the enjoyment of Ishvara.

(vii) While there are others who believe that creation is for the sport of Ishvara.[23]

Gaudapada disposes of the theories where God is taken as creator by saying that creation is God's nature, for what desire is possible for Him, whose desires are always in the state of perfect fulfillment.[24]

As regards creation, there are numerous *Shrutis* to the effect that creation is from the existent or from the non-existent.[25] But logically neither of these two is tenable. Of what is existent, birth through *maya* alone is possible and not in reality.[26] And what is non-existent cannot be born either really or illusorily. The son of a barren is born neither in reality nor through *maya*.[27]

But how are the passages in the *Shrutis* declaring creation to be interpreted? Are they nonsensical? If they are so, their authority is challenged. Gaudapada does not say that the *Shrutis* declaring creation are nonsense. He assigns a definite purpose to them. The creation-texts are but a device (*Upaya*) to introduce the Absolute. The creation, which is described in different ways with the illustrations of earth, metal, and sparks, etc., is only a means to the recognition of the Absolute. There is in no way anything different from the Absolute.[28] Then again, he maintains that the vedantic masters have been talking to the students of the mediocre type in terms of creation only because of their anxiety to serve the lesser aspirants. The new initiates may get confounded if they are suddenly accosted with Acosmism.[29]

As a matter of fact, even to say that the truth is *ajati* would be meaningless, for *ajati* is meaningful only so long as *jati* carries a meaning. And that is so in the empirical world alone.[30] Cosmology is thus a myth or allegory, which shows that the first principle is everything everywhere.

2. THE WORLD AS MAYA

Gaudapada's Mayavada is the direct corollary of his denial of causation. It makes two statements. First, all productions are empirical (*samvritya jayate sarvam*); secondly, everything in itself is unborn (*svabhavena hyajam sarvam*).[31]

Gaudapada says that ultimate Reality is only Advaita, the world is *maya-matra*, mere illusion.[32] Besides the word *maya*, he employs several words to indicate the illusory nature of the world: —*vaitathya, mithya, kalpita, viparyaya, abhasa,* and *samvrti,* etc. The second *prakarana* of *Agamashastra* is significantly termed *vaitathya*; the sole object of this *prakarana* is to establish the illusoriness of the world. It is because of *maya* that we have this world of differentiation (*mayaya bhidyate hyetad*).[33] The world is differentiated into name, form, and function because of *maya*.[34] Only empirically and practically, the objects of phenomena have substantiality, causality, and motion.[35]

The universe of multiplicity is only a product of *maya*.[36] Whatever is perceived is nothing but the creation of mind, for the plurality is not perceived when the mind is transcended.[37] So long there is belief in causality, the endless *samsara* (chain of birth and death) will be there. When that is destroyed by knowledge *samsara* becomes non-existent.[38]

The illusoriness of the world is established by Gaudapada on the analogy of dream world. The objects seen in the dream are illusory. In the waking experience too objects are seen. So they are illusory.[39]

Gaudapada says that the waking experience is on a par with the dream experience.[40]

We cannot differentiate the two states on the ground of practical efficiency. It is true that dream-water cannot quench actual thirst, but it is equally true that the so-called actual water cannot quench the dream thirst. It cannot thus be said that the things of the waking alone are fruitful. If they are fruitful in the waking state, the things of the dream are fruitful in the dreaming state.[41]

It may be asked: how can the contents of dream constitute the illustration for proving the illusoriness of the world when they are so strange and abnormal? One may dream, for instance, of a person endowed with eight arms and seated on a elephant with four tusks.[42] Hence it is illogical to compare the objects of the waking state with those of the dreaming state. But this objection does not stand. In the dream state the objects are not realized to be strange and abnormal. The dream contents appear to be strange and abnormal from the side of the waking state, but in themselves they are quite normal.

It does not mean that Gaudapada has altogether denied the empirical difference between the waking and the dreaming states. From the standpoint of waking the dream occurrences seem to take place within the body in the small confined space while the objects of waking experience appear to belong to the external world.[43]

Secondly, the contents of dream, being related to the mind alone, are un-manifest (*avyakta*); while the objects of waking which are related to the outer sense organs also are manifest (*sphuta*).

Thirdly, while in the experience of former, the external senses, are inactive, in the cognition of the latter, they are active.[44]

Lastly, while the dream-contents last only till the mind of the dreamer imagines them (*chittakalah*), the objects of the external world extend to two points in time (*dvayakalah*)[45]. Thus according to Gaudapada, no doubt there is empirical difference between the two, but from the ultimate standpoint they are on a par.[46]

If the contents of dream and the objects of waking are unreal, what else is real? The answer is that on the ground of illusion, the self cannot be unreal. It is not possible to deny the self for the one who denies is of the very nature of the self.[47] It is the self that posits through *maya* the dream-contents as well as the external world. The things created in the mind within and those posited in the world without, both these are the illusory imagination of the *Atman*. This is the settled view of Vedanta, so says Gaudapada.[48] Thus mayavada leads to *Atmadvaitavada*.

The above arguments of Gaudapada try to show that our sensuous experiences whether that o dreams or of the waking life have a common characteristic. Both have *nama-rupa* and *kriya*. Dream experience is short-lived whereas the waking experience is more enduring. But if a man dreams for many years and his waking experiences are short-lived he may accept his dream world as real and the world of his waking experience as illusory. That is to say, except in the duration of time the dream experience and the waking experience both are made up of the same type of the sensuous data. Again, it may be true that the dream experience is private and individual whereas the waking experience is universal and objective. But according to Gaudapada that does not make the waking experience something different from illusion, because, the criterion of unreality, or *mithyatva* is contradictoriness. Whether it is the world of dream or the world of the waking experience, contradictoriness is there. Moreover, these two worlds contradict each other, the dream experience is contradicted by the waking experience, for example, a beggar's being a king in a dream is contradicted when he awakes. Similarly, the waking experience is contradicted in a dream, for example, a millionaire finds himself a pauper in his dream. By implication, therefore, Gaudapada suggests that that alone is real, which is never contradicted. Reality, therefore, is necessarily the Advaita; the world of multiplicity is mithya or unreal.

3. JIVATMAN AND REALITY

Ayam atma Brahma[49] provides the basic theme of the Advaita view. This Advaita view of the Upanishad has been accepted by Gaudapada, which he has elaborated in his own way. In the Advaita philosophy of Gaudapada, there is ultimately no difference between the individual and the Absolute (*Jivatmanorananyatvam*).[50] The birth and death of the individual are illusory.[51] The individual in itself is eternal and infinite. Its apparent finitude is because of *maya*.

Gaudapada refers to the theory of *Koshas*, which is discussed in the *Taittiriya* Upanishad. He holds that the purpose of inquiry about the theory of *koshas* is to disentangle the self from the non-real *koshas* and to realize its non-dual nature.[52]

While explaining the relation between the *jiva* and *Atman* Gaudapada mostly gives the analogy of *ghatakasa* and *mahakasa*. He says that as the *ghatakasa* springs up from the *mahakasa* (space) so the *jiva* (individual) springs up from Atman.[53] As jars, etc., being destroyed in space, are completely merged into space, so are the *jivas* merged into the *Atman*.[54] Here a question naturally arises: the *Atman* that springs up as different *jivas* being one, if one *jiva* feels happiness or suffers pain, all the *jivas* should have the same state of mind. But in fact it is not so. Gaudapada answers the objection in the following manner. As one *ghatakasa* (space occupied by a jar) being connected with dust, and smoke, etc., not all are connected with them, so are the jivas reference to happiness etc.[55] On this point T.M.P. Mahadevan observes: —

As we have already remarked his view is *ekatmavada* and not *ekajivavada*. The empirical plurality of *jivas* is recognized by him. So far as the self per se is concerned there is neither birth nor death, for it is neither action nor enjoyment. These refer only to the jives which are many; and their many-ness along with their varied nature and condition are due to the psycho-physical complexes that limit them. Just as when one part is produced, all parts are not produced, and when one is broken, all are not broken, when one soul is born, all souls are not born, and when one dies, all do not die.[56]

As between *ghatakasa* and *mahakasa* there is only apparent difference, so is the case with regard to *jiva* and *Atman*.[57]

As the *ghatakasa* is neither a transformation nor a part of *akasha*, so is also a *jiva*, neither a transformation, nor a limitation of *Atman*.[58] It is the ignorant to whom the sky appears to be soiled with dirt, who regards the *Atman* as affected by birth etc., the unenlightened sees impurities in *Atman*.[59] As in the origination and destruction of the *ghatakasa*, the *mahakasa* is not affected so is the case with *Atman* in regard to death, birth, etc., which are concerned only with bodies.[60] The *sanghatas*, or bodies with which the *Atman* is born in the form of *jivas* are like the *ghatas* of *ghatakasas*. These sanghatas have, however, no real existence.[61] Gaudapada maintains complete identity between *jiva* and *Atman* (*jivatmanorananyatvam*).[62] While concluding the third chapter of *Agamashastra*, Gaudapada observes: —No individual souls is born, nor is there any possibility of it. This is the highest reality where nothing is born.[63]

When the veil of *avidya* falls off (*avaranachyuti*)[64] the world of plurality which is *vitatha*, (*asat*)[65] naturally disappears (*dvaitasyopashamam prapancopashamam*)[66] and it is then that mind becomes non-mind (*amanibhava, amanasta*)[67] and then one realises in this state of the non-difference of *jiva* from the self.[68] This state is the state of non-duality (*advaitaprapti*),[69] which is the truth (*tattvibhuta*)[70]. This is the realisation of immortality (*amritatva*),[71] freedom (*moksha*)[72] and perfection (*nirvana*).[73]

We thus find something unique in the philosophy of Gaudapada, which, so far has not been stated in such a bold manner by any other Indian philosopher. It is indeed a very striking statement that this world of our everyday life has no reality at all. To negate this world is really a very bold statement, because it is something, which is contradictory to our normal experience.

If we want to find out the relation between man and Nature, we are certainly in a fix because from the standpoint of

Gaudapada Nature or the world does not really exist. But man so long as he does not know his real nature is part and parcel of *Prakriti* or the world. Thus, man has two aspects, one as a part of Nature functioning through body, senses, and mind—a jivatman and the second man in his true nature, not a part and parcel of *Prakriti*, not with any name and form but the transcendental *Atman*. When we are trying to understand the relation between man and the world, it means therefore, that we want to understand the relation between the *jivatman* and the world.

Though according to Gaudapada the ultimate nature of man is *Atman* or pure consciousness, he has not created a sharp opposition between Reality as beyond all qualities or *nirguna* and the Reality that appears with qualities or *saguna*. The controversy in regard to *saguna* and *nirguna* had not yet become so much important for man in his religious life. Gaudapada himself was conscious of the religious demand of the *jivatman* and the value of worship in life and, therefore, he suggested a gradual realisation of the one through the different qualitative stages. The *saguna* is prescribed as a means to realise the *nirguna*. Human mind cannot jump at once to the nameless and formless. It must work through qualities and forms. The idea is that the *jivatman* must penetrate through the gross sheaths or *koshas* and reach the pure *Atman* by gradually making the mind functionless. This is possible through knowledge.[74]

In Gaudapada's analysis in regard to the nature of *jivatman* we find him mentioning the different levels of consciousness when he talks about the *vishva*, *tejas* and *prajna* states of *Atman* and shows that beyond all these *jagrat*, *svapna* and *susupti* states, there exists the *turiya* Atman which is *nityaprakashasvarupa*. This man who is a composite entity realises when he knows his real nature. All these lower levels of empirical consciousness do not exist for him and, therefore, this world of *nama* and *rupa* vanishes. It is in this sense that the world including the jivatman is *mayamatra* according to Gaudapada. Man's essential business in life, therefore, is to understand the nature of this maya. Man, therefore, must try to understand the truth and Reality behind this *Prakriti* by gradually discovering the root principle that works through mind projecting the one into many. Thus, by implication man's life is not a passive resignation after being baffled and despaired on account of sufferings of life, but it is accepting a challenge thrown by *Prakriti* to him. He must analyse and understand the manifold appearances of Nature and discover the ground behind it—the Reality as his true end.

B

1. THE ADVAITA VEDANTA OF SHAMKARA

The Concept of Adhyasa

In the philosophy of Shamkara we find the concept of Advaita of Gaudapada explained in greater detail and with elaborate arguments. For Shamkara the world is ultimately unreal. The only Reality for him is Brahman.

The reality of this world of many and varied objects, the *nama-rupamayajagat* is accepted universally as real; and this reality is based on the universally accepted ground that we perceive it directly with our senses. It is *pratyakshagochara*. If one questions the reality of this world one must therefore question the adequacy of our normal *pratyaksha-jnana*. Does our *pratyaksha-jnana* give us false knowledge? If so, how?

This was the task before Shamkara, as he wanted to show the ultimate unreality of this world. This has been done by him in his discussion on adhyasa.

Shamkara opens his celebrated commentary on the *Brahmasutra* with an elaborate discussion of the nature of

Adhyasa. Adhyasa explains at once the phenomenality of the universe and non-duality of the absolute *Brahman*. Shamkara maintains that the *yushmad pratyaya* and the *asmad pratyaya*, i.e., the object and the subject are opposed to each other like light and darkness.[75] *Adhyasa* is the attributing of the subject and its aspects to the object and its aspects and vice-versa. It is thus the coupling of the real and the unreal. Shamkara holds that in spite of this, it is on the part of man a natural procedure (*Naisargikoyam lokavyavaharah*).[76] Shamkara defines *adhyasa* very precisely: — "The apparent presentation in the form of remembrance, to consciousness of something previously observed in some other thing."[77] And yet more precisely: "Superimposition is the cognition as something of what is not that."[78]

Shamkara himself raises a question regarding the possibility of *adhyasa* about the self. All definitions of *adhyasa* agree in so far as they represent superimposition as the apparent presentation of the attributes of one thing in another thing, for example, mother of pearl appears like silver, the moon, although one only appears as if she were double. But how is it possible in the case of the subject which is just opposite of object? In superimposition one object is attributed on another, which is before us. Shamkara advances three answers to this question. First, he holds, the self is not non-object in the absolute sense. Secondly, subject or self is well known to exist on account of immediate intuition. Finally, he declares: "Nor is it a rule without exception that object can be superimposed only on such other object as are before us, i.e., in contact with our sense organs, for non-discerning men superimpose on the ether which is not the object of sensuous presentation, dark-blue colour.[79]

On the soil of this natural ignorance stands, according to Shamkara, all human knowledge, empirical as well as Vedic. Shamkara cannot explain the world of multiplicity without the assistance of this natural ignorance. T.R.V. Murti rightly observes: —"An enquiry about Ajnana is, therefore, an investigation into the *a priori* conditions of experience.[80]

Shamkara points out that there are standard means of valid knowledge, like perception, inference, and testimony, etc., which have been accepted by all; and therefore there must be some ground why all these should be placed under the sphere of natural and universal ignorance—*adhyasa*. Shamkara explains that whether it is perceptual knowledge or it is knowledge which we get from testimony, such knowledge is essentially based with the "not I" or the body. This is obvious because knowledge or action whether perceptual or belonging to testimony necessarily belongs to a subject. Thus all knowledge with which a man is normally concerned is relational. The subject is always associated with its opposite, the object. Pure subject, therefore, is beyond this relational knowledge. All types of empirical knowledge, Shamkara points out, are inadequate and are only distinguished from that of animals only in degree because of man's superior intelligence, but in kind they are similar.

Actions of animals and men both are guided and controlled by desires to accept or to avoid. Such actions, therefore, are always related to the gain or loss, pleasure or status in life. But it has been advocated in the *Shruti*, Shamkara points out, that pure subject or the self has nothing to do with such gain or loss. Self is never interested in all these. So in all cases of empirical knowledge or knowledge from testimony the subject is associated with the object and, therefore, the pure subject is represented in a relational form which is nothing but its appearance. Thus Shamkara observes: — "In this way, there goes on this natural, beginningless and endless superimposition, which appears in the form of wrong conception, and which is the cause of individual souls appearing as agents and enjoyers and is observed by everyone."[81] And "to remove this root of

the evil and to teach the knowledge of the unity of the soul—
this is the aim of all the texts of the Vedanta."[82]

2. THE STATUS OF THE WORLD

(ii) Reality and Unreality

In the Advaita Vedanta of Shamkara, the world of sense-and-
intellect is generally dubbed as '*maya*'—'illusion' in the sense
of 'imagination' or 'hallucination'. But rarely does '*maya*' mean
to Indian philosophers, even for Shamkara, that the world is
illusion in the sense that it does not exist. *Maya* is philosophical concept employed by Shamkara as the basic postulate for
the explanation of the physical world. In general, the concept
of maya basically means that the physical world is neither real
nor unreal, but is indeterminate (*Sada-sad-Vilakshana*). The
much-abused analogy of the rope and the snake is employed
by Shamkara to illustrate the difficulty of the world problem.
Dr. Radhakrishnan very pertinently observes: —"The riddle
of the rope is the riddle of the universe. Why does rope appear
as the snake is a question, which school-boys raise and philosophers fail to answer."[83]

Here, we will critically examine the status of the snake, in
the rope-snake illusion, in detail.

Illusion as conceived by Shamkara is an identification of
the unreal (snake) with the real (rope) (*Satyanrite
mithunikaranam*). This identification is mutual (*itaretara*) i.e.,
one term cannot be held aloof from the other. The unreal is
superimposed on the real. Identification is the only relation
that can subsist between the real and the unreal. The unreal
appears as if it is real. In the rope-snake illusion, the snake is
taken as real, then negated and finally rejected as unreal. To
begin with, 'This is a snake' is for all practical purposes a

legitimate presentation. The relation of the 'this' to the 'snake' is one of complete identification. This state may be called the state of illusion. Here the snake is taken as real. After the first presentation is the second one, 'This is not a real snake'— 'This is but a rope'. Here 'This' serves as a nexus between 'This is a snake' and 'This is but a rope'. Both refer to the same subject. The latter judgment cancels or negates the identity of the 'rope' with the 'snake'. It is not true that the snake was real when it was apprehended and became unreal later when cancelled. 'This is but a rope' here the snake is, of course, negated but it is not mere nothing. It has certain 'given-ness'. The snake is although illusory, it cannot be said that it is not 'given' at all. And so far as it has this appearance of 'given-ness' it is not altogether non-existent like the purely self-contradictory terms such as 'square circle' or the son of a barren woman.

Now, we shall examine the category of illusory as analysed by Shamkara. It is a new category, the category of the indeterminate. The illusory (snake) is neither real nor unreal it is *anirvachaniya*. Why? Nothing can be predicated of the illusory object. Can we say that the snake was of such and such nature? All these characters are now definitely known to have belonged, even then, to the rope. The temporal and spatial positions, which the snake occupies, actually belong to the rope. Dr. T.R.V. Murti observes: —"The reflected image in the mirror has not any size, and colour, etc., of its own; for they all belong to the original object or to the mirror (*Upadhi*). These characters, the would-be predicates do not and cannot get related to the snake or the virtual image for they are not existent subjects."[84]

As we have seen the illusory snake cannot be the subject of any proposition; can it be the predicate of any subject? No! Its relationship with any existent subject is not possible. The real entity does not accommodate as a matter of fact within its bosom an illusory object. The illusory object, thus, neither characterises anything nor is characterised by anything. All attempts to characterise in terms of others, to define it, and to explain it causally or by way of identity have proved futile. It is not expressible in terms of others, so it is indeterminate, *anirvachaniya*. It is neither the subject nor the predicate of any proposition. It is utterly unrelated. It is what it is. That it appeared in knowledge is to say nothing intrinsic about it. Its character and existence are entirely exhausted in the appearance (*Pratibhasha matrashariratvam*). Dr. Murti well observes: "The vedantic definition of the illusory is but a paraphrase of the reason given for its illusoriness, the world is illusory because it is given, because it is an object (*drayatvat, jadatvat*)." This can be expressed as a case of immediate inference-obversion, 'the given' is not the not given, it is different from the 'not given'. Of the 'not given' we can conceive only two types, the subject which knows, but is not known and the utterly unreal, e.g., the son of a barren woman. As the indubitable and independent, the subject is real, while the other about which no question of truth or falsity is suggested even, is utterly non-existent.[85] the illusory, the given (snake) is given as an object, it cannot be either real—*sat* or unreal—*asat*. To express it in simple language, the object of illusion (snake) is not real, for the latter it is sublated, and the real can never be negated. It is not unreal for it is cognised as existent and the unreal can never be cognised. Therefore, Shamkara concludes that the contents of illusion are indeterminate, *anirvachaniya*, inexplicable as either real or unreal. On the other hand, the fact that the real can never be sublated and the unreal can never be cognised is attested to by normal cognitive experience. It is, therefore, in the logic of the Vedanta, only the *anirvachaniya* object that can be a content of perception and an object of negation also. Vedanta does not hold that *sat* or real and *asat* or unreal are contradictory terms; but are independent of such mutual exclusion and cannot be defined in contradictory term. Thus, no contradiction or violation of the Excluded Middle is to be apprehended for the *Asat* is not conceived as the very negation of *Sat* but as that which does not confront us as real. Had the *Sat* and the *Asat* been conceived as mutual contradictories, e.g., the *Sat* as the un-contradictable and the *Asat* as the contradicted, the acceptance of the one would have *ipso facto* meant the rejection of the other and vice-versa. *Anirvachaniya* thus is different from the 'not given'— from the *Sat* and the *Asat* (*Sad-a-sadvilakshana*). It is the *anirvachaniya* alone, the inexplicable as either real or unreal that can be both revealed and rejected.

Can any cause for illusion be assigned? The question is not whether the illusory appearances, e.g., has the snake any cause, for we have already seen that it is unique and unrelated. If the illusion were uncaused or had any cause other than the ignorance of the real, it would prove permanent and in no case would cease on our attaining the knowledge of the real.

The contention of Shamkara, on this issue, is that in all illusions, Ignorance of the Real (the *Adhisthana*, the locus) is the only cause of the origin and sustenance of the illusion. The snake is seen on the locus of the rope.

By the analysis of the rope-snake illusion, we may trace the following factors involved in it: First, the absence of the correct knowledge of the locus, *adhisthana*. Here, in this case, the rope is not known. Technically, this is the *Avarana*. There is thus necessary connection between the illusion and ignorance.

Secondly, to identify the unreal with the real, something must also crop up. The appearance of the snake gives a content, and a character to the illusion. This is the *vikshepa*.

Thirdly, it is the knowledge and non-knowledge of the locus (rope), which cancels and allows the illusion (snake).

Fourthly, a consciousness is to be granted which knows both the illusion and its cancellation.

Finally, there are some other factors too. A knowledge of similarity (*Sadrishyajnana*), sense contact, and some defect either in the sense organ, such as jaundice or some environmental defect as darkness, the refractory medium, and distance are also assigned as causes.[86] It is possible to maintain with a show of plausibility that in illusion like rope-snake, the knowledge of similarity is operative. This, however, is not true of others, e.g., the blueness of the sky.

Contact of senses with a real object is considered necessary in the case of perceptual illusion. But this rule is violated in the illusion 'the sky is blue'.

It is more difficult to dispose of the claim that some defect, physical or physiological, is to be found in all cases of illusion, Darkness, for instance. Is responsible for the mischief of the snake. But how can I know that the presence of certain factor, say darkness, engenders illusions or its removal cancels it or in some way contributes to either? I may know darkness, but darkness as conditioning the illusory presentation of the snake I do not know.

Dr. Radhakrishnan rightly observes: —

The Root of the illusion is logical and psychological and not metaphysical. The pluralistic universe is an error of judgement. Correction of error means change of opinion. The rope appears as a snake and when the illusion is over, the snake returns to the rope.[87]

At one place he observes: "Unreal the world is, illusory it is not."[88] It is not convincing. The world is illusory it is not unreal, if it is not real. T.M.P. Mahadevan rightly observes: —

"Nor is it unreal in the sense of void. Maya is existent but not real."[89] Shamkara is not so much negating the physical world, as he is re-interpreting it. Shamkara does not assert the absolute oneness-identity of Brahman and the physical world. By non-difference '*ananyatva*', Shamkara does not mean identity but only denies this difference."[90]

Shamkara criticises the *Shunyavada* on the ground that it negates the physical world without posing another reality. To negate an error is to accept the truth on which it is based.[91] Here the error is only negated and corrected and it is not reduced to a mere 'nothing', because its 'given-ness' is a fact. G. R. Malkani is quite pertinent in his observation: —

> Even though the illusory does not exist, the perception of that illusory does exist: I perceive a rope to be a snake. The snake is non-existent in the rope. It appears, therefore, that while the illusory does not exist, the perception of the illusory cannot be denied to be a fact of reality.[92]

Shamkara employs the simile of the rope and snake and the like to suggest the one-sided dependence of the world on Brahman. In the rope-snake illusion whereas the appearance of the snake is dependent on the existence of the rope, the existence of the rope does not depend on the appearance of the snake. In the same way, the world is dependent on Brahman in the sense that there will be no world without Brahman. The non-existence of the world does not make any difference to Brahman. Brahman is the original of which the world, as it has been said, may be regarded as a 'translation at the plans of space-time'; and Brahman depends as little for its being on the world as an original work does on its translation.[93]

Shamkara does not allow the employment of causation to Brahman. The category of causation applies in the realm of phenomena. The world is the realm of causes and effects and we cannot, strictly speaking, say that Brahman is the cause of the world. An essentially non-empirical Being Brahman is absolutely beyond the approach of an empirical category like causation.

Shamkara never denies the existence of the physical world. Dr. S.K. Das observes: —

Thus the standing problem of philosophy—the relation of finite to the Infinite—does not arise for Shamkara at all. The situation is further reinforced by a resolute carrying out of the dialectic of causation, which unequivocally denies the metaphysical reality and independence of the effect as distinct from the cause. This does not, however, amount to a denial of the empirical reality of he finite world of things as an appearance of reality.[94]

Again he observes: —"Well, as Shamkara might equally urge in the very worlds of Dean Jnge, the world of names and forms, this *maya*, is a solid fact which we have to accept as such and not to account for."[95] To sum up the doctrine of *Maya* recognises the reality of the physical world from the relative standpoint. When it declares the physical world to be '*mithya*' (unreal) it is only from the standpoint of ultimate Reality. This unreality in the Vedanta of Shamkara does not signify a mere construction of fancy (*alika*) but is used in the sense of *anirvachaniya* (logically indefinable). Thus we see that Brahman cannot be *anirvachaniya* for, although it is distinct from unreal, it is not distinct from Real, because it is Reality. And by the same logic, the unreal (such as the hare's horn) also cannot be regarded as *anirvachaniya*, for although it is distinct from the real, it is not distinct from the unreal, for it is unreality. The physical world, therefore, is pragmatically and conventionally existent and it is non-existent only from an ultimate point of view. Shamkara frankly admits that the existence of the physical world is unquestioned: —"For this apparent world whose existence is guaranteed by all the means of knowledge cannot be denied unless some new truth (based on which he could impugn its existence) for a general principle by the absence of contrary instances."[96]

A careful study of Shamkara's philosophy as we find it in his *Sariraka bhashya* and the commentaries on the Upanishads shows that the world has a peculiar status and significance. For Shamkara, the world is *mithya*. But this term *mithya* is to be understood not in its ordinary sense as is found in a dictionary. To understand clearly his concept of *mithyatva* is to understand the status of this empirical world according to Shamkara.

Unfortunately, *mithya-satya*, *sat-asat*, or their English equivalents frequently used, have invariably a sense of contradiction, that is to say from the standpoint of common sense what is *mithya* cannot be *satya* or if anything is real it cannot be unreal. Our common sense logic is based on this sense of contradiction. But *mithya* in Shamkara's philosophy cannot be brought under such a traditional dichotomy of opposition.

To understand the status of this empirical world, therefore, we must keep ourselves aloof from the traditional meaning of *mithya* and *satya*. This is necessary because the two terms *satya* and *mithya* are products of our empirical consciousness and they are brought up in the context of relational validity. But when we are evaluating this world from the transcendental standpoint such terms really cannot convey our meaning. We cannot avoid them either when we express ourselves through language. This, in fact, is source of confusion in regard to the understanding of Shamkara's philosophy. The status of the world cannot be spoken about or described, it can only be understood. The world is *mithya* or illusory not exactly like a dream or a mirage or a *bandhya-putra*. Such a comparison though very often made, is ill chosen. All that which is referred to by these terms belong to the empirical world, that is to say, real or unreal, true or false—both belong to the empirical world. Not only that the person who refers to them also belongs to this empirical world, but when we try to understand the status of this world from the standpoint of Brahman, and accept Brahman as the only Reality, we use 'Reality' in two different senses. For example, when we say 'the rope is real', and 'the snake is unreal' the meaning of the 'real' here is not the same as the meaning of it when we say 'Brahman is real and the world is unreal'. The reality and unreality of the rope and the snake respectively belong to the world. If this world is unreal then the reality of the rope and the unreality of the snake both belong to unreal world. Thus we may say that our experience of a snake in a rope is a *mithyajnana*, of a *mithyajnana*—the unreality in an unreal world or an illusion in an illusory world. For all practical purposes and transactions in human knowledge the world is the base to determine the truth and falsity of anything. In other words, the world is the ground, upon which both the truth of the rope and the falsity of the snake are determined. To call this world as unreal or illusory like the snake is, therefore, meaningless because that on account of which the reality and unreality of objects are determined cannot itself be unreal. This is what Shamkara has tried to suggest when he says that this world has a peculiar status, neither *sat* nor *asat* in the accepted sense of the terms. If the snake is unreal or an illusion, the world cannot be unreal or an illusion in the same sense.

Shamkara's concept of '*maya*' has a great significance in the Advaita philosophy. But unfortunately '*maya*' has created a peculiar psychology for not only a layman but also intelligent educated individuals. It seems people are afraid of 'maya' because they think that if they accept this principle the world loses all its importance and man has nothing to do with it. As we have seen '*maya*', of Shamkara does not mean something unreal in the ordinary sense of the term. The term '*mithya*'has been used for explaining the nature of '*maya*', and that has created a great deal of confusion. The fact is that *maya* can be expressed through '*maya*', and its exact synonym is not available. *Maya* is maya because it is *anirvachaniya*. Truly speaking, we should not say that the world is unreal or *mithya*, but we should say that world is *maya*—meaning thereby that the world is not what we take it to be through our empirical consciousness. To understand its real nature, we must have the *paramarthika drishti.*

Difficulty in regard to understanding of the nature of this empirical world is that we who want to understand it do it with our empirical consciousness. To understand the empirical world with our empirical consciousness is to walk through a blind alley.

The approach to understand the nature and status of this world, therefore, must necessarily be different. The discussion on this approach will be at the proper place later.

(ii) *The Manifestation—real or illusory*

We have seen that according to Shamkara the world is not a mere illusion in the sense that it does not exist. The entire universe is inconceivably vast and contains a series of small worlds or *lokas* as *Bhu*, etc.[97] According to their good and bad actions people go after their death to heaven and hell respectively to reap the fruits of *karma* by different paths.[98]

At some places Shamkara has classified the contents of the world into stationary and mobile (*achara* and *chara*, or *sthavara* and *jangama*),[99] while at others into the animate and inanimate objects,[100] or into enjoyers and the objects of enjoyment.[101]

While commenting on *Prashna Upanishad*, he mentions the five gross elements along with their qualities and causes, viz., five subtle elements (*tanmatras*), the five sense organs and the five motor organs along with their objects, the inner organ with its four forms—*manas buddhi*, *chitta*, and *ahamkara*—together with their objects, the thread-like vital air (*sutratmaka prana*) and all that which it connects and illuminates and the reflection of the universal Self, which, like the reflection of the sun in water, has entered (the different bodies) and appears to be an agent and enjoyer.[102] in short, according to Shamkara, all names and forms, agent s and actions and their fruits form the constituents of the empirical world.[103]

In the *tarkapada*, Shamkara maintains that the *Samkhya pradhana* and the *vaisheshika paramanus*, apart from other difficulties involved in their conception as the ultimate cause of the world, cannot explain the orderly arrangement and harmony experienced in the world. The ultimate cause of this vast, wonderful and well-designed world must be both intelligent and powerful enough to account for it. He, therefore, rightly says that the omniscient and omnipotent *Brahman* alone can be the ultimate cause of this world.[104]

Brahman is the *Adhishthana*—substratum underlying the whole world of phenomena. The second aphorism of the *Brahma Sutra* states the *tatastha laksana* of *Brahman* as the cause whence result the origination, sustenation and destruction of the world. Causality of the universe is the qualification par accidence of *Brahman* and it constitutes the essential nature of *Ishvara*. *Ishvara* is *Brahman* seen under the limitations of *Maya*. Creation in the Advaita Vedanta is not an event in time done once for all. The fact of the world being without a beginning is seen in *Shruti* and *Smriti*.[195] As a matter of fact creation is a myth in the system of Advaita Vedanta. Shamkara takes the idea from Gaudapada and declares: "*Paramarthachintakah* have no respect for cosmology which matters much for cosmologists".[106] in his commentary on the Brahmasutra he substantiates these observations with arguments which are as follows: —

> To consider the matter thoroughly a conflict of statements regarding the world would not even matter greatly, since the creation of the world and similar topics are not at all what the scripture wishes to teach. For we neither observe nor are told by the scripture that the welfare of man depends on these matters in any way, nor have we the right to assume such a thing, because we conclude from the introductory and concluding clauses that the passages about creation and the like form only subordinate members of passages treating of Brahman. That all the passages setting for the creation and so on observe the purpose of teaching Brahman, the scripture itself declares.[107]

Now what kind of causality is recognized in respect of *Ishvara*—is He efficient cause or the material cause or both? The first and the second are not possible. Since if *Ishvara* were either the efficient or the material cause alone, He would be finite; His infinitude will be affected. Hence it must be admitted that He is the material cause as well as the efficient cause (*abhinna-nimittopadana-karanam*). There is no inconsistency whatever in the material cause being itself the efficient cause. The world has a material cause which is non-different from the efficient, since it is generated as preceded by knowledge like the happiness, misery, attachment, aversion, etc., present in the self. That the dual causality belongs to *Brahman* qualified by *maya* is established by the creational text, which declares efficient causality in "that desired" and material causality in "May I become many?"[108] The Nyaya-vaisheshika maintains that *Brahman* evidently is the operative cause (efficient) of the world. Shamkara replies: —

> *Brahman* is to be acknowledged as the material cause as well as the operative cause, because this latter view does not conflict with the promissory statements and the illustrative instances. The promissory statement chiefly meant as the following one. Have you ever asked or that instruction by which that which is not heard becomes heard, that which is not perceived, perceived, and that which is not known, known? (Kh. Up. VI. 1.3)

The illustrative example referred to, is the one mentioned (Kh. Up. VI. 1.4) 'My dear, as by one clod of clay all that is made of clay is known, the mode, the modification (i.e., the effect) being a name merely, which has its origin in speech, while the truth is that it is clay merely.[109] "The fact of the sacred texts declaring that the self reflected likewise shows that it is the operative as well as the material cause. Passages like 'He wished, may I be many, may I grow forth,' show in the first place that the self is the agent in the independent activity which is preceded by the self-reflection; and in the second place, that it is the material cause also, since the words, 'May I be many' intimate that the reflective desire of multiplying itself has the inward self for its object."[110]

Brahman of the Advaitin is not the creator of the world in the sense that a potter creates a pot; nor is creation of the world an emanation from nothing. The non-existent can never create anything out of it. If an effect were really nonexistent prior to its creation (a position held by the Nyaya-vaisheshika School), no agency whatever could bring it out. The Samkhya criticises the Nyaya position and points out that the effect is found in a potential form in the cause. This effect is not non-existent prior to the cause. Shamkara appreciates the Samkhya criticism of Nyaya views but points out further that the Samkhya view also cannot be accepted. He attacks the very intelligibility of the category of cause. The Samkhya explanation that the effect is merely a transformation of the cause fares no better than the Nyaya theory in the hands of Shamkara: —

> The Advaitin rightly believes in the progressive develop-ment of knowledge. He would concede the doctrine that the effect is pre-existent in the cause in order to lead the pupil on to deny the separate existence of the effect from the cause. He would concede the doctrine of the con-crete universal transforming itself into the particulars, in order to lead the pupil to conceive this transformation as nothing but an illusory manifestation. Cause and effect are illusory manifestation of *Brahman*. *Brahman* is nei-ther the cause of the world nor is he transformed into the world.[111]

The dual causality of *Brahman* is declared as His *tatastha lakshana* according to *Vivartavada*. Shamkara is emphatic on the point so that he may not be misunderstood. The material causality of *Brahman* consists neither in origination as by the primal atoms, nor in the transformation, as of Primal Nature. The Nyaya-vaisheshikas and others who hold the view of abso-lute creation say that something originates from something else and they attribute the creation of the world to the conjunction of primal atoms. The Samkhya and those who are in sympathy with their view of transformation characterize the world as a transformation of Primal Nature, as curd is of milk. To the question regarding the difference between transformation (*Parinama*) and illusory manifestation (*vivarta*) it is said when a thing attains a state which is different from its present one it is called transformation; when a thing while not abandoning its prior state, appears to be of different state it is known as illusory manifestation.

Now the objection that this world is different in nature from *Brahman* and hence cannot have it for its material cause. To this Shamkara's reply is: —"For we see that from man, who is acknowledged to be intelligent, non-intelligent things such as hair and nails originate and that on the other hand, from avowedly non-intelligent matter such as cow-dung, scorpions and similar animals are produced."[112]

According to Shamkara, the reasoning of the Shunyavadin also is inconclusive. There is an objection that in some places scripture speaks of the effect before its production as that which is not; for instance, 'In the beginning this was that only which is not' (Kh. Up. III. 19.17) and 'Non-existent indeed this was in the beginning' (Tatt. Up. II.7). Shamkara replies: "This we deny for by the Non-existence of the effect previous to its production is not meant absolute Non-existence; but only a different quality or state, viz., the state of name and form being unevolved, which state is different from the state of name and form being evolved."[113]

In the commentaries, the *nama-rupa*—evolving and emerging changes are always described as accompanied by the underlying causal power, i.e., *Brahman*. Whenever and whatever changes emerge, they can never emerge separated or detached from the underlying *Atman* or *Brahman*, "Can a transformed state of the earth stand even for a moment if severed or disconnected from clay? What is produced by something remains inseparably connected with it, it cannot be separated out of it."[114] If such be the case, if under all circumstances, the *nama-rupa* are found to be accompanied by the underlying causal reality and if this causal reality maintains its unity in the

successive changes, it follows that the underlying *Brahman*
which is the source of all these varieties of the evolving changes
can never be looked upon as purely transcendental and as
unrelated to and cut from these changes. In the Advaita Vedanta
Brahman is always looked upon as *adhisthana* because it sustains all.

In an important passage occurring in the Bhasya on the
Taittariya Upanishad, Brahman is defined as *Samanya*—i.e.,
as universal.[115] This universal, this *samanya* is the idea of Being in general, pure being (*Sat*). It is obtained by abstracting
all specific determinations whatsoever. As it is the absence of
everything, Shamkara points out, it should not be taken as pure
nothing as the 'being', 'isness', cannot be removed. But a doubt
may arise that what is devoid of all determinations is merely a
non-existent thing.[116] Shamkara resolves this doubt by remark-
ing that as *Brahman* is the cause, it cannot be said to be non-
existent: "*Brahman* free from space, attributes, motion, frui-
tion, and difference, being in the highest sense and without a
second seems to the dull witted as no more than non-being."[117]
Brahman is held to be the locus of the universe. But in what
did form the *nama-rupa* exist in *Brahman*? Did the actual di-
versities of *nama-rupa*; the actual determinations exist in the
cause? No. There was not yet any differentiation, there was as
yet no separation of *nama-rupa* into space and time.[118] Shamkara
has well described this condition by the following illustration.[119]
(*Madhunirasavatghrite madhuryavat...gachchhanti*).

Now we shall see how the *nama-rupa* came out. The being
distinguishes itself from itself and becomes its other. It was
simply cause' before, now the cause comes out in the form of
'effect'. The universal is inflated with a determination, a difference. It is evident from these that Shamkara did not altogether
deny distinction between the cause and its effect. But is this
distinction an absolute distinction? The particulars and the de-

terminations, which are produced, are in reality not utterly and absolutely different and absolutely and utterly other (*anya*) from the Being (*Sat*). Shamkara observes that it is our *avidya*, which sees absolute distinction between the cause and effect. It is *Brahman*, the universal, the Being, which evolves all its determinations and difference of *nama-rupa* out of its own being. In putting forth its own particulars, it has not lost itself, nor has it become something else (anya) for its other, its opposite is only itself Brahman. It follows that the other is only itself, another form of the cause, the mere manifestation of its nature, it is in reality only itself.[120] Therefore, the world is at bottom no other than *Brahman*.

Shamkara makes some very weighty observations while explaining the term Infinite (*Ananta*). All finite objects Shamkara observes are limited. The limit of a thing can be known only by knowing what lies beyond the limit. To be finite means, which has a limit.[121] But limit always involves negation. A horse is a horse and not a cow, because it possesses the determinations or qualities of a horse and not those of a cow. It is in this negative aspect that qualities limit.[122] Thus one finite object negates another finite object. Now can any of the finite objects exclude or negate the Infinite? No, it cannot. Why? Because, according to Shamkara, the Infinite is the cause of all finite objects. Hence none of the finite objects can negate their cause.[123] Even when Infinite passes over to its opposite-finite, it still remains the same. A lump of earth negates an earthen pot and vice-versa but do the lump of earth and the earthen pot negate the very earth.[124]

Shamkara makes no distinction between *Brahman* and *Ishvara* as some scholars ascribe it to him. The act of creation, he says ought not to be regarded as a separate and distinct act by which *Brahman* has become something other than its own self; as if it was *Brahman* first and then became a creator. As regards the view of the two *Brahmans*, it has been shown very clearly by R.P. Singh. "There are not two metaphysical principles in Shamkara, one to account for the existence of the universe and the other to insure the attainment of the summum bonum of life."[125] Such a manner of thought would introduce a false difference in the nature of *Brahman*, which is always a real unity. *Brahman* and *Ishvara* are one.[126] The immanent God is in reality nothing but the transcendent *Brahman*,[127] Shamkara has definitely condemned those who would make the slightest distinction between Brahman and *Ishvara*.[128] Shamkara uses the pair of terms '*Ishvara*' and '*Brahman*' as well as the other pair, '*Maya*' and '*Avidya*' rather indiscriminately.

It is not correct to make a rigid distinction between the Acosmic *Brahman* (*Nirguna*) and the Cosmic *Brahman* (*Saguna*). It has been shown that behind the multiplicity of *nama-rupa* there is the underlying unity *Brahman*. To show that this unity is not reduced to the multiplicity the acosmic aspect is emphasised, which shows that *Brahman* is unaffected by the changing *nama-rupa*. On the other hand, having shown that *Brahman* devoid of all particular determinations, it may not be supposed to be void, the cosmic aspect (*Saguna*) has been emphasised.

Having shown the material causality of *Brahman* a few observations are here made by Shamkara on the efficient causality of Brahman. The universe is a cosmos and not chaos. The rhythmic movement of the sun, the moon and the stars, the music of the spheres, the enchanting song of the nightingale, the beautiful form of the black antelope—all these cannot be the handiwork of either a blind force or of a chance coincidence of atoms collecting together. Without the postulation of an intelligent being possessing omniscience, and omnipotence, the regulated creation of the Universe is not intelligible. Shamkara observes: —

That omniscient, omnipotent cause from which proceed the origin, sustenance, and dissolution of this world— which world is differentiated by names and forms, contains many agents and enjoyers, is the abode of the fruits of actions, these fruits having their definite places, time and causes, and the nature of whose arrangement cannot even be conceived by the mind—that cause we say is *Brahman*.[129]

In the same continuation he further observes: —

The origin etc. of a world possessing the attributes stated above cannot possibly proceed from anything else but a Lord possessing the stated qualities; not either from a non intelligent *pradhana*, or from atoms or from non-being or from a being subject to transmigration nor again, can it proceed from its own nature (i.e., spontaneously without a cause) since we observe that (for the production of the effects) special places, times and causes have invariably to be emphasized.[130]

Finally, Shamkara concludes: —

The teacher has now refuted all the objections such as difference of character and the like, which other teachers have brought forward against what he had established as the real sense of the Veda, viz., that the intelligent *Brahman* is the cause and matter of this world.[131]

3. MAN'S UNIQUE STATUS IN THE ADVAITA VEDANTA

Man occupies the central position in the philosophy of Shamkara. Man's empirical self is called *jivatman*. As such he is the agent and enjoyer, acquires merit and demerit, experience pleasure and pain.[132] His power and knowledge are finite.[133] He is subject to attachment and hatred etc.[134] Shamkara refers to the passage...of *Mundaka Upanishad* where the *jivatman* or man has been compared to a bird that eats sweet fruit. *Shruti* refers to man as a *bhokta*...[135] In his essential nature, man is the transcendental self (*atman*) but because of ignorance he identifies himself with the body, the sense organs and the internal organ etc., or superimposes on the self the attributes of the body, the sense organs and the internal organ etc., Shamkara observes: —

> Attributes of the body are superimposed on the self, if a man thinks of himself (his self) as stout, lean, and fair, or as standing, walking or jumping. Attributes of the sense organs, if he thinks 'I am mute, or deaf, or one eyed, or blind. Attributes of the internal organ when he considers himself subject to desire, intention, doubt, determination, and so on.[136]

And then again he observes: "In this way there goes on this natural beginningless—and endless superimposition, which appears in the form of wrong conception, and is the cause of individual souls appearing as agents and enjoyers (of the results of their actions), and is observed by every one.[137]

As man's self is different from the body, the sense organs, and the internal organ, it is different from his vital air (*prana*) and the mind (*manas*) as well. Shamkara tells us: —"You are neither mind, nor vital breath; for, both of them are something unconscious. The distinction of the self from the mind is seen from such expressions as my mind has gone elsewhere."[138] The vital breath is affected by hunger and thirst and you are their witness. Just as the knower of the pot is different from it, so you are also different from these states of vital breath, which is experienced as mine (and not as 'I').[139]

In the *anandamayadhi prakarana*, while dealing with the implications of *Brahma puchchham pratishtha—Brahman* is its tail, its support, Shamkara tells us that man's true self is different from all the sheaths of body (*annamaya*), vital air (*pranamaya*), mind (*manomaya*), understanding (*vijnanamaya*), and even bliss (*anandamaya*). But in his essential nature man is bliss itself; other *Koshas* are only appearances.

Shamkara recognizes the three states of *jivatman*—the waking, the dreaming, and the sleeping. In the waking state he identifies himself with the gross body and sense organs and is called *vishva*, perhaps because here in this state he is in contact with the external world (*vishva*). In the dreaming state, he identifies himself with the subtle body and is called *Tejas* (vital). And in the sleeping state (*sushupti*) he identifies himself with the karana *sharira* and is called *prajna*.[140] Underlying all these states there is a permanent witness which is termed by Shamkara as *sakshin*, which means a seer, a spectator or an onlooker [141] while it witnesses all objects, it itself is witnessed by none. It is rightly observed: —"While the *jiva* may become the object of self-consciousness on account of the objective element it includes, it is wrong to speak of the *sakshin* as knowable, for it is the pure element of consciousness in all knowing, and to assume that it is knowable would be to imply another knowing element—a process which leads to the fallacy of infinite regress. But the *sakshin* does not therefore remain unrealised, for being self-luminous by its very nature it does not require to be made known at all. Its presence is necessarily equivalent to its revelation and it is, therefore, never missed."[142]

Regarding the controversy of *Ekajivavada* or *Anekajivavada*, Shamkara undoubtedly subscribes to the view of *Anekajivavada*. The existence of a *jivatman* is an empirical fact, and so is, according to Shamkara, the existence of many individual souls. He has repeatedly spoken of their plurality and differences.[143]

To explain the relation between jivatman and Brahman Shamkara often employed two analogies, the one is the sun's reflection in water contained in different receptacles of it, which is termed as *Pratibimbavada*, the other is the limitation of ubiquitous space within a jar or other such objects, which is termed as *Avachchhedavada*—(doctrine of limitation). In their essential nature all the *jivas* are pure consciousness. But on account of the differences of their limiting adjuncts they only appear to be different. Just as the pure or impure nature of water affects the sun's reflection only and not the sun itself, so is the case with the individual souls also which are affected by the good or bad qualities of the internal organ and not *Brahman*, the pure consciousness. Just as one and the same unaffected ubiquitous space appears to be different due to its apparent limitation by a jar, etc., even so the same universal consciousness appears as different individual souls due to its being conditioned by different internal organs.

Shamkara following the upanishadic teaching establishes the essential identity between *Atman*, which is the innermost self of *jivatman* and *Brahman*. That is to say, from within *jivatman* is *Atman*, which is identical with *Brahman*—the cosmic Reality. This identity is well brought out in the great sayings of the Upanishads such as '*Tat tvamasi*',[144] '*Ayamatma Brahma*'[145] etc. The empirical life of the *jivatman* is solely due to *adhyasa* and when this obstacle of *ajnana* is removed by *jnana*, *jivatman* realises its identity with *Brahman*. This realisation of identity in Advaita philosophy of Shamkara is called *moksha*. This is the highest goal, according to Shamkara, of human life.[146] One who realises it in one's present life makes the best of it while one who fails to realise it is the greatest loser.[147] There is no better attainment than that of the self. It is this that all Vedic assertions and scriptural prescriptions have for their ultimate end.[148] *Moksha* is the state of *Brahmanhood*.[149]

This realisation of *moksha* is not the attainment of something new but it is the realisation of that which is one's very nature. Shamkara does not talk of a heaven, which is apart from us but a heaven, which is already with us but which we have forgotten for the time being. Thus it does not involve the process of becoming *Brahman* but it is the realisation of being *Brahman*. It is rightly observed by Deussen: —"Accordingly, in liberation there is no question of becoming something, which does not already exist, but only of the attainment of the knowledge of what has existed from all eternity."[150] That is why Shamkara very lucidly emphasises that *moksha* is not the fruit of *dharma* or *karma*. He observes: "But this (*moksha*) is eternal in the true sense, eternal without undergoing any change (*kutastha nitya*), omnipresent as ether, free from all modifications, absolutely self-sufficient, not composed of parts, of self luminous nature. That bodiless entity in fact, to which merit and demerit with their consequences and threefold time do not apply, is called release."[151]

Thus according to the Advaita Vedanta of Shamkara man has a unique position in the universe. He is confronted with Nature within and without. He has to deal with two worlds the external world, which is full of things and situations and the internal world, which is full of ideas, drives expectations and aspirations. This internal world is far more complex than the external world. It is this world that makes man reflective and forces him to philosophise. It is this world, which leads man to an attitude of an enquiry about his own nature. Thus there arises in the innermost soul of man a desire to know his true being.

This is because man cannot accept himself as an object among other objects of the world—just produced and then after sometime destroyed. He tries to discover whether there is any meaning and purpose of his being a man born in the universe. Even if there were a purpose of man's being a part of universe, this is not enough to satisfy his demand. A small nut in a machine has a purpose yet the nut is unconscious of it. Is man like a nut having a purpose and not knowing it? This is for man not a dignified status that he can accept. He is not only determined but wants to have his freedom also. He wants to create.

But man does not like this creation to be a blind expression of his vital energy. This inner necessity to fulfil the creative demand of the soul when analysed and reflected upon, leads man to the discovery of the central core of his being. Man then realises that his essential nature is beyond the empirical coverings of Nature. He discovers the self or *Atman* and recognises those elements that make him a *jivatman.*

Man is, thus, embodied spirit in Nature. This fact is to be remembered by man and hen only his status in the world can be understood. Man is the bridge that connects the *vyavaharika* and the *paramarthika.* But the *paramarthika* cannot be related to the *vyavaharika.* Human intellect, there fore, abundantly used metaphors an analogies to bring the non-relational in to the manifold of relations. This is what the Advaita Vedanta tries to show when it uses both the *tarka* and the *Shruti* to explain the nature and status of man and the world.

C

THE VISHISTADVAITA OF RAMANUJA

1. Parinamavada of Ramanuja

In the Advaita Vedanta we have seen that the Reality behind the whole universe and the innermost principle in man is *Brahman* or *Atman.* The highest end for man is the realisation of *Atman.* God occupies a place of secondary importance. The aspiration here is to discover the ultimate Reality, as the one. For a true Advaita vedantin, therefore, religion and all other aspects of life, though important for practical life, are just superficial, to be discarded for the sake of the ultimate Truth. No doubt the world is not to be neglected, nor are ethics and social relationship valueless, yet the significance of all these alters so much when a man realises the Advaita Truth, that they become shadowy and far away from the Truth.

In the theistic Vedanta we have a different view of man and his universe. In this philosophy the natural human attitude has been accepted and the emotional demands of the souls have been valued. Religion, therefore, comes back with a creator God. The philosophy of Ramanuja, the basis of Vaishanava Vedanta gives a philosophy of life where man and the world are as important as God. For Ramanuja creation is a fact. The ultimate Reality Brahman creates this world out of His own being. The creator is the *Karana Brahma* and the created is *Karya-Brahma*. Ramanuja explains creation with his doctrine of *parinamavada*.

Ramanuja's conception of the causal principle, i.e., *Satkaryavada* is different from that of the atheistic *Samkhya*. The term 'cause' is not merely used in the logical sense of an invariable and essential antecedent or *avastha* of a phenomenon. "Every cause is 'because' and is identified with the ground."[152] Ramanuja's Satkaryavada connotes immanent causality. The apt illustrations of causal principle are not clay and its modifications or the different vital airs which form the one air but the development of life from childhood to youth.[153] personality implies inner growth and the unfolding of the infinite consciousness that belong to the *jiva*. Causality thus connotes immanent unity and freedom.

According to it nothing new comes into being, nor is anything created out of nothing. Ramanuja quoting *Chhandogya Upanishad* points out that all beings are rooted in the Truth; all beings exist because of Truth and all beings that have their root in the being. Finally go back to the Truth. Ramanuja holds: "Being alone becomes and is the cause of the becoming. The one alone becomes the many and is the cause of the manifold. The absolute broods and becomes the many by evolving"[154]

All the vedantins agree in denouncing the *asatkaryavada* of the Nyaya-vaisheshika school and its doctrine of *samavaya*. They also agree in disproving the Buddhistic *kshanabhangavada*. Buddhistic theory of momentary-ness makes life impossible. Ramanuja shows the absurdity of the principle thus. If every thing is momentary the sentient subject perishes and has no continued existence of a person. The objects of sensation are also momentary and do not retain a structure enduring more than a moment for recognition. What has been apprehended in the next moment, because it is momentary becomes the experience of another person.

The causal principle in Ramanuja refers to the real modification of *Prakriti*, the free causality of the finite self or jiva and the supra-personal identity or *Brahman* as the inner ground of the system of nature and society of selves.[155] Ramanuja's *parinamavada* has a significant metaphysics behind it. Thus Shri P.N. Nivasachari rightly observes: —

The cosmological is the three-fold problem of philosophy relating to nature, self, and God. It is by the will of *Ishvara* that nature changes and the self-progresses and it is by knowing Him as the inner self of all beings that all beings are known. *Brahman* is the ultimate meaning of the universe and the philosophy of nature and that of the self have their foundation only in the vedantic knowledge of *Brahman*. Thus understood, causality is not an altar to the unknown God but is an adequate idea which the nature of *Brahman* as the world-ground.[156]

2. THE QUALIFIED ADVAITA

Like Shamkara, Ramanuja's conception of *Brahman* is as one without a second in the sense that there exists nothing outside or independent of Him. But unlike Shamkara, Ramanuja makes no distinction between *nirguna Brahma* and *saguna Brahma*. To him *Brahman* is *saguna* only. He possesses all good qualities such as perfect bliss, infinite knowledge, inconceivable powers, unlimited filial affection, kindness, valour, and benevolence, etc.[157] He is the source of all values, which man aspires for. He creates, sustains, and destroys the entire universe as a matter of mere sport of *lila*.[158] All the conscious and unconscious objects exist in Him. They constitute in a way the body of *Brahma*, Ramanuja's *Brahma*. Is thus *Purushottama*— a personal God. Ramanuja names Him Vishnu. The school has been called Vaishanava Vedanta. This *Purushottama* is, no doubt, one without a second but it is qualified by two modes, *chit*, and *achit*, the *jivas* and the *prakriti*.[159] That is why Ramanuja's philosophy is known as *vishishtadvaita*.

The entire philosophy of *vishishtadvaita* is contained in the very benedictory verse of the *Vedantasara*. Ramanuja saluting Lord Vishnu observes: "I bow unto Vishnu who has for his body all the sentient and the non-sentient beings, who is the self of all objects, who is associated with the Goddess, Shri, who is the ocean of Bliss untainted with impurities." In this verse, we find all he fundamental features of Ramanuja's Qualified Advaita. The Supreme Being according to Ramanuja is Vishnu. All the *jivas* and the material things and the Lord are distinct from each other. The Lord, Vishnu possesses a host of auspicious qualities free from all evils. The Lord could be approached only through *Bhakti* or *Prapatti*, which is only a form of *Bhakti*.

The concept of *Brahman*, as the *Sharirin* and of the world as the *Sharira*, serve as the very foundation of the philosophy of Ramanuja. Ramanuja observes: "There is, for example the text in the *Brihadaranyaka* which declares that the whole world constructs the body of *Brahman* and that *Brahman* is its self. That text teaches that earth, water, fire, sky, air, heaven, sun, the regions, moon, and stars, either, darkness, light, all being's breath, speech, eye, ears, mind, skin, and knowledge, form the body of *Brahman,* which abide within them as their self and Ruler."[160] This *Sharira* view of the world is revealed in the *Sadvidya* and is developed by the *Satkaryavada* already explained. *Brahman* enters into the world of *achit* along with the finite selves and evolves the names and forms that constitute the world of space-time. *Brahman*, the cause being real, the world the effect, which is a *parinama* of the cause, is also real. The *Sharira* view of the world is rooted in the dual causality of *Brahman*: —"I am the origin and the dissolution of the whole universe. Higher than I there is none else; all this is strung on me as pearls on a thread. (Bh. G. VII, 4.7)."[161] "*Brahman* alone is the material as well as operative cause of the universe."[162] *Brahman* with *chit-achit* as its *Sharira* in the undifferentiated state becomes *Brahman* with *chit-achit* as the *Sharira* in the effect state of differentiation. As *Brahman*, the cause is not different from the cosmic order, the effect, so by knowing *Brahman*—*natura naturans*, the cosmic order as *natura naturata* is likewise known.

Ramanuja tries to explain the *Sharira-Shariri* relation between the world and *Brahman* by the utilization of the grammatical rule of *Samanadhikaranya*. It means that one thing being equally qualified by several attributes each of which has its own distinctive meaning and embodies the unity of difference.[163] In the term 'blue-lotus', the adjective 'blue' qualifies the noun 'lotus' and there is no discrepancy between the blue colour of the lotus and its sweet fragrance. The keynote of *Samanadhikaranya* is that the same thing can be qualified by several attributes each of which has its own meaning and context. They can co-exist side by side in the same substance without suffering from self-contradiction.

This grammatical rule of *Samanadhikaranya,* which is the logic of Ramanuja's philosophy, enables us to understand the epistemological exposition that the world of matter and soul is the *aprithaksiddha visheshana* of *Brahman.* There can be no *visheshana* without a *visheshya.* The proposition 'The lotus is blue' refers to the substance or *vishishta,* namely, the lotus having the quality or *visheshana* of blueness. The substance or the *vishishta* is the organic unity of the *visheshana-visheshya* relation and the two are distinguishable but not divisible. "The unity of *Brahman* and the world as *visheshya* and *visheshana* is *vishishtaikya* and not *svarupaikya.*"[164]

Ramanuja defines the *Sharirin* and the *Sharira* terms in the following way. That is called *atman* or *Sharirin,* which is always the containing (*adhara*) and controlling (*niyanta*) of another and which uses it for its own satisfaction. The *Sharira* is so-called by reason of its being in its entirety the *adheya,* the *niyamya* and the *shesha*; it is inseparable from the *Sharirin* and forms its *aprithakasiddha visheshana* or *prakara.* Any substance, which a sentient self can completely control and support for its own purposes and which stands in an entirely dependent relation is called *Sharira:* —"In this sense, then all sentient and non-sentient beings together constitute the body of supreme Reason, for they are completely controlled and supported by him for his own ends and are absolutely subordinate to him."[165]

In the *Vedartha Samgrah* Ramanuja concludes that the *Sharira-Shariri bhava* is a reconciliation of the extremes of vedantic doctrines like the schools of *abheda, bhedabheda,* and *bheda.* It establishes *Abheda* by the idea of *Brahman* as the unity of the *Sharira-Shariri* relation in which the *Sharirin* is the one without a second that sustains the manifold of *chit* and *achit*. It supports truth of *bhedabheda* by the view that the *prakarin* is the one that exists as the many *prakaras*. And *bheda* is proved by the fact of the eternal distinction between the *chit* and *achit*— and *Ishvara* in their nature and character (*Svarupa* and *Svabhava*). The relation between *Brahman* and the world as *Sharirin* and *Sharira* is defined in terms of *adhara* and *adheya*, *niyanta* and *niyamya* and *sheshi* and *shesha*, which are only logically distinguishable and not separable.

3. CREATION OF THE WORLD

It has been already stated that according to Ramanuja God is the material as well as the efficient cause of this world.[166] When he wills, *Prakriti* begins its manifestation. Ramanuja maintains that the *Purushottama* remembers at the termination of *pralaya*, the constitution of the preceding universe, wills to become manifold and creates the world.[167] God wills to be many and it is at His will that *Prakriti* begins to manifest. The manifestation of *Prakriti* may be studied in the light of the principle of *parinama* or transformation. *Prakriti* is differently spoken as *akshara*, *avidya*, and *maya* and has been defined as the sub-stratum of the three *gunas*, *sattva*, *rajas*, and *tamas* by Ramanuja. *Prakriti* is eternal or *akshara*. It is ever changing in its form and function. It is called as *avidya*, as it obscures and obstructs the knowledge of *Brahman* and it is also known as *maya* as it connotes the wonders of creation. Before *Srishti*, it remains in the state of creation called *avyakta* or the un-manifest when *Srishti* begins, of the *avyakta* is born the *mahat tattva*. *Mahat tattva* produces *ahamkara*, which is tree-fold—the *sattvik*, *rajas*, and *tamas*. They are also known as *Vaikarika*, *Tejas*, and *Bhutadi* respectively. Eleven *indriyas* emerge from the *Sattvika* aspect: five *jnanendriyas*, five *karmendriyas*, and manas or mind.[168]

The *tamas ahamkara* causes the tanmatra of *Shabda* from which comes *Akasha*. *Akasha* produces the *tanmatra* of *sparsha* whence comes *vayu*. *Vayu* produces the *tanmatra* or *rupa*, which in its turn causes *teja*. *Teja* produces the *tanmatra* of *rasa* from which emerges *ap*. *Ap* produces the *tanmatra* of *gandha*, which gives rise to *prithvi*.

The divine act of triplication is quintuplication. Quintuplication is a process, which consists in the inclusion of all the qualities in all the elements. Each of the five elements is divided into two parts and one half of each is combined with one eighth of the remaining elements.

The universe is composed of the five mixed elements and each substance is so called because of the preponderance of one or other element.

Therefore, according to Ramanuja, the ultimate elements combine together to form the different objects of the world. In all the objects of the world there are these ultimate elements only one of them is in greater proportion in one object than the others. Thus, the qualitative variations have become possible. This quintuplication or *panchikarana* is not by *Brahma* according to Ramanuja by *Brahman* because *Brahma* himself is a product of such combination of creation and dissolution goes on repeating itself *kalpa* after *kalpa*. There is no end of this cycle. The motive, which prompts it, is nothing but sport.[170]

4. THE STATUS OF THE WORLD

The world has a distinct status in the philosophy of Ramanuja. It is crated with a purpose. The purpose is to provide for the souls an opportunity to work out their destiny according to the merits and demerits of their *karma*. Both the conscious and unconscious are parts of *Brahman*. The world is a manifestation from subtle to the gross. When the created world fails to provide proper environment for the *jivatman* the whole manifestation is withdrawn and *pralaya* takes place. This is nothing but going back to the original subtle state where everything existed in the un-manifested or *avyaktavastha*. The divine will then create a new *srishti*. Thus in Ramanuja we have a cyclic conception of creation and dissolution and this cycle is endless.[171]

As the world is a manifestation of a part of God, it in no sense can be unreal. The world is not only real but also in its essence it has the divine in it, only manifested in such a gross state of the bhutas that it seems to be mere matter. The world contains in it things and events which are the cause of man's suffering. The rough and cruel aspects of Nature, untimely death and disease all these are there in the world which have made it not a very happy place for a suffering man. In other words, there is evil in the world and if the world is a manifestation of God, and the part of the Reality, evil must be real. Thus in the philosophy of Ramanuja the problem of evil must be solved.

From the standpoint of Absolute Idealism, though evil has significance it has no reality. Evil is relative, for example seawater is bad for man for drinking purposes; it is good for the water animals. Thus good, bad, cruel, and kindness etc., are just relative. Everything is all right at its proper place. It is evil because we do not know. Of these relative conditions we consider something as good or bad. Evil, therefore, is a product of ignorance. When real knowledge comes, all these relative conditions vanish and with the perspective of absolute oneness we do not find evil anywhere. This is the position of the Advaita Vedanta. From the standpoint of the ultimate Reality or *paramarthika drishti* evil does not exist.

But in the philosophy o Ramanuja we have not only perspective of oneness but also that of many-ness—both being

real. Therefore, Ramanuja must explain the reality of evil in
this world. Man has to face evil in this life, because he is to
deal with the world, which is full of three kinds of sufferings,
adhibhautika adhidaivika and *adhyatmika*. It has been said
that this world is a moral stage. Man who is involved in good
and bad actions constantly suffers from the conflict between
the 'is' and the 'ought'. This is the basic feature of man as a
moral being. This conflict has made human life tragic no doubt
but it is this feature that has made his life human also. Man has
to purify himself and for the self-purification or *atmasuddhi* a
world is necessary. This world, therefore, is a place, which
allures him, provokes him and tends to make him a slave of his
passions and desires. Thus the world has its importance for
man because here in the world his ability to conquer over his
gross or lower nature grows and is tested. This is from the
standpoint of Ramanuja's philosophy a part of the divine plan.
Thus, the world has its importance and significance for man
who has to deal with this world, to understand its significance,
to conquer it and then to be a master of it. A *jivatman*, therefore, cannot be without a world. The world is an essential place
for man to make him conscious of his true end.

   Ramanuja accepts reality of the world and, therefore, it is
natural that as an interpreter of *Brahmasutras* he must reject
Shamkara's doctrine of *maya*. He rejects Shamkara's
'*mayavada*' by raising seven objections against it known as
Sapta-anutapatti.[172] The first objection is the impossibility to
determine the *ashraya* of *maya*, because *Brahman* who is
jnanasvarupa cannot be the *ashraya* of *maya*, neither *jiva* can
be, because it is already a product of *maya*. Later followers of
Shamkara have tried to suggest different *ashrayas* of *maya*, for
example Vachaspati Mishra[173] suggests *jiva* as the *ashraya* of
maya, whereas Amalananda in his *Vedantakalpataru* suggests
reciprocal dependence between *jiva* and *maya*. These are

parasparashrita. This suggestion is true to meet the difficulty regarding the priority of *jiva* and *maya.* If *jiva* is source of *maya* it must be prior to *maya* but that cannot be because *jiva* is *jiva* on account of *maya.* Again maya cannot be prior to *jiva* because in that case it must exist either in *Brahman* or as an independent entity beside *Brahman.* To solve this difficulty Amalananda suggests reciprocal dependence. But Madhusudana Sarasvati in his *Advaita Siddhi* says that reciprocal dependence between *maya* and *jiva* is not possible, because we cannot prove that one's existence depends on the existence of the other.

According to Vidyaranya[174] the source of *maya* is pure *chit. Maya* is superimposed on *Brahman* but it does not influence *Brahman.* The writer of *Tattvasuddhi* suggests that *Ishvara* is the source of *maya.* Another unknown writer of *Prakatartha Vivarana* suggests that *maya* is different from *avidya. Maya* is in *Ishvara,* and *avidya* is in *jiva. Maya* can only project but *avidya* can project and conceal. Madhusudana Sarasvati seems to be not quite clear about the *ashraya* of *maya.*

For him *jiva, Ishvara* and *Brahman,* each may be regarded as the source.

The discussions in regard to the source of *maya* by the philosophers who came after Ramanuja show that Ramanuja's objection cannot be properly met. The question however may be raised whether Ramanuja's objection is a valid one. What we feel is that Ramanuja's objection in regard to the *ashraya* of *maya* and the answers to this objection by the later Advaita philosophers—all these are discussions made by *buddhi,* which functions in the relational world of logic. The nature of *maya* cannot be understood through Logic. It is not a logical conclusion, which establishes the nature of '*maya*'. It is rather an experience, which at once reveals to us its nature. We have taken only one objection of Ramanuja to show this limit of

Logic. No discussion can settle the issue. Other objections need
not be taken here because they suffer from the same difficulty.
To understand the nature of *maya* and for that matter the status of the world, we must penetrate beyond Shamkara's verbal
statements and try to understand his suggested meaning of
bhavarupa ajnanam. We shall try in the concluding chapter to
show that the Advaita Vedanta and the theistic Vedanta need
not necessarily have opposition with respect to the status of the
world, which has been so commonly accepted.

5. MAN AND HIS RELATION WITH THE WORLD

Ramanuja maintains that individual souls are really conscious entities and that they are essentially of the nature of
bliss, and atomic in size.[175] Though he does admit that individual souls are like *Brahman* they are really distinct from
Brahman who is their Lord and object of worship.[176] The
upanishadic great sayings such as '*Tattvamasi*' mean to
Ramanuja only similarity between the nature of *Brahman* and
the individual soul (*jnanaikakarataya Brahmprakarta*) and not
the identity between them. According to Ramanuja, the identity propounded by the upanishadic texts is the identity of one
and the same differently qualified entities (*vishishtasyaikyam*).[177]
A soul is eternal, it was never created and it will never be
destroyed.[178] It is beyond creation and destruction which actuality belong to the material body for eternality and changeless-
ness are its essential nature.[179] The souls though finite in form,
are infinite in number. Thus their mutual difference and their
difference from God is real.[180] They are both *karta* and
bhokta.[181] Their bondage is because of their own deeds.[182]
Among them they are of various types—high, middle and low.
But God is not open to the charge of cruelty and partiality.
Ramanuja maintains that inequality of creatures depends upon
the deeds of individual souls.[183]

It is already stated that according to Ramanuja, not only consciousness but also bliss constitutes the essential nature of *atman*.[184] But its bliss and infinite intelligence are obscured because of its own beginningless karma, which are of the nature of *avidya*.[185] Ramanuja holds that *atman* is different from the twenty-four categories of *Prakriti* and is eternal, self-luminous and morally free.[186] Like Shamkara, Ramanuja also maintains that it is because of *avidya* that *atman* mistakes itself for body, is imprisoned in embodiment and migrates from body to body.[187] He opines that for the performance of one's duties, the knowledge of one's self as a distinct and separate entity from body is a necessary condition.[188] And these duties are essential for the termination of one's bondage.[189]

Thus, according to Ramanuja, the individual souls in the state of purity possess the qualities in common with *Brahman*. But they differ from *Brahman* in two ways, one, for the creation and control of the world they have no power, only *Brahman* has got this power.[190] Two, the individual souls are atomic in size,[191] whereas *Brahman* is all-pervading. As they are atomic in size, the individual souls are infinite in number and different as they have different bodies. It is because of ignorance that the individual souls are associated with material bodies and because of this association they suffer. The souls can realise liberation and can get rid of their suffering, when they have knowledge of the nature of *Brahman*, and from this knowledge results *Bhakti*. Thus the devotion as the result of knowledge brings the soul its liberation.[192] But before getting this knowledge of *Brahman* the individual soul must perform his duties as enjoined by the Vedas.[193] The performance of such duties must be without any reward like heaven as we have it in *Purva-Mimamsa*. It must be *nishkama karma*. Through *nishkama karma*, the accumulated effects of the past actions are destroyed. This destruction is necessary before getting true knowledge.

This knowledge makes him understand that God is the creator, sustainer and controller of all beings and that he is really a part of God who controls his soul from within. Through his devotion to God he must have His grace and then God chooses him for liberation. Intense devotion to God and constant meditation on Him as the dearest object of love ultimately leads to an immediate knowledge or *sakshatkara* of Him.

Man's status as a being in the universe is of a profound interest. He is essentially a spirit yet a part of *Prakriti*. He possesses all the animal qualities like instincts and emotions but he is also endowed with the sense of duty and the sense of incompleteness. He is finite but he is conscious of his limitations. Not only this, he is capable of analysing his situations and evaluating his status as an unfulfilled suffering individual.

Not only this but he is endowed with a higher type of emotions, which make him more than an animal. Because of these emotions, he is human. He gradually realises that he is not only human but also possesses spark of divinity in him. Thus the human world is a place where Nature and Spirit are functioning together. As *Brahman* is the abode of *chit* and *achit*, similarly man also is an abode of *chit* and *achit* in a miniature scale. Only what is to be achieved by him is to be conscious of this truth.

But to begin with man is not at all conscious of the presence of spirit in him. He considers himself as a part of *Prakriti* and behaves accordingly. He is guided by his *indriyas* and conditioned by the laws of causation. So long as he is working under the causal principle of Nature, he is not acquainted with the fact that he is free. When man finds that his relation with *Prakriti* in the physical, vital and mental plane only conceals his true nature, he feels a sense of helplessness.

Man's struggle with his limitation due to his being controlled by *Prakriti* makes human life intensely subjective. This subjectivity forces him to find out a support as it were, which can help him to go through this struggle for an ultimate victory. Thus man tries to discover the purpose of his life, which draws him towards a faith that he has his saviour—God. Man's relation with Nature is such that he becomes reflective and gradually learns to understand that there is a subtle power which can alter this relation so that man remains no more a slave but a master of *Prakriti.*

Thus, man's primary business while in this world, is to discover this subtle power, which will change the complexion and significance of his life. This subtle power is his *antaryamin*— his God. When man discovers his *antaryamin* within his own being, he as it were gets a new life. The old one, which he has been accustomed to live, becomes then superficial and meaningless. Thus the understanding of man's relation with *Prakriti,* leads man to the understanding of the subtle power behind *Prakriti.* This again leads to the finding that this subtle power resides in him as his *antaryamin.* Then a new relation grows between man and his *antaryamin* whom he has discovered. In the beginning, according to Ramanuja it is a mere knowledge but not a realisation. The knowledge that man has God within him is not enough. This knowledge brings an intense devotion to God so much so that all other things and events of his daily life of normal existence become unimportant. He becomes incapable of concentrating on these things. His whole attention is constantly directed towards God. A new emotional life emerges, which is qualitatively different from the normal one with which he is acquainted as a creature of *Prakriti.* This is what Ramanuja calls *Prapatti* or *Bhakti.* This devotion to God works as a new force, which draws man towards God as the magnet draws a piece of iron.

This new life of the *Bhakta* calms down the manifold material desires of the human mind and consequently brings to him a life of peace. Not only this but after some time there emerges a new quality which the devotee experiences that draws him closer to his God. This is Love. The devotee has not yet experienced his God directly. But he feels that he is near Him. Still there exists a thin curtain that separates man from God. When this Love grows, it reaches ultimately to a point where man directly experiences God as his ultimate reality. This *sakshatakara* is the highest end to be realized by man.

The *Vaishnava Vedanta*, therefore, gives man a new approach towards the realisation of the ultimate Reality. It is through Love. This love to God provides human society an ideal, which may be deduced as a corollary. The Vaishnava philosophy suggests that love for God can be easily realised through man's love for man. In the present world man does not love his fellow beings otherwise there would not have been any quarrel, any aggression, or any war. Love is a potent force to bind one man with another, to bind man with God. Thus theistic Vedanta gives a practical and concrete philosophy of life for man.

D

OTHER SCHOOLS OF THEISTIC VEDANTA

There are schools of theistic Vedanta other than Ramanuja's. Each school has its own interpretation of the Upanishad, the *Bhagavad-Gita*, and the *Brahmasutras*. Some like the Vallabha School accept the Bhagavata as the fourth *prasthana*. The other schools are that of Nimbarka, Madhva, Chaitanyadeva and Jivagosvami.

But all these theistic schools accept *Brahman* as *Ishvara* who possesses an infinite number of suspicious attributes. They also maintain that this world is real. They also believe that the individual souls are infinite in number and atomic in size. All these schools also emphasize that *Bhakti* is the means of attaining liberation; after liberation the individual soul is not merged into God or the absolute Reality losing identity. But it retains its identity throughout—even after liberation.

The Nimbarka school has also been called the *Bhedabhedavada* because it suggests and tries to prove that there is both a difference and a non-difference between the *dharmin* and the *dharma* for example, *agni* and its *dahika shakti*—the burning power of the fire is not different from the fire yet it cannot be the same as fire. A similar relation is between the soul as a knower and his attribute as knowledge. It is not possible to prove either the absolute identity or the absolute difference between them. The same thing may be said in regard to God and the soul.[194] They are non-different because the soul is a real manifestation of God; again they are not identical because the soul is different from God as God alone is the *niyanta*.

The doctrine of Vallabha is generally known as *Suddha Advaitavada*,[195] that is, *Brahman* is *Suddha* or pure in the sense that He is free from *maya*. Thus the *jiva* and this world where he lives are essentially the same as *Brahman* without involving any idea of *maya*. The world according to Vallabha is *brahmatmaka* only its qualities of *Chaitanya* or consciousness and *ananda* or bliss are obscured. The relation between *jivatman* and God is that of a part and a whole—*ansha* and *anshin*.[196] For Vallabha *abheda* or non-difference alone is real whereas difference is simply for the sake of *lila*. Here the Vallabha School is different from both that of Ramanuja and Nimbarka because for the later schools the emphasis is more on the difference, which is really real. The non-difference is because of the similarity of nature between *jiva* and *Brahman*. Thus 'that thou art' (*tattvamasi*) is literally true for Vallabha, whereas for Ramanuja and Nimbarka that is to be understood metaphorically.

For Vallabha *Bhakti* is of two kinds, one, *maryada bhakti*
and two, *pushti bhakti. Pushti bhakti* is a higher kind of *bhakti,*
which is nothing but the core of God. This higher *bhakti* cannot be gained by *sadhana* but can only be obtained by God's
grace.

The school of Madhva though belongs to the theistic systems of Vedanta yet it stands apart because of certain characteristics that are not to be found in the other schools.
Madhvacharya is an ardent advocate of the philosophy of *bheda*
(difference), which is generally called *dvaitavada* (dualism)
perhaps because Madhva has drawn a clear-cut line of demar-
cation between his two types of ultimate reals—one *svatantra*
(independent) and the other *asvatantra* (dependent). The Lord
Vishnu is Madhva's only independent Reality whom he desig-
nates as *Purushottama Paramatman* or *Brahman.*[197] Everything else is dependent on Him. But technically speaking
Madhva is an advocate of pluralistic realism as under his
asvatantra tattva he propounds a number of beginningless and
endless real entities. Lakshami, the Vedic sounds, the
avyaktakasha (uncreated space), the *jivas* (individual souls),
and the primordial matter, etc., are held to be as eternal as
Brahman Himself. All eternals, whether *svatantra* or *asvatantra*
are equally real and so are the difference between them.

Thus the most striking feature of Madhva's philosophy is
his teaching of *bheda.* It is because of *bheda* or difference that
all the entities of the world are unique in their nature and they
are different from one another.[198] Madhva has recognised five
kinds of fundamental differences in the world.[199] They are the
differences between the *jivas* and *Ishvara,* the *jivas* and the
material substance, the material substance and *Ishvara,* and
the mutual differences between the different *jivas* as well as
among the material objects themselves.[200] These differences
constitute the very nature of the things. It is because of the
difference that one thing is distinguished from another. That is

why the followers of Madhva urge that the seeker of a cow does not move to catch hold of a *'gavaya'* when he sees it.[201] These differences are real as they are possessed by the great Lord Himself.[202] Had the world of five-fold differences been illusory, it would have been sublated, or, if it had a beginning it should have an end. But it is neither sublated nor destroyed; so with all its differences it is real and beginningless.[203]

Madhva's theory of causation has a peculiarity. He has tried to combine both the doctrines of *Satkaryavada* and *asatkaryavada* and calls it *Sadasadkaryavada*. It has been also termed as *'bhedabheda'* and *'savisheshabheda'*. Causation is meaningless without a cause—stuff (*upaddnadravya*) to that extent it is *satkaryavada* or rather *satkaranavada*. A particular cause makes a particular effect possible. This means that the effect has an intrinsic relation to the cause. From this point of view the relation between cause and effect is identity—*abheda*. A jar is essentially clay to that extent it is identical with the cause. But the effect is not pre-existent in the cause it is a new thing and has come there *do novo*. To this extent, it is *asatkaryavada*, that an effect has a form, which its cause has not is also a fact, otherwise there is no meaning why one thing is called cause and another thing effect. From this point of view the effect must be considered to be a new thing. A jar in its form is purely a new creation and is different from its cause, the clay.

According to Madhva the world is real, because what is revealed by *pramana* is real. The world so far is revealed, by pramana is real. It is real in the sense that it is not non-existent.

The Advaitin holds that since the world is sublated so it is *sadasadvilakshana*. Against it, Madhva holds that the world is revealed by *pramana* and, therefore, is not sublated. He asserts that the superimposition of a thing requires the reality of the same thing together with the reality of something else. Without real silver and real shell, the superimposition of silver is not possible. In the same manner without two real worlds the superimposition of the world is not possible. So the reality of the world cannot be denied.

For Madhva God or the Supreme Being is the one and only Independent principle and all finite realities comprising the *Prakriti*, *Purusha*, *kala*, *Karma*, and *Svabhava* etc., are dependent (*Paratantra*). This concept of two orders of reality viz., '*Svatantra* and *Paratantra*' is the keynote of Madhva philosophy.[204] The world is dependent. Its reality is in every sense of the term dependent. Madhva takes a thing to be real in three senses. If it has existence of its own, it is real. Existence is called '*satta*'. So *satta* is reality. If it has any function, then it is real. A function is called *pravritti*. So *pravritti* is reality. To have knowledge is to be real. Knowledge is called *pramiti*, so *pramiti* is reality. If a thing has no existence, has no function and has no knowledge then it is not real.

Everything in the world has reality in a dependent way. We may take for instance a jar. Its existence has to be given by an outside agent. It is made to have a function by an outside agent. Similar is the consideration with regard to all *anitya* things. The world has a derived reality.

The fact that everything of the world is subject to changes imposed on it by the things that are external to it implies that it is not self-established or self-sufficient. The dependent is the proof of the Independent. It is only through the Independent that the dependent is explained.

As the source of all, Independent is accepted as self-established and self-sufficient, infinite and perfect by Madhva. It is presupposed by the world. Madhva's contention is that it is not the creator of the world in the sense that a pot-maker makes a pot. The perfection of *Brahman* makes the world possible. One who has an overflow of joy, sings, dances and so on. Similarly, the overflow of *ananda* from *Brahman* has its expression in the reality of the world.

The Independent is that which has *satta*, *pramiti*, and *pravritti* independently of other things. It is not the material cause of the world. Its mere immanence directs the world process. In this sense it is the efficient cause of the world. It directs the world in accordance with the *karma* of the *jivas* who are benefited by the world.

Like Ramanuja, Madhva's *Brahman* is the embodiment of all auspicious qualities.[205] As the sole director of all It has none equal or better. It is in all. It has all. It is in the world. It knows all. It is all-powerful. Everything, however, bad it may be, is a means for the perfection of the world. In the *achetana* thing *sattva* is good and *rajas* and *tamas* are bad. But the last two help the realisation of the first. Badness is the way to goodness. But *Brahman* is free from all evils and impurities and possesses all excellence.[206] When the scriptures declare of Him as *nirguna* it does not mean that He is devoid of even good qualities; it simply means that He is free from all evils. It is perhaps to emphasise the perfect defect-less-ness of *Brahman* that Madhva has dwelt so much on His difference from the finite *jivas* and the world alike.

According to this school, creation is a fact and the world is real. The world according to it is produced out of *Prakriti*, its material cause, which is subject to the will of the Lord.[207] It is the will of the Lord that is the primary cause in the production of the world. Though, the *Paramatman*, being *aptakama*, has no desire for anything it is because of His sportive mood or *lila* that He creates the world.[208] The creation of the Lord is explained in the Madhva system by citing the example of a man who in his joyous mood dances and sings.[209] The creation in Madhva philosophy occurs at the time when the Lord is overwhelmed with the feeling of promoting the good of the *jivas*.

The Madhva argument in favour of the reality of creation is quite similar to the method followed by either Gauda or Shamkara for discrediting its ultimate metaphysical value. Just as both Shamkara and Gauda argue that because the world is a false appearance, creation is not a real creation, the Madhva philosophers contend that because the reality of world is unassailable the creation is to be admitted as a real event. The Madhva refutation of the Shamkarite philosophy of creation is naturally, therefore, mostly a criticism against the vedantic argument about the falsity of world.

According to Madhva souls are atomic in size. Wisdom and bliss constitute their very nature; but they are generally ignorant of them. There are three kinds of souls: —*nitya, mukta,* and *baddha*. The *nitya* souls are those, which are, like Lakshami eternally free and have never been in bondage. The *mukta* souls are those, which though not eternally free, have ultimately attained freedom from bondage. The '*baddha*' souls are those, which are in bondage.[210]

As already stated Madhva is an ardent advocate of the concept of *bheda*. So the souls are in no state identical with *Brahman*. They retain their difference even in the state of liberation.[211] The text '*advaitam paramarthatah*' has been interpreted by Madhva as the absence of an equal or superior being to Vishnu who is said to be the most perfect, the best and the highest of all beings or entities.[212] The well-known assertion '*Tattvamasi*' has been taken to mean only some sort of resemblance between the *jiva* and *Brahman*. The world '*Tat*', it is maintained, always refers to a distant object, while the word '*tvam*' refers a person who is quite near. Therefore, it is concluded, identity of the one with the other is inconceivable.[213] Thus, the independent and perfect *Brahman* can never be the same as the finite and dependent *jiva*.[214] Not only this, Madhva and his followers have gone to the extent of reading the text '*Tattvamasi*' as '*atattvamas*' which reverses the meaning of the original text in order to seek a scriptural support for their hypothesis of difference between the *jiva* and *Brahman*.

While according to Shamkara liberation can be attained only through the knowledge of one's identity with *Brahman,* according to Madhva it is possible through the 'knowledge of one's difference from the omniscient Lord'.[215] It is through the knowledge of the innumerable good qualities of *Brahman* that one attains liberation and not through the realisation of one's identity with Him. The most essential condition for one's release from bondage is devotion to God. Without it liberation from bondage is never possible.[216] But His grace is the essential condition for liberation. Radhakrishnan observes: —

The author of the *Nyayamrita* argues that he who has the vision of the truth but not the grace of God necessary to effect freedom, continues to live in the flesh..."Complete freedom can be achieved only through the grace of God."[217] What is the most peculiar aspect of Madhva's *moksha* is that his 'released soul is liable to experience of miseries. [218]

What has been stated above is that for Madhva *Brahman* or God is only the efficient cause and not the material cause of the world. All other theistic schools accept that God is both the efficient and the material cause. This shows that though Madhva accepts the authority of the *Upanishads* and the *Brahmasutras,* he rejects the most fundamental idea, which is propounded there, namely the one manifesting as the many. Ontologically his ultimate entities are independent eternals. As a consequence, therefore, *Ishvara* cannot be said to be the creator in the true sense of the term, nor can He be called omnipotent. The system suffers from weak logic, and its too much in alliance with the *Puranas* from where concepts are freely taken and used for the purpose of illustration.

The theistic Vedanta School, which was based on the teachings of Chaitanyadeva and Jivagosvami, takes its material from the writings of Madhva, Nimbarka and Vallabha; it is known as *achintyabhedabhedavada*.

This school emphasises the infinite *shaktis* of *Brahman* or *Krishna*. Of these, three are main, namely, *svarupashakti*, *mayashakti* and *jivashakti*. The *svarupashakti* is also known as *chitshakti*. This is God's *antaranga-shakti*. It has three aspects, namely *sandhini*, *samvit* and *ahladini* corresponding respectively to *sat*, *chit*, and *ananda*. The first is responsible for the existence of everything, His own existence and that of others. By the second, He knows and makes others know. And by the third, He enjoys and makes others enjoy bliss. These are, however, inseparable. These three together are called *suddha sattva* or pure existence, which is untouched by maya.

Mayashakti is that aspect of God's power, which is insentient and material and it cannot function without the *svarupa shakti*. This *maya* has been further divided into two aspects, one *gunamaya* consisting of *sattva*, *rajas* and *tamas* and *jivamaya*. At the time of creation *guna maya* is transformed into the constituents of the material world. *Jiva maya* makes the *jiva* forget his real nature and attracts him towards material pleasures.

God's *Jivashakti* is manifested into all created beings, human or otherwise. This is also known as *tatastha shakti*. This school points out that God is both *saguna* and *nirguna*. This school accepts *Brahman* or *Shri Krishna* as *Rasa* as stated in the *Upanishads*.[219] This has been further elaborated by this school by making *Krishna* as the transcendental *Rasika*. In *Shri Krishna*, the *Parama Ishvara*, His *svarupa shakti* and *rasahood* find most perfect expression. But in the un-manifested state it is known as *nirvishesha Brahman*. It is this *Brahman*, which is generally referred to in the scriptures. Of the intermediate manifestations the one which is nearest to *nirvishesha Brahman* is known as *Paramatman* or the *antaryamin*. Between the un-manifested *svarupa shakti*, and the fully manifested *Shri Krishna* there exist innumerable higher expressions of *svarupa shakti* in different degrees. These are divine beings known as *bhagavata svarupa* sharing the *Lila* of the Lord. Thus according to this school ultimate Reality appears in three aspects, *Brahman*, *Paramatman*, and *Bhagavata*.

In this Bengal school of theistic Vedanta, *Jivatman* is a *shakti* of God superior to *maya shakti* and is *chit* by nature. It is, therefore, an *ansha* of God on account of its being His *Shakti*, and is a knower and a doer. Because jivatman is a *shakti* and *ansha* of God, its duty is to serve God.

This school is known as *achintybhedabhedavada* because it points out that the relation between the *jiva* and *Brahman* as we find in the *Upanishads* can be interpreted as that of *bheda*, as that of *abheda*, and also as that of *bheda* and *abheda* both. All these views can be supported by the statements from the *Upanishads*. But the fact is that the nature of this relation though it can be interpreted and explained in the above three ways, yet it cannot be really described in language and cannot be grasped by reason. The nature of this relation is not thinkable; it can be only experienced. A man who has experienced it agrees to accept all the three views simultaneously.

A careful observation of Indian tradition and culture in their varied expressions through human behaviours, either individual or social, shows that the philosophy of life, which is consciously or unconsciously practiced in India is more influenced by the theistic Vedanta than by the *Advaita Vedanta*. The Advaita philosophy is practiced and discussed only in a limited circle of some professional philosophers and a few *sanyasins*.

This is very natural because the human mind is generally associated with the senses, and, therefore, man's acceptance of the world as real is, but inevitable. The association of the human mind with this world of many pleasurable and painful objects has become intensely complex and subtle owing to the

desires and aspirations that make man conscious of his existence. Religious urge, social relationship like affection, and
friendship, etc., get their fulfillment only when man accepts a
theistic type of humanism as his philosophy of life. This the
theistic Vedanta has supplied to the general body of people in
India.

Man wants a God, because it is his nature. Man tries to
bring dignity in life through peace and love. Hence, it is natural that man aspires for a life of *ahimsa* so that the whole world
may be his home and all human beings his brothers. This outlook throughout the world is found to be not in abstract technical philosophy but in religious philosophies The Vaishnava
Vedanta and Christianity both have inspired men in this world
because of this fact.

Coming to the relation between man and the world in the
theistic Vedanta schools we find that the world or Nature has
not been taken as an enemy of man to be discarded, but rather
an interesting and important place where Nature can help man
to purify his soul so that he may know his authentic nature.
According to the theistic Vedanta schools man and Nature are
two aspects of the same Reality and all human behaviours are
to be guided by this key-principle. Man functions in Nature
and Nature functions in man. Through knowledge and finally
through devotion to the ultimate Reality, good man controls
the functioning of Nature in him and gives a new complexion
and meaning to his functioning in Nature. The highest aim for
him is to realise God as a Person—Vishnu or Krishna or Hari.
Man's attempt for this realization is just making a homeward
journey.

Man being a social being, his responsibility is great. He is
primarily a moral creature choosing between good and evil.
The theistic Vedanta makes man conscious of his ethical responsibility. It has its prescriptions for man's behaviour to his
fellow beings. It supplies a social philosophy for man based on

love and good will. It emphasises human love as a step to the divine love. This indeed has a great appeal for man everywhere in the world unless he is a positivist of a dogmatic type.

REFERENCES

1. A.S. IV. 22—a, b
2. A.S. IV. 22—c, d
3. A.S. IV. 38 & 40
4. A.S. IV. 3 .
5. A.S. IV. 4
6. A.S. IV. 6
7. A.S. IV. 7
8. A.S. IV. 11-12
9. A.S. IV. 13
10. *The Central Conception of Buddhism* Stcherbatsky, pp 23-4
11. A.S. IV. 14
12. A.S. IV. 15
13. A.S. IV. 16
14. A.S. IV. 17, 18
15. A.S. IV. 19
16. *Gaudapada,* p. 138
17. Op. Cit. p. 25
18. A.S. IV. 25
19. A.S. IV. 26-27
20. A.S. IV. 28
21. A.S. IV. 54
22. A.S. IV. 55
23. A.S. I. 7-9
24. A.S. I. 9
25. A.S. III. 23
26. A.S. III. 27
27. A.S. III. 28
28. A.S. III. 15
29. A.S. IV. 42

30. A.S. IV. 74
31. A.S. IV. 57
32. A.S. IV. 17
33. A.S. III. 19
34. A.S. III. 6
35. A.S. IV. 44. III-9
36. A.S. II. 19
37. A.S. III. 31
38. A.S. IV. 56
39. A.S. II. 4
40. A.S. II. 5
41. A.S. II. 7, IV. 32
42. T.M.P. Mahadevan, *Gaudapada*, p. 118
43. A.S. II. 4
44. A.S. II. 15
45. A.S. II. 14
46. A.S. II. 5
47. A.S. II. 11
48. A.S. II. 12
49. Mand, upa. 2
50. A.S. III. 13
51. A.S. IV. 68. 70,
52. A.S. III. 11
53. A.S. III. 3
54. A.S. III. 4
55. A.S. III. 5
56. *Gaudapada*, p. 160
57. A.S. III. 6
58. A.S. III. 7
59. A.S. III. 8
60. A.S. III. 9
61. A.S. III. 10
62. A.S. III. 13
63. A.S. III. 48, IV. 71
64. A.S. IV. 97

65. A.S. II. 1
66. A.S. I. 29; II. 35
67. A.S. III. 31-32
68. A.S. III. 13
69. A.S. II. 36
70. A.S. II. 38
71. A.S. IV. 92
72. A.S. IV. 30
73. A.S. III. 47
74. A.S. III. 33
75. SBS. P. 3 (G. Thibaut)
76. SBS. P. 3
77. SBS. P. 4. (*Smritarupah paratra purva drisravabhasah*)
78. Ibid. p. 5 (*Atasminstadbuddhih*)
79. Ibid. p. 6
80. Ajnana, p. 123
81. SBS, p. 9
82. Ibid
83. *Indian philosophy*, Vol. II, p. 587
84. Ajnana, p. 138
85. Ajnana, p. 139
86. *Samkshepa Shariraka*, 1, 28-30
87. *Indian Philosophy*, Vol. II. P. 583
88. *Indian Philosophy*, Vol. II, p. 583
89. *The Philosophy, of Advaita*, p. 235
90. Bhamati on the *Vedanta Sutra Bhashya*, II. 1. 14
91. Vedanta Sutra *Bhashya*, II, 2-31
92. Ajnana, p. 14
93. S. Radhakrishnan, *Indian Philosophy*, Vol. II, 570
94. *A Systematic Study of Vedanta*, P. 163
95. *A Systematic Study of Vedanta*, p. 163
96. SBS. II. 2-31, p. 427
97. SBS. I.3.30 (*bhuradilokaprabaha*); SBG. VIII. 16-17; SB, Isha Upa. 4
98. S.B. Isha. Upa. 10, 18; SBG. IX. 3

99.   SBG. IX. 10

100. SB. Brihad Upa. 1.5.2

101. SBS. II. 1. 13

102. SB. Prashna Upa. IV. 8

103. SB. Chh. Upa VII. 24-1 (*Kaiyakar akaphala bhedo hi samsarah*)

104. SBS. 1.1.2. II. 1.22

105. SBS. 2.1.36

106. AS. B. 1.7

107. SBS. 1-4. 14, p. 265-6

108. S. Chh. Upa. VI. 2-3

109. SBS. 1.4. 23, p. 284, 285

110. I-4-225; p. 286

111. S.S. Surya Narayana Sastri, *Bhamati Catussutri*, p. 28-9

112. SBS. 2.1.6, p. 305

113. SBS. 2-1-17, p. 333

114. S. Brih. Up. 1.6

115. S. Taitt. Upa. 2.6

116. Ibid. 2.6. (*Tasmat visheshato' grahanat nastiti*)

117. S.   Chha.   Up.   VIII.   I.   17. (*Digdeshagunagatibhedashunyam hi paramarthasad advayam Brahma mandabuddhinam asadiva pratibhati.*)

118. *S. Taitt. Upa* 2-6, 2-1

119. *Prashna up.* 4.1

120. S. Brih. Upa. 1.6.1. (*Nakaryam namakaranat vyatiriktamastikinchit*)

121. *S. Taitt. Up.* 2.1

122. *S. Taitt. Upa.* 2-1

123. *S. Taitt. Upa.* 2

124. *S. Chha. Upa.* 6.2.2. (*Pindahghatam vyabhicharati ghatashcha pindam, kintu, pindaghatau mritvam na vyabhicharatah*)

125. *The Vedanta of Shamkara*

126. Skena. Upa. 3.1. (*Brahmshabdavachya Ishvara iti avastyate*)

127. *S. Mund. Upa.* 2.1.3

128. *S. Taitt. Upa.* 2.7. (*Na bhedadrishtimishvarakhyam tadeva Brahma alpamapyantaramkurvate bhayam bhavati*)

129. 1.1.2. p. 16

130. SBS. 1.1.2. p. 16-17

131. SBS. 2.1. 37. p. 361

132. SBS. I. 2. 8

133. SBG. IV. 5

134. Ibid. VII. 13. 27

135. *Mundaka Upa.* III. 1.1

136. SBS. I. 1.1

137. Ibid.

138. *Tattvopadesha.* 9

139. Ibid. 10

140. S.A. S. 1.2

141. *SB. Sveta. Upa.* VI. 11. (*Shakshi drasita*)

142. Hiriyanna *Outlines of Indian Phil.*, p. 343

142. A. *Anekajivavada*=cf. R.R. Pandey, 'Some philosophical problems of Vedantasiddhanta muktavali, WZKSXX (1976), pp. 172-175

143. SBS: 1.3.15, II. 3.43; SBG 11.12; IV.10.11, *Katha Upa.* 1.2.24; 1.3.5-9

144. *S. Chh. Upa.* VI. 8.7

145. *S. Brihad Upa.* II. 5. 19

146. *S. Taitt upa.* II. I, SBS. 1.1.1. (*Brahmavagatirhipurusarthah*)

147. *S. Kena upa.* 11.5

148. *Upadesha Sahari*, XVIII. 4

149. SBS. 1.1.4. (*Brahmabhavashcha mokshah*)

150. *The System of Vedanta*, p. 401

151. SBS. 1.1.4

152. P.N. Nivasachari, *The Philosophy of Vishishtadvaita*, p. 260

153. RBS. 2-1. 16

154. RBS. 1. 4. 27
155. RBS. 2. 1-22
156. *The Phil. Of Vishishtadvaita*, p. 261
157. RBS. II. 1.37
158. RBS. II. 1-33
159. RBS. 1.1.1. (*Prakaradvaya vishishtaikavastu...*)
160. RBS. 1,4.27. p. 403
161. RBS. 1,4.3. p. 259
162. RBS. 1,4.23, p. 401
163. RBS. 1.1.13
164. P.N. Nivasachari; *The Philosophy of visheshtadvaita*
165. RBS. 2-11.9. p. 424
166. RBS. 1.1.2
167. RBS. 1.3.2
168. RBG. XV. V
169. RBS. 2. 4.17
170. RBS. 2.1.33 (*Sargelilaiva prayojanam*)
171. RBS. II.1.33
172. RBS. 1.1.1
173. Bhamati, 1.1.1
174. VPS. p. 18
175. RGB. II. 17, RBS. II. 3.20
176. RBS. II. 1.22
177. RBS. I. 1.1
178. RBG. II. 11, 18; RBS. II. 3. 18
179. Ibid. II. 15
180. RBG. II. 12
181. RBS. II. 3. 33-39
182. RBG. II. 14
183. RBS. II. 1. 34
184. RBG. II. 59
185. RBG. XV. 7
186. II. 3-19, 33
187. RBS. 1.1.1. (*Shariragochara chahambuddhiravidaiva*)
188. 188. RBG. II. 10

189. RBG. II. 13

190. RBS. IV. 4. 17

191. RBS. II. 3. 20

192. RBG. VII. 14

193. RBS. 1.1.1

194. NBS. III. 2.28

195. *Shuddhadvaitamartanda*, p. 24

196. VBS. II. 3. 43

197. SDS. V.I. (*Dvividhatattvam svatantrasvatantrabhedat svatantrabhagavan Vishnuh*)

198. *Vishnutattva—nirnaya* (*Prayah sarvatovilakshanam padarthasvarupam drishyate*)

199. *Vishnutattva—nirnaya* (*Prakrishtah panchvidhobhedah prapanchah*)

200. SDS. V.22

201. Ibid. V.6

202. Ibid. V.22

203. Ibid. V.22

204. *Tattvasankhyana* (*Svatantramasvatantram dvividham tattvamishyate*)

205. SDS. V. 34

206. SDS. V. 1; V. 43

207. *Muktimallika shloka* (4.70)

208. *Tattvaprakashika* on *Sutra lakavattu lila kaivalyam*

209. *Muktimallika*, p. 442

210. IP. Vol. II. P. 744. (Radhakrishnan)

211. SDS. V. 29

212. SDS. 21. 23

213. SDS. V. 28

214. SDS. V. 29

215. *Nyaya-Sudha*, 1. 230

216. SDS. V. 27

217. IP. Vol. II. P. 748

218. AHIP. Vol. II. Pp. 698-99

219. *Taitt. Upa.* II. 7

7

VEDIC COSMOLOGY IN THE LIGHT OF MODERN ASTROPHYSICAL THEORIES

The question as to how this universe came into being has been poetically posed in the Veda: What was the tree, what wood in sooth produced it...he established all things.[1]

In the Vedas there is a tendency to present every god as the supreme at one time or other and as the supreme god he must have made heaven and earth. At times the world has been presented as a beautiful piece of architectural art. In the Rigveda God Vishnu has been presented as having measured out three worlds with his three steps: —

> I will proclaim the mighty deeds of Vishnu
> of him who measured out the earthly space;
> ...stood out in triple regions widely pacing.[2]

At places gods like Vishvedevas, Indra, Agni, Maruts and Trastar are spoken of as having made firm the earthly and the heavenly regions: —

> What was that one who in the unborn's
> image hath stabilized and fixed
> firm these worlds six religious (regions)[3]

But behind the plurality of the Vedic gods, there is something real of which Agni, Indra, and Varuna etc. were only the forms. The oft-quoted lines in this connection are as follows: —

> The real is one, the learned
> call it by various names
> Agni, Yama and Matarishvan.[4]

Among the architects of the universe Vishvakarman, Hiranyagarbha and the Person are important. The Vishvakarman is the maker of all. There are two hymns about him in the Rigvedic text. These hymns simply describe the process of the formation of the world by Vishvakarman as the active agent in giving the form to the world: —

In the first hymn a question is raised as to which abode could he have been in when he created the world. He has eyes all round he has his face turned in all directions. He the one god created the Heaven and the Earth, and in so doing he blew out with both his arms, with wings... Vishvakarman is asked to perform a sacrifice with the Heaven and the Earth.[5]

In the second hymn the different qualities of Vishvakarman have been mentioned. He is the creator and the author of the diversification in the world. He sees all, knows all the worlds, bearing the one name of the gods. The waters are spoken of the bearing the first "Law' where all the gods had the vision.[6]

The hymn attributed to Hiranyagarbha starts with the glorification of Hiranyagarbha as the one who existed in the beginning at the head of all, the one lord of all that have come into existence. This hymn contains ten verses and in the first nine of them there is a refrain at the end, 'To which god may we make offerings?'...He was one God above all the gods.[7]

In the Sukta attributed to '*Purusha*' a significant change is seen. In the case of Vishvakarman and Hiranyagarbha they are only the active agents and the material cause is external. But in the case of the 'Supreme Person' for the first time a monistic theory in which the efficient and material cause got united. There are sixteen verses in this Sukta. In this Sukta *Purusha* himself is infinite and transforms himself into the phenomenal world.

This Sukta also begins with the glorification of the *Purusha* as having a thousand heads, a thousand eyes and a thousand feet. He encompasses the whole world and stands out ten fingers beyond the cosmos. This all is *Purusha*, whatever had been and whatever will be. He lords over immortality. Such is his greatness and the *Purusha* is greater than that; the whole world is just one quarter of His and the three quarters of His, the immortal, is in the Heaven.

This Sukta maintains that what is termed as *Virat* is said to have come out from the 'Supreme Person'. And another person was produced out of it. This person being born surpassed the world both before and behind. When this person sacrificed, all the beings in the air, in the woods and in the villages were born. The Vedas arose out of this sacrifice. The various animals like the horses and the cows and the goats and sheep were also produced in this sacrifice. Here the entire process of creation is spoken of as a sacrifice (*yajna*). Here a question is raised about this *Purusha* that was transformed into material at the sacrifice by the gods as to what became of his face, arms, thighs and feet. The reply that is given is that the wise people were his face, the warriors were his arms, the thighs became the traders and out of his feet were produced the manual labourers. The moon was born out of his mind and the sun from his two eyes. Air and breath came out of his ear. Fire came out of his face. The *antariksha* was produced out of his navel; and heaven from his head. The earth was born out of his two feet and the cardinal points came out of his ears. In this sacrifice, the spring season became ghee, summer season the fuel and the autumn became the oblation. The whole world was produced in this way. This is what happened when the gods performed the sacrifice with the *Purusha*.

This Sukta concludes with a verse in which it is maintained that this sacrifice performed by the gods became the first prin- ciples of law. It is also described in this hymn that in this sacrifice, the demi-gods (*Sadhyas*) and the poet-sages (*Rishis*) also participated.[8]

There is another theory of the creation of the world in the Vedas, which is highly philosophical in nature but stated in beautiful poetic language. It is called the 'Song of creation' (*Nasadiyasukta*). This Sukta starts with a description of the state of the universe prior to its appearance as a bewildering mass of phenomena, when there could be no distinction be- tween what is and what is not. There was neither atmospheric region nor the celestial region beyond. In such a condition what is it that can cover up, and the where, in whose support? There was no indication of night and day. All opposites like being and non-being, death and life, good and evil were viewed as developing from within and, therefore, had the possibilities of being reconcilable again in this fundamental principle. In the beginning there was darkness hidden in darkness. All this was a sea of water with no mark or indication. On this there arose a will in the beginning, which was the first germ for the mind. The rays of light stretched across, was it below or was it above? Who then knows, who can explain, whence there arose this manifold creation? Even gods appeared only after this manifolding process. Hence who knows whence that came into being? Listen, this manifold came from something whether it created this or did not create it. That supreme lord in the high- est heaven it is that is such a something and perhaps he knows; perhaps he too does not known it.[9]

In this Sukta the expression, '*Tad Ekam*' is very significant. It shows how the notion of a monistic principle is tending to emerge out.

Till quite recently Vedic cosmology was never taken seriously. What is this Vedic cosmological concept? It is the cyclic concept, i.e., the concept of creation (*srishti*) and dissolution (*pralaya*). Let us have a look into the recent theories of Astrophysics.

According to the epoch making discovery made by two Astrophysicists, Edwin Hubble and Humason, the universe is undergoing expansion after a primeval explosion which they called the 'Big Bang'. According to George Gamow of George Washington University, after the 'Big-Bang' the universe will continue to expand for about two billion years.[10] Lincoln Barnett opines that the universe in this picture is like a balloon in which cycles of expansion and contraction succeed each other through eternity.[11]

According to the second law of Thermodynamics, the universe is progressing towards a 'heat death' when all the galaxies and stars will have given away their energy in the form of heat and radiation and the whole universe will have attained a uniform temperature. What is this heat death? It is somewhat similar to our concept of dissolution (*Pralaya*). Lincoln Barett describes: —

All space will be at the same temperature. No energy can be used because all of it will be uniformly distributed through the cosmos. There will be no light, no life, no warmth-nothing but perpetual and irrevocable stagnation. Time itself will come to an end. For entropy is the measure of randomness. When all system and order in the universe have vanished, when randomness is at its maximum, and entropy cannot be increased, when there no longer is any sequence of cause and effect in short when the universe has run down, there will be no direction to time, there will be no time. And there is no way of avoiding this destiny.[12]

The important philosophical corollary and 'the inescapable inference' from this running down of the universe to a state beyond time and energy flow is, writes Lincoln Barnett, that everything had a beginning.[13]

New discoveries confirm the fact that the universe had a beginning in some remote 'Big-Bang' and will have an eventual 'collapse' in a "Big Crunch' in some remote future. It is this fact that made Einstein withdraw his concept of the 'cosmological constant'. He was said to invent the theory of a Static Universe.[14]

According to Chandrasekhar, who made a rare contribution to the knowledge of the collapse and 'death of stars', the collapse in its turn triggers thermonuclear explosion inside them. In that process hydrogen is converted to helium. In the case of heavy stars, even helium is converted into carbon and oxygen and eventually into iron, which releases no energy, and the nuclear alchemy stops there. What happens to a star, which has exhausted all its nuclear fuel? Will such a star be able to keep up its equilibrium against the powerful gravitational force? The existence of the stars called 'white dwarfs' which are visibly faint but highly dense and compact gives us the answer 'yes'. Chandrasekhar has explained how black wholes could be made. The behaviour of '*black holes*' has created a great debate with contradictory findings.

J.V. Narlikar is opposed to the "Big Bang' theory and he supports the Steady-State theory. He maintains that the odds that the universe emerged from a state of zero volume turned to be zero.[15]

It is assumed that the universe exploded 4,500 million years ago from a super dense state: —This is the story of the beginning of our present universe. After the explosion, the elastic forces which sent the fragments flying with velocities of at least one fifth of that of light could not have originated anywhere but in the most condensed state of matter known to the physicist, the so-called nuclear fluid. This is the substance that fills the interior of atomic nuclei; one cubic centimeter of nuclear fluid weighs 250 million tons. At that density the whole universe— which is believed rightly or not to be of finite mass—would have been squeezed into a volume equal to that of a sphere of 220 million kilometers radius or about that of the orbit of Mars. Lemaitre was the first to visualize such an initial state of the universe; he pointed out that at the density of nuclear fluid, this would correspond to one giant atom. This 'primeval atom', 'the egg from which the universe was hatched', must have been unstable, in the same manner as all atoms heavier than bismuth are radioactively unstable. It must have decayed spontaneously, exploding the instant it was formed. Our present universe would thus consist of the debris of radioactive decay of one single atom.[16]

How did the primeval atom come into being? In the case of no predecessor it must have been created on the spot. In the case of the opposite assumption a previous state, a collapsing universe, which crashed from all directions into one spot. The collapse was stopped at the maximum possible density of matter, that of nuclear fluid, whose elastic forces not only broke the impact, but also sent the universe expanding, like a rubber ball rebounding from a wall.

The question arises: where did the previous collapsing universe come from? We are forced to arrive at the picture of an oscillating universe, the 'cosmic pendulum' which expands to a certain maximum volume then contracts and rebounds from the point like state of maximum density to start the next stage of expansion, and so forth.[17]

The Inflationary Theory is just like a rubber tube under great pressure of air leaks when put in water bubbles come out. Let us examine these theories one by one in the light of our Vedic cosmology.

1. BIG BANG THEORY

According to this theory at the point of singularity the dimensions of the cosmos is 0 but its mass is infinite. When there is a big bang—great explosion—there is an interaction between two forces, radiation force and gravitational force. At the first stage radiation force predominates over the gravitational force, which is almost 0. After some time the gravitational force predominates over the radiation force. This stage is called critical point. Then expansion caused due to the radiation force after some time begins to contract. At the critical point the cosmos returns back to its original stage. It is cyclic. The *Nasadiya Sukta*, 'Song of Creation' provides a far better explanation than this BIG BANG THEORY. According to the *Sukta* all opposites like being and non-being, death and life, and good and evil are viewed as absent in the beginning. It was all darkness hidden in darkness. Even gods appeared after the manifolding process. Hence, who knows whence that came into being? There arose a will in the beginning, which was the first germ of mind. In this *Sukta* the expression '*Tad Ekam*' is very significant. It is a beautiful description of acosmic *Brahman* How acosmic *Brahman* becomes cosmic *Brahman* is shown in a typical philosophical manner.

2. STUDY STATE THEORY

This theory is opposed to the BIG BANG theory. One of its advocates is J.V. Narlikar. He writes that the odds that the universe emerges out of a state of zero volume turns out to be zero. According to this theory the BIG BANG is a local and temporal phenomenon. We know only the visible universe, which is covered by the rays of sun, but what about the infinite number of galaxies, which remain invisible? Creation and dissolution are going on without affecting the Absolute. Even the Oscillating Universe theory simply supports our cyclic concept of creation and dissolution.

New discoveries confirm the fact that the universe had a beginning in some remote Big Bang and it will have a collapse in a 'BIG CRUNCH' in some remote future. It is this fact that made Einstein withdraw his concept of the 'cosmological constant'. He was said to have invented the theory of a 'static universe'.[18]

3. INFLATIONARY THEORY

This theory is like the vibration or *spanda* of *Parama Shiva* of *Kashmira Shaivism*. Creation and dissolution are freedom (*swatantraya*) of *Parama Shiva*.

Astrophysics has its own limitations. It has to work and speculate within its boundary conditions or what Roger Penrose calls the 'point of singularity' or 'the event horizon' of a '*black hole*'. Its solution could only be given by the Advaitins through their concept of Acosmic *Brahman* and Cosmic *Brahman*. The *Nasadiya Sukta* gives its Acosmic state—"He who surveys in the highest heaven, He only knows or happy he may know not. This 'Song of Creation' is through and through poetic and equally philosophical. It is a rare and unique Vedic contribution to the world of literature. The other three *Suktas* devoted to Vishvakarma, Hiranyagarbha and *Purusha Sukta* provide beautiful cosmological theories. In these theories the concept of '*Tad Ekam*' is very relevant. In this connection the remarks of A. De Reincourt are very relevant: —'This void is emptiness; far from it; it is indeed creative potentiality, one which can presumably be experienced by mystical insight although science cannot penetrate beyond the ultimate barrier. The mystical emphasis always put on the ultimate non-reality of the material world and on the all-pervading reality of un-individualized consciousness (such as is postulated by the logical mind of Erwin Schrodinger), which underlies all physical appearances—but physical science can only stand on the threshold of this 'otherwise' or 'beyond' of the visible universe.[19]

REFERENCES

[1] C. Kunhan Raja, *Some Fundamental Problems in Indian Philosophy*, p. 118

[2] R.V., I.154.1; A. A. Macdonell, *Hymns from the Rigveda*, 1923

[3] R.V., I.164.6; C.R.T.H. Griffith, *The Hymns of the Rigveda* (Benaras, Lazarus & Co., 3rd ed., 1920-6)

[4] R.V., I.164.46 (Griffith)

[5] R.V., X.81.1-7 (Griffith)

[6] R.V., X.82.1-7 (Griffith)

[7] R.V., X.121.1-10, A.I. Thomas, *Vedic Hymns?* London: John Murray, 1923

[8] R.V., X.90.1-16 (Thomas)

[9] R.V., X.129.1-7 (Macdonell)

[10] L. Barnet, *The Universe and Dr. Einstein* (London: Comet Books / Collins, 1956), p. 106

[11] Ibid

[12] Ibid., p. 107

[13] Ibid., p. 110

[14] Nigel Calder, *Einstein's Universe* (New York: The Viking Pressing, 1979). pp. 147, 123

[15] J.V. Narlikar, *The Exploding Universe*, Illustrated Weekly of India, Nov. 6-12, 1983, p. 12

16 Ernst, J., Opik, *The Oscillating Universe*, A. Mentor Book, published by the New American Library, First Ed. 1960, p. 120

17 Ibid, p.121

18 Nigel Calder, *Einstein's Universe*, pp. 147-123

19 Amaury De Reincourt, *The Eye of Shiva* (New York: William Morrow & Co., 1981), p. 172-73

8

CONCLUSION

In The different systems of Indian Philosophy we find statements and explanations in regard to the origin and nature of
Prakriti or the world we also find that man belongs to this
world. But if one tries to understand what exactly is the relation between man and the world so that human life may be
guided by that understanding, one does not find any clear picture of this relationship in the systems so that the working out
of a plan for realising the highest end may be possible. Yet
there is enough information and suggestions in these classical
systems of Indian philosophy from which we may draw certain
conclusions. By analysing and understanding the implications
of certain statements we can have an idea of what exactly is
man's position in the universe. No doubt, in many cases statements are aphoristic and therefore are liable to be differently
interpreted, yet if one tries to understand the underlying spirit
of Indian philosophy as such with an insight one will feel that
there is the possibility of getting the general idea about the
nature, status, and significance of the world.

I think it will be out place to mention here that a modern
man bought up in the atmosphere of utility-oriented society
and with a thoroughgoing positivistic outlook may not be able
to possess this insight, which helps him in discovering the true
spirit of Indian philosophy. That is why in Indian systems par-

ticularly in the Vedanta the question of '*adhikari*' has been raised. A particular outlook is to be developed, which is an essential prerequisite for understanding the Vedanta—or as a matter of that the spirit of Indian philosophy.

It is certainly a wrong approach if *Prakriti* or the world and man are taken as distinct and separate entities to begin with, and then to find out their relationship. In Western philosophy, Descartes is believed to have introduced this dualistic concept. Whitehead has rightly shown that such a bifurcation is arbitrary and artificial. This dualistic approach has created a lot of confusion both in the Western as well as Indian philosophy. But the true tradition of Indian philosophy is not of this nature. The Upanishads, which are the source of the different systems have repeatedly emphasised oneness—though diversity has not been overlooked or neglected. Man and *Prakriti* or the world are related but the relation is not that of exclusive polarity. In man there is opposition between the conscious and the non-conscious, the chit and the achit, but this is only apparent, and its significance when understood reveals that they are complementary to each other in a particular sense. They are distinct but not different and opposing. Our superficial understanding treats them as such. Man and *Prakriti* or the world are complementary in the sense that the more we understand *Prakriti* the better we understand man, and the more we understand man the better we understand *Prakriti*. In fact, neither can be treated and under stood in isolation.

We have studied in the preceding chapters the different theories of the creation of the world. Barring a few exceptions, we have found that generally the world is taken to be a gradual manifestation. This manifestation may be non-conscious though with a purpose, as in the Samkhya; or it may be the manifestation of God or Reality as in the theistic Vedanta. In the Advaita Vedanta of Shamkara there is no manifestation at all and the world has only an apparent existence but as for all practical purposes this apparent world has been discussed by Shamkara seriously and we may accept the manifestation theory as a general view for explaining man and his world. I feel, the Upanishads are to be taken as our best guide for this view. For example in the *Prashnopanishad Prana* the manifestation has been called *Vaishvanara* and *Vishvarupi*. Shamkara has interpreted this by saying that the fundamental principle is manifested in different beings in different forms like the sun manifesting with its infinite number of rays. In the Upanishads, there are enough hints suggesting that the search for the ultimate reality *Atman* is to be made by advancing from the gross to the subtle levels of the manifestation. One has to rise from the material to the vital plane, from the vital to the mental, from the mental to the intellectual and from the intellectual to the blissful. One has to transcend the *annamaya, pranamaya, manomaya, vijnanamaya,* and even the *anandamaya kosha* in order to reach the ultimate end, which is beyond all these levels of existences According to the Upanishads Reality is not only the '*ekam*', but also the '*vibhu*'. This means the ultimate Reality is not only the macrocosm or the *virat* but also the microcosm or the *anu*. This again means that the one is in the many and the many are in the one. The world, therefore, may be accepted as a manifestation of the ultimate Reality.

In Samkhya-yoga the same manifestation is explained in terms of *Prakriti-parinama*. The subtle *avyakta* becomes *vyakta*, and gradually from the *mahat tattva* the different levels of existences emerge culminating ultimately into the *panchamahabhutas*. In the yoga system not only that of Patanjali, but also in other systems these *tattvas* are to be experienced directly in order to know and understand their significance. Hence, in Indian tradition *Darshana* is not verbal discussions and theoretical explanations as Western philosophy is; but it is the direct realisation o the tattvas. It is *Tattvasakshatkara*. The reality is a manifestation from subtle to the gross existences. Therefore, the key-principle of any kind of yoga system is to rise from the gross to the subtle. If the deferent levels of existences are in a descending order, man in his search for the subtle Reality must ascend. In the yoga system this ascent of man is through the direct realisation of different *tattvas*.

In the Vedanta philosophy *manana* and *nididyasana* prepare the ground for the onward journey towards the subtle Reality as the One. It is not finding out the prime genus through logical process. But it is a concrete experience of the One, which is present in the many. It will be a mistake if we accept the ultimate One as the culmination of an intellectual process. Because though the search begins in the world of names and forms it goes beyond the domain of mind and, therefore, it transcends any conceptual or intellectual process. The experiencing of the subtle Reality in the gross manifestation is possible not by *buddhi* but by *bodhi*. *Aparoksha anubhuti* is a new state which is supramental. Thus the achievements in the yoga system can be explained only in terms of the gradual manifestation of the subtle one into the gross many. In the theistic Vedanta system the world is the manifestation of God. The world being the manifestation of God the highest end for man is to realize this God in these many manifestations.

In the Advaita Vedanta, however, the world of names and forms has been explained in terms of superimposition or *adhyasa*. But if it is said that this world of names and forms exists only for the mind and not for that experience in which except oneness nothing can be distinguished, we may say that the gross manifestations of the ultimate Reality cannot be known when the mind does not function. That is to say from the supramental level, the gross existences cannot be experienced as the subtle existence cannot be experienced by the mind. To experience the subtle Reality, there must necessarily be a subtle instrument and to experience the gross, there must be a gross instrument of knowledge. We, therefore, should not misunderstand the Advaita Vedanta standpoint. When it is said by the Advaita vedantin that the *namarupamayam jagat* does not exist, it means that from the standpoint of a subtle experience (*paramarthika drishti*) the gross existences do not exist. A gross existence like that of our empirical world does not exist because it cannot be experienced in *aparoksha anubhuti*. Thus we may say from the standpoint of the Advaita vedantin whatever is not experienced through *aparoksha anubhuti* does not exist; and whatever is experienced through *aparoksha anubhuti* alone exists.

Thus even from the Advaita standpoint the world may be taken as a manifestation of the ultimate Reality, and the manifestation is from the subtle to the gross. The realisation of the One in the *jnanamarga* of the Advaita vedantin is a gradual discovery of the supramental subtle experiences through which there arises the gradual disappearance of the gross realities in their varied names and forms.

It is because of this gradual disappearance of this world of many names and forms from the domain of a higher type of experience, and a kind of conviction due to the self-evidence of the Reality as the one, that this world has been called by Shamkara as unreal, illusory or *maya. Maya* is a special category of existence introduced in philosophy by the Advaita vedantin. Its significance is to be understood properly. When understood properly, we find that there is no real contradiction between the Advaita and the theistic Vedanta or the *nirguna* and the *saguna* view of God. But this cannot be logically shown. It can only be experienced.

In our study of Kashmira Shaivism we find the principle of manifestation from the subtle to the gross has been explained

in a more tangible way, maintaining though its Advaita character. According to this system the universe with all its infinite
variety of objects is a manifestation of the ultimate Reality known
as *Parama Shiva*. This manifestation is of His immanent aspect called *Shakti*. But *Shakti* or the creative power of *Shiva* is
not different from *Shiva*. This *Shakti* again functions in different ways as the Cit *Shakti*, Ananda *Shakti*, the *Ichchha Shakti*,
the *Jnana Shakti*, and the *Kriya Shakti*. These may be described as pure consciousness, pure joy, divine will, the power
of knowledge and the power of assuming any creative form.
Parama Shiva, or the ultimate Reality manifests His *Shakti*
and we have this world, *Parama Shiva* as the ultimate Reality
becomes and pervades the universe and yet remains the transcendent pure consciousness unaffected by the manifestation.
Countless universes may be formed and may be withdrawn but
one is linked with the other by a causal relation. The manifestation has been called *Srishti* or *abhasana* and the withdrawal
or the *pralaya*.

While describing the manifestation of the gross reality this
system mentions the different *tattvas* as we find in the Samkhya.
Over and above them, it accepts other *tattvas* as well such as
Ishvara tattva, and *Shakti tattva*, etc.

We need not go into the details in regard to the system but
what we want to suggest is that in this system we find the
upanishadic view elaborated as a definite theory where the
world is a manifestation of the ultimate Reality. The manifestations here have been called as *abhasa* or appearances, but the
appearances are considered here real in the sense that they
are the aspects of the ultimate Reality, *Parama Shiva*. This
world of names and forms does not exist as such in *Parama
Shiva*. But it exists in *Parama Shiva* in its essence. Therefore,
this world cannot be called unreal. The meaning of *abhasa* in
this Trika philosophy is that the one becomes the many but

even after becoming the many the one remains unaffected. Hence, the manifestation has been sometimes called 'an experiencing out'. Reality or *Parama Shiva* experiences out when His *Shakti* manifests into different existences.

The meaning of the 'Advaita' and the significance of *maya* must be understood properly. It has been already said that the true nature of Reality cannot be known through Logic. It must be experienced as a *Tattva.* 'Advaita' has often been referred to as a principle, but we prefer to call it not a principle of logic but rather a *tattva*. Thus 'Advaita *Tattva* ' must be experienced.

This experience is the experience of the One in the many. Thus when a man through the process of yoga tries to experience the reality of the different objects of the world, he gradually discovers that these objects of many forms and many names contain within themselves a single principle, which reveals their inner nature. When man makes this discovery namely the one Reality is manifesting into these names and forms the distinctness and variety gradually disappears. He then as it were becomes a part of that Reality itself and as his mind is not functioning as an instrument of knowledge he becomes unconscious of the different objects of the world. Figuratively we may say that as the one comes nearer and nearer to us, the many goes away and gradually disappears. This does not mean that the many does not exist. It only means that the many has no existence in the supramental consciousness of the individual who has discovered the one in the many through his sadhana. This is the experience of the Advaita. This is the meaning of the 'Advaita Tattva'.

At the time when the world of names and forms is gradually fading out of existence in a man's consciousness, he actually feels that the world is rather like a dream. This is the experience of the world as *maya*. *Maya* has been experienced by the yogi as a *tattva*. The significance of maya can never be

understood if we take it as a logical concept. It, therefore, cannot be treated as an ordinary illusion. All empirical existences
are real from the *vyavaharika* standpoint and this is the standpoint, which a philosopher cannot avoid if his philosophy is
discursive. That is why the meaning of the Advaita has generally been misunderstood, and the term *maya* frightens a man
of common sense for whom to talk of the unreality of this world
is a shear nonsense. If one can understand properly the significance of *maya*, one can realize the existence of the one in the
many. Then only it is possible for one to understand the nature
of this world, which is a manifested form of Reality. This understanding, I believe, alone can help our understanding of
not only of *Prakriti* or the world, but also of man and his relation with this world. We shall then have the true picture of man
who has to realize his end while living in this world.

It may be noted that one of the great contributions of Indian philosophy especially of Advaita Vedanta and Samkhya is
the conception of *Jivanmukti*. The goal of life is not something,
which is to be attained only after death. It can be attained
rather realised here and now if the necessary Sadhana is properly pursued. In other words, the goal of life is not the object of
mere faith but something, which can be realised right in this
life and all doubts with regard to it can be eliminated. That is
an ideal, which is not found in some of the systems of even
Indian Philosophy and much less in the systems of Western
Philosophy.

Man or *jivatman* is not entirely a product of *Prakriti* though
he is under the influence of *Prakriti*. This influence is so great
that he not only is ignorant about his true nature but also he is
unconcerned with respect to the question whether man is some
thing more than what he is taken to be at the ordinary empirical level of consciousness. *Prakriti* or the world has such an
influence upon man that he cannot think of himself as some-

thing other than as a part of the world. The moment when man feels that he is something more than a part of nature he becomes reflective and he begins philosophising. Thus man at some stage of his existence in the world feels that his innermost self cannot be explained in terms of physical or biological entities. This philosophic attitude then forces man to search for his own essence or reality. At this stage he considers himself as the subject and the world as the object.

As the Upanishads have shown man's search begins as an empirical subject, and the process is a gradual discovery of the pure subject through the rejection of its empirical coverings or *koshas*. Thus the world exists not only outside but also inside the man. He has his body functioning under the physical laws. This body is controlled by the life principle functioning under the biological laws. He has his mind also functioning under the psychological laws. But all these are the laws of *Prakriti*.

Even though controlled by all these empirical laws of *Prakriti*, the reflective man feels his innermost being is something more than what is being controlled by these laws. Thus in man there is *Prakriti* and there is something other than this *Prakriti*. This 'something other than *Prakriti*', is not yet discovered as the concrete reality, but remains at the beginning a possibility, which gets its sustenance through faith. But as faith is strengthened. It produces a conviction that man is the meeting ground of Nature and Spirit. Spirit is that 'something other than *prakriti*', which is yet to be discovered in man as his *antaryamin*.

But for the reflective man the fact that he is the meeting ground of Nature and Spirit has a tremendous significance. It is this conviction that alone can help him in understanding his ultimate purpose in this world and so to have a philosophy of life that will guide him through his worldly activities.

There is nature working in man, but if man understands her method and the consequences of her laws and then learns the technique of keeping himself unaffected by them, he is able to get nearer the spiritual essence of his being. Thus, it is through Nature that man can move towards the Spirit. Nature is not to be rejected. It is to be understood and then conquered in the sense of bringing her under a higher and subtler type of laws—the laws of the Spirit.

When this happens man discovers a world of facts and the world of values in a new perspective. These two worlds, which are for the common man constantly producing disharmony and conflict would be properly understood and correlated in life. Values take their origin from facts. That is why knowledge of facts must be a preliminary condition for the knowledge of values *Prakriti* supplies us with facts; and from these facts originate multifarious empirical values. When man realises that these empirical values cannot stand by themselves but must have their locus or ground, the revaluation of values begins. We may say, therefore, that man's search for Reality beyond the domain of *Prakriti* or the empirical world is a continuous revaluation of values. This revaluation is not in terms of only values but always in terms of facts that is, ultimately the facts are to be interpreted and reinterpreted with the help of the values that have been newly discovered. What is suggested here is that our knowledge of the spirit helps us in getting a more thorough and better understanding of Nature. A proper understanding of Nature is not possible from the standpoint of Nature. It is only possible from the standpoint of Spirit. The '*chit*' alone can explain the '*achit*'.

This is because as we have already suggested that *Prakriti* or the world is a manifestation of Reality from the subtle to the gross; our understanding of the subtle alone can give us an understanding of the gross. In other words if man can discover the *Sukshma* transcendental Reality in him, he can understand the functioning of the same Reality in its *sthula rupa,* which is also in him. This means, therefore, that a man is not necessarily required to deal with the two worlds as opposed to each other. It is for the ignorant that *Prakriti* is considered as a place where man is entangled and loses his freedom. But with knowledge man gets a new vision and finds out that it is in this world that he can regain his freedom. From the very beginning, therefore, we must get rid of the concept of bifurcation of Reality or that of opposition between Nature and Spirit. Man alone can do it because in him the two are felt as distinct. Man, therefore, has a unique status and his responsibility has a profound significance.

So far as the Indian systems of Philosophy are concerned, we, therefore, find that Nature, man and Reality or God are so interelated that the understanding of all the three is involved in the understanding of any one of them. Man cannot be known properly if *Prakriti* or the world remains unknown because *Prakriti* operates in man. Also man cannot be known if God remains unknown, because the Divine operates in man. If Reality is a gradual manifestation of the subtle to the gross, and if man is a being where the subtle and the gross appear as conflicting realities, human destiny or the highest end must necessarily be the discovery of Reality or God in every particle of this manifestation. This is what I believe to be the discovery of oneness, the fundamental principle of the Vedanta school of philosophy.

ABOUT THE AUTHOR

Born on 2 April, 1942 Professor Rewati Raman Pandey was educated at Alahabad University where he was awarded M.A. (Phil.) in the year 1962 and D. Phil. in 1969.He did his post doctoral research at Munster/Hamburg Universities in West Germany during the years 1972-74. In 1972 he was awarded the Darsanacharya from Sampurnanad Sanskrit University Varanasi.

Professor Pandey is a resident of Nand Nagar Colony near B H U Varanasi and has served Banaras Hindu University in various capacities for thirty-three years. He until recently held the seat of Professor in the Department of Philosophy and Religion at the Banaras Hindu University. At present professor Pandey holds the prestigious position of Vice-Chancellor of Deen Dayal Upadhyaya University, Gorakhpur, one of the premiere educational institutions in India.

Of the many publications to his name '*Samagra Yoga; Scientific Temper and Advaita Vedanta*', '*Man and the Universe*' and '*Amritasya Putrah*' are the most outstanding. He has also published many papers and lectures.

BIBLIOGRAPHY

A.A. Macdonell
—*Hymns from the Rigveda*, Associate Press, Calcutta
—*Vedic Mythology*, Indological Book House, U.N.S., 1963.
A.B. Keith
—*The Religion and Philosophy of the Veda and Upanishads*,
 Harvard University Press, 1925
—*Indian Logic and Atomism*, Oxford, 1921
—*The Samkhya System*, YMCA Pub. House, Calcutta, 1949
—*The Karma Mimamsa*
A.C. Mukerji
—*The Nature of Self*, The Indian Press, 1943
—*Self Thought and Reality*, The Indian Press, 1943
A.E. Gough
—*The Philosophy of the Upanishads and Ancient Indian Meta-
 physics*
Amalananda
—*Kalpataru* (Nirnayasagar Press, Bombay), 1927
Appaya Dikshit
—*Parimala*, Nirnayasagar Press, Bombay, 1927
—*Siddhantaleshasangraha* (Achyuta Granthamala Karyalaya,
 Kashi, First Ed.) Samvat 2011
Aurobindo
—*On the Veda*, Aurobindo Ashrama, Pondicherry, 1964

—*Life Divine*, Aurobindo Ashrama, Pondicherry, 1970
—*Human Cycle*, Aurobindo Ashrama, Pondicherry,   1949
Annam Bhatta
—*Tarkasangraha with Dipika* (Athalye's Ed.)
A.Kaegi
—*The Rigveda: The oldest literature of the Indians*
A.K. Majumdar
—*The Samkhya Conception of Personality*
A.P. Mishra
—*Samkhyatattva-Kaumudi-prabha*
Bhojaraja
—*Yoga-Sutra-Vritti*
B.N.K. Sharma
—*A History of Dvaita School of Vedanta and its Literature*—2
    Vols.
Chitsukhacharya
—*Tattvapradipika* (Nirnayasagar Press, Bombay, 1927)
C.Kunhan Raja
—*Some Fundamental Problems in Indian Philosophy*
D.N. Shastri
—*Critique of Indian Realism*, Agra University, Agra, 1964
Sharmaraja Adhvarin
—*Vedantaparibhasa*, Ed. S.S. Suryanarain Sastry, Adyar Li-
    brary, 1942
Debiprasad Chattopadhyaya
—*Indian Philosophy*
Dale Riepe
—*The Naturalistic Tradition in Indian Thought*, Motial Banarsi
    Dass, Varanasi, 1964
E. J. Thomas
—*Vedic Hymns*. London, John Murray, 1923
F. Max 1
—*The Vedas*, Sushil Gupta (India) Ltd., Calcutta, 1956

—*The Upanishads*, SBE, 1879

Gautam

—*Nyayasutra* (Eng. Tr. By S. C. Vidyabhusana), The Panini Office, Alld., 1913

Ganganath Jha—*Nyayasutras with Vatsyayana's Bhashya and udyotkara's vartika* (Eng. Tr. Indian Thought, Alld.)

—*Prabhakara School of Purva-Mimamsa*

—*Purva-Mimamsa in its sources with a critical bibliography by U. Mishra*

—*Shamkara-Vedanta*

Gaudapada

—*Samkhya-Karika-bhashya*, CSS, 1953

—*Mandukya-Karika* (Gita Press, Gorakhpur)

G. Thibaut

—*The Vedantasutras with the commentaries of Shamkara and Ramanuja* (Eng. Tr. SBE)

G.N. Mallika

—*Philosophy of Vaishnava Religion*

G.R. Malkani, R. B. Das and T.R.V. Murti

—*Ajnana*

H.D.W. Griswold

—*The Religion of the Rigveda*

H.G. Narhari

—*Atman in pre-upanishadic literature*

Hariharananda Aranya

—*Patanjala-yoga-Darshana*

H. Zimmer

—*Philosophies of India*

Ishvarakrishna

—*Samkhya-Karika with Mathara Vritti*, CSS, 1922

Jayanta Bhatta

—*Nyayamanjari*, Medical Hall Press, Banaras

J. C. Chatterjee

—*The Hindu Realism*, Allahabad, 1912
J. Ghosh
—*Sankhya and Modern Thought*
Jaimini
—*Mimamsa-Sutra* (Eng. Tr. By G.N. Jha)
Jayatirtha
—*Nyayasudha*
Jiva Gosvami
—*Satsandarbha with the Com. Sarvasamvadini*
J.C. Chatterjee
—*The Hindu Realism*, Allahabad, 1912
J. Kirtikar
—*Studies in Vedanta*
J. Sinha
—*A History of Indian Philosophy*
Kshemaraj-shrikrishnadasa
—*Astatransadupanishadah* (Sri Benkatesvara Yantralaya, Sam.
    1966
K. Narayanasvami Aiyar
—(Tr.) *Thirty minor Upanishads*, Madras, 1914
K.S. Murti
—*Revelation and Reason in Advaita Vedanta*
Kanada
—*Vaisheshika-Sutra* (Eng. Tr. By S.C. Vidyabhasana), Lazaraus
    & Co., Banaras, 1973
Keshava Mishra
—*Tarkabhasa*, Ed. Bss, 1937
Kapila
—*Sankhya-pravachana-sutra*, Bhartiya Vidya Prakashanh,
    Samvat 2022
Kumarila Bhatta
—*Shloka-Vartika* (Eng. Tr. By G.N. Jha)—Ed by Kunhan Raja,
    Madras University Press, 1946

—*Tantra vartika*
Kokileshvara Sastri
—*The Introduction to Advaita Philosophy*
Krishnasvami Aiyar
—*Shri Madhva and Madhvism*
Kshemaraja
—*Shivasutravimarisini*
K.C. Bhattacharya
—*Studies in Philosophy*, 2 Vols., Progressive Pub., Calcutta,
     1956
K.D. Bharadwaj
—*The Philosophy of Ramanuja*,
Shankarlal Lokacharya
—*Tattvatraya*
M. Bloomfield
—*Hymns of the Atharvaveda* (Tr.) SBE, 1897
M. Hiriyanna
—*Outlines of Indian Philosophy*, George Allcn & Unwin Ltd.,
     1959
—*Kenopanishad with the com. of Shamkara* (Tr.)
Mandana Mishra
—*Brahmasiddhi*, Govt. Press, Madras, 1937
Madhusudana Sarasvati
—*Advaitasiddhi* (Bombay Ed.)
M.N. Sirkar
—*The System of Vedantic Thought and Culture*
Madhva
—*Brahmasutrabhashya*, Akhila Bharata Madhva Mahamandala,
     Udipi, Shaka 1879
—*Gitabhashya*
—*Anuvyakhyana*
—*Tattvadyota*
Madhavacharya

—*Sarvadarsanasangraha*, Hemaraj Shri Krishnadas, Bombay, Shaka 1827

Nandalal Sinha
—*The Sankhya System*

N.K. Brahma
—*The Philosophy of Hindu Sadhana*

Nimbarka
—*Vedanta-parijata-saurabha*

N.K. Devaraja
—*An Introduction to Shamkara's Theory of Knowledge*

P. Peterson—*Hymns from the Rigveda* (Tr.)

Paul Deusson
—*The Philosophy of Upanishads* (Eng. Tr. By A.S. Gedden)
—*The System of the Vedanta* (Eng. Tr. By C. Johnston)

Prashastapada
—*Padartha-dharma-sangraha*, CSS, 1924-31

Patanjali
—*Yoga-Sutra*, Ajmer, 1961

Prabhakara
—*Brihati*, Madras University, 1934

Pashupatinatha Shastri
—*Introduction to the Purva-Mimamsa*

Parthasarathi
—*Shastradipika Tarkapada* (Nirnayasagar Ed.)

P.V. Kane
—*A brief sketch of the Purva-Mimamsa System*, Poona, 1924

P.D. Devanandan
—*The Concept of Maya*

Padmapadacharya
—*Panchapadika* (Ed. By Rama Shastri, 1891)

P.N. Srinivasachari
—*Philosophy of Vishishtadvaita*

Prakashananda

— *Vedantasiddhantamuktavali* (Achyuta Granthmala, Benaras), Samvat 1993

P.T. Raju

— *Thought and Reality*, George Allen & Unwin Ltd., London, 1937

R.T.H. Griffith

— *The Hymns of Rigveda*, 2 Vols. (3rd Ed.), Lazarus & Co., Banaras, 1920-6

R.D. Ranade

— *A Constructive Survey of Upanishadic Philosophy*, (Oriental Book Agency, Poona, 1926)

Ramanuja

— *Sribhashya*, Shri Bhagvadramanuja Granthmala, Annangacharya, Kanchipuram, 1956

— *Gitabhasya*, Shri Bhagvadramanuja Granthmala, Annangacharya, Kanchipuram

— *Vedantasara*, Shri Bhagvadramanuja Granthmala, Annangacharya, Kanchipuram

— *Vedantadipa*, Shri Bhagvadramanuja Granthmala, Annangacharya, Kanchipuram

— *Vedarthasangraha*, Shri Bhagvadramanuja Granthmala, Annangacharya, Kanchipuram

R.G. Bandarkar

— *Vaishnavism, Shaivism and Minor Religious Sects*, Varanasi, 1965

R.P. Singh

— *Vedanta of Shamkara*, Jaipur, 1949

R. Reyna

— *The Concept of Maya*

— *The Philosophy of Matter*

R.S. Shastri

— *Hindi Tr. Of Vedantasara*

R.K. Tripathi

—*Spinoza in the light of Vedanta*, BHU, 1957
S.D. Santabalekara
—*Rigveda-Samhita* (Svadhyaya-mandala, 1940)
S.N. Dasgupta
—*A History of Indian Philosophy*, 4 Vols., Cambridge, 1932
—*Yoga Philosophy and Religion*
S. Radhakrishnan
—*Indian Philosophy*, 2 Vols., George Allen & Unwin Ltd., London, 1940
—*Philosophy Eastern and Western*, 2 Vols.
—*Source Book of Indian Philosophy*
Swami Nikhilananda
—*The Upanishada*, 2 Vols. (Tr.)
Shridhara
—*Nyayakandali* (Eng. Tr. By Jha)
S Bhaduri
—*Studies in Nyaya-Vaisheshika*
—*Metaphysics*, Bori, Poona, 1947
S.C. Banerjee
—*The Sankhya Philosophy*
S.S. Suryanarayana Sastri
—Edited and Translated. *The Sankhyakarika of Ishvarakrishna*
—*Bhamati* (Eng. Tr.)
—*Vedantapraibhashya* (Eng. Tr.)
Swami Vijnanashrama
—*Hindi Tr. Of Patanjalayoga-darsana, with the comm. of Vyasa and Vriti of Bhojadeva*, Shri Madanlal Lakshmi Niwas Chandaka, Ajmer, 1961
Shabara
—*Shabara bhasha*
Shalikanatha
—*Prakarana-panchika* (Chowkhamba, Banaras)
Shamkaracharya

—*Sharirakabhashya* (Nirnayasagar Press, Bombay, 1927)

—*Shamkara's bhashya on: Isha; Prashna; Kena; Katha; Mundaka; Mandukya; Taittiriya; Aitareya; Chhadogya; Brihadaranyaka; Shvetashvatara*; Gita (Gita Press, Gorakhpur)

—*Minor Works of Shamkara*, 2 Vols. (Ashtekar and Co., Poona)

Sarvajnatmamuni

—*Sankshepa Sariraka*, Udasina Sons, Vidyalaya, VNS

Sadananda

—*Vedantasara*, Poona, 1929

S.M. Srinivasachari

—*Advaita and Vishishtadvaita*

S.K. Balvelkar

—*Vedanta Philosophy*

S.S. Hasurkar

—*Vachaspati Mishra on Advaita Vedanta* (Mithila Institute, Darbhanga, 1954)

Saddhusantinatha

—*Mayavada*

T.R.V. Murti

—*The Central Philosophy of Buddhism*, George Allen & Unwin Co., London, 1959

T.M.P. Mahadevan

—*The Upanishads* (Selection), G.A. Natesan & Co., Madras, 1940

—*Gaudapada*, University of Madras, 1960

—*The Philosophy of Advaita*, Luzac & Co., London, 1938

Th. Stcherbatsky

—*Buddhist Logic*, 2 Vols., Dover, Publication, New York, 1962

Udyotakara

—*Nyayavartika*

Udayana

—*Nyayakusumanjali Kiranavali*, Sriniwas Press, 1941

U. Mishra
—*The Concept of the Matter*, Allahabad, 1936
Vidwan H.N. Raghavendrachar
—*The Dvaita Philosophy and its place in Vedanta*
V.S. Sukthamkara
—*Ghate's Lectures on the Rigveda*
Vatsyayana
—*Nyaya-Sutra-bhashya*, O.B. Agency, Poona, 1939
Vishvanatha
—*Nyaya Siddhantamuktavali*, CSS, 1937
Vallabha
—*Nyayalilavati*, Nirnayasagar Press, 1915
Vachaspati Mishra
—*Bhamati*, Nirnayasagar Press, Bombay, 1927
—*Nyayavartikatatparyatika*, CSS, 1925
—*Sankhya-tattva-kaumudi*, Shri Rama Press, Gaya, Shaka
    1852
—*Tattva Vaisharidi*
Vijnanabhiksu
—*Sankhya Pravachana-bhashya* (Chowkhamba, Banaras)
Vyasa
—*Yoga-Sutra-bhashya* (Ed. P. Vedanta, Calcutta)
Vallabhacharya
—*Anubhashya*, The Govt. Central Press, 1921
Venkatnatha or Vedantadeshika
—*Shatadusini* (Ed. By Anantacharya, Conjeevaram)
Vyasatirtha
—*Nyayamrita*
Vidyaranya
—*Panchadashi* (Achyuta K. Banaras)
—*Vivarana-prameya-sangraha* (Achyuta K. Banaras)
V.S. Ghate
—*The Vedanta*

V.S. Urguhart
— *The Vedanta and Modern Thought,* Humphrey, Milford, 1928
V. Bhattacharya
— *The Agamashastra of Gaudapada,* University of Calcutta, 1943.
W. Norman Brown
— *Man in the Universe*
W.D. Whitney
— *Atharva Vedasamhita* (Tr.)

INDEX

OTHER TITLES ON INDIAN PHILOSOPHY
FROM PILGRIMS PUBLISHING

www.pilgrimsbooks.com

For Catalog and more Information Mail or Fax to:

PILGRIMS BOOK HOUSE
Mail Order, P. O. Box 3872, Kathmandu, Nepal
Tel: 977-1-424942   Fax: 977-1-424943
E-mail: mailorder@pilgrims.wlink.com.np